THE TED BUNDY FILES

THE TED BUNDY FILES

A 1976 Companion

Development of the Violent Mind
Book 5

AL CARLISLE, PHD

The Ted Bundy Files:

A 1976 Companion

Al Carlisle, PhD

Book Five in the *Development of the Violent Mind* Series

The information in this book is authentic, and much is part of public record. Some names and identifying details have been removed to protect the privacy of individuals involved.

ISBN: 978-1-952043-15-4

Library of Congress Control Number: 2024931440

Edited by Jess Lindsay & Steve Harmon

Cover designed by C. Lindsay Carlisle

Created with Vellum

Introduction

From his work with Ted Bundy in 1976 to his passing in 2018, Dr. Carlisle collected tapes, letters, interviews, and other information by and about Ted Bundy. This was the beginning of Dr. Carlisle's research on the development of the violent mind.

The contents of this book come from Dr. Carlisle's Ted Bundy files. For years many of them were thought destroyed in a basement flood. They were found after his death.

Part of his Bundy files were included in "The Psychological Assessment of Ted Bundy."We have included several chapters from that book here..

Dr. Carlisle hoped to one day gather enough research on enough serial killers to find a measurable pattern of behavior that led good people, through a series of choices, to become serial killers.

He believed that if a person on this path could be identified and given the help they need, they would never become killers.

His goal was to protect children from serial killers and also prevent them from becoming violent offenders.

Like Dr. Carlisle, we hope that, through his books, others will want to continue his research so that someday we can break this pattern.

We also hope this book will help correct some of the misinformation that has spread about Ted over the years and facilitate further research into the development of the violent mind.

Part I: The Utah Investigation

Information from the initial investigation of Ted Bundy in Utah.

ONE

Elementary Police Report

ELEMENTARY REPORT

Bountiful Police Department
Case No. 9340-74
ATTEMPT TO LOCATE
TUESDAY, NOV. 26, 1974

At 1130 hours Detective Vrainnes and myself contacted Carol DaRonch at the Telephone Company office located at xxxxx.

She was shown photos furnished by driver's license division of six men, names as shown below:

1. Michael R. Driver's license xxxxx. Murray, Utah
2. Ronald A. Driver's license xxxxx. Park city, Utah
3. Kenneth C. Driver's license xxxxx. Salt Lake City.
4. Michael M. Driver's license xxxxx. Salt Lake City.
5. Alan K. Driver's license xxxxx. Provo, UT.
6. Larry M. Driver's license xxxxx. Midvale, UT

The photo of Ronald A. was second. At the time the photos were shown we were seated at a table in the northwest corner of the building. Detective Vrainnes on my left, Carol on my right. She was asked to look at the photos and see if she thought any of them resembled the man who tried to abduct her.

She picked the photos up from the table and placed them in her lap. She looked at the top photo and then placed it under the others. As she looked at the second photo, she showed a reaction by raising her eyebrows and looked hard at the photo. She then placed this photo on her left knee and continued looking at the other photos rather fast.

After she looked at the photos, I asked her if she liked any of them. She said no, then picked up the photo from her knee, placed in back into the pile on the bottom. She then put the photos back on the table. I again asked if she saw anyone she liked. She said no. I asked about the one on her knee. She smiled, pulled it from the bottom and stated that the hair is too long and not dark enough. She was asked to pick another photo that might look like the hair, if she could, from the group. She picked the photo of Larry M. and said the hair looked more like this. The hair in this photo is combed back and darker.

Case No. 9340-74

ATTEMPT TO LOCATE
THURSDAY, Sept. 4, 1975
COMPLAINANT: DEAN KENT

Reporting officer and Sgt. Collard went to the Murray Police Department where contact was made with Sgt. Paul Forbes of Murray city police.

Reporting officer obtained custody of a handcuff key which had been turned over to Murray Police Department to be sent back to the FBI lab which was not done. Also reporting officer requested custody of the handcuffs which they had obtained in an attempted abduction case in Murray on November 8, 1974 involving one Carol DaRonch.

Sgt. Forbes gave the reporting officer both the handcuffs and the handcuff key and this officer signed the receipt for them.

Reporting officer then contacted Carol DaRonch and requested that she accompany this officer and Sgt. Collard to view a possible suspect vehicle which she agreed to do.

She was transported to the location where the suspect vehicle was last seen, however, upon arrival it was discovered that the vehicle had since been removed from that location.

Miss DaRonch was then returned to her place of employment.

Also, reporting officer requested of Miss DaRonch that if the vehicle was located if it would be all right to contact her at home to have her view it and she agreed that this would be all right.

Reporting officer and Sgt. Collard will attempt to locate the vehicle first thing in the morning and is located will contact Miss DaRonch and have her view the vehicle.

Typed by BRUSCHKE

Copies to FILES/INVESTIGATORS

Officer assigned and writing report: DETECTIVE BEAL

ABDUCTION

Case #: 9340-74

FRIDAY, Sept. Five, 1975

COMPLAINANT: DEAN KENT

On 9/4/75 reporting officer met with Jerry Thompson of Salt Lake County Sheriff's Office where additional information in the Debra Kent case was received.

This information is in relation to a Theodore Bundy who resides in Salt Lake City at xxxxx. The information received was in regards to the Volkswagen he is operating which is a 1968 Volkswagen Bug, license number xxxxx registered to Mr. Bundy.

This vehicle is thought to be the same vehicle that was used in the attempted abduction of a Carol DaRonch who resides at xxxxx, Murray.

On 9/4/75 reporting officer and officer Beal made contact with Carol at her place of employment which is Mountain Bell in Murray. Her supervisor consented to her leaving for one hour at which time we took her to the residence of Mr. Bundy and attempted to observe his vehicle, however, upon arrival it was found that the vehicle had been moved.

On this date, 9/5/75 this officer will again attempt to contact the Bundy vehicle and then contact Miss DaRonch.

Additional information was given and this information was placed into the master file.

This information is in regards to various murders, abductions in the states of California, Colorado, New Mexico, Oregon, Washington and Utah. The individuals' names, ages, when they were missing and when found along with where they were found.

This information will be charted along with other coordinated evidence received from Mr. Bundy's use of his gasoline credit card.

Typed by: BRUSCHKE

Copies to: FILES/INVESTIGATORS

Officers assigned and writing report: DETECTIVE SGT. COLLARD

ATTEMPT TO LOCATE

Case #: 9340-74

THURSDAY, SEPT. 4, 1975

COMPLAINANT: DEAN KENT

Victim: DEBRA KENT

#1- Ernest A., Utah driver's license #xxxxx, date of issue xx/xx/xx.

DOB: xx-xx-xx

#2- Arthur M., Utah driver's license #xxxxx, date of issue xx/xx/xx.

DOB: xx-xx-xx

#3- Donald H., Utah driver's license, #xxxxx, date of issue xx/xx/xx

DOB xx-xx-xx

#4- Theodore Robert Bundy, Utah driver's license, #xxxxx, Date of issue xx/xx/74

DOB 11-24-46

#5- J. Robert G., Utah driver's license, xxxxx, date of issue #xx/xx/xx

DOB xx-xx-xx

#6- Clarence Y., Utah driver's license, #xxxxx, date of issue xx/xx/xx

DOB xx-xx-xx

#7- Alfred G., Utah driver's license, #xxxxx, date of issue xx/xx/xx

DOB xx-xx-xx

#8- Steven L., Utah driver's license, #xxxxx, date of issue xx/xx/xx

DOB xx-xx-xx

#9- Greg L., Utah driver's license, #xxxxx, date of issue xx/xx/xx

DOB xx-xx-xx

Reporting officer, Sgt. collard, Lieut. Ballantyne contacted Carol DaRonch and showed her the above listed pictures. Carol went through the pictures and then went to picture #4 pulling this picture out stating this looks like the individual.

Reporting officer asked Carol if she was sure and she stated she was sure this looked like the man as she remembered him on the date of the occurrence last year.

She did state however at that time he had a mustache.

Typed by BRUSCHKE

Copies to FILES/INVESTIGATORS

Officers assigned and writing report: DETECTIVE BEAL

ATTEMPT TO LOCATE

Case #: 9340-74

THURSDAY, SEPT. 24, 1975

COMPLAINANT: DEAN KENT
Victim: DEBRA KENT

Reporting officer, Lieut. Ballantyne accompanied by Capt. Hayward, Jerry Thompson of Salt Lake County Sheriff's office met with the Salt Lake County Attorney's office to present the facts in this case to determine whether or not there was sufficient evidence to proceed by Salt Lake County on the attempted abduction of Carol DaRonch from Murray.

After discussing the case County attorney's office determined they wished to take it under advisement overnight and would make the decision by morning.

They will contact Capt. Hayward and advise him.

Typed by BRUSCHKE

Copies to FILES/INVESTIGATORS

Officers assigned and writing report: DETECTIVE BEAL

The below interview was conducted by Detective Jerry Thompson. The interview is with CHARLES and ROSEMARY SHEARER, conducted on 11-26-75 at the Se Rancho Motel, room 52, where both subjects are now residing.

Q: (Detective Thompson) Go ahead.

A: Well anyway, I was getting a little frustrated, 'cuz Ted was telling me not to do this and that around my house and watch out for the cops, so I went over to his apartment one day and knocked on the door and he answered the door and he'd been drinking, he offered me some beer when I went in, and I said no I didn't want anything, and I sat down and I was real blunt and I says I want to know what's going on, I want to find out why the cops are after you and I want to know why. You're telling me that I can't do this and that around my house. So, he staggered in and we sat down in the living room. I asked him what the deal was, and he says well they pulled me over on some burglary tools, or something like that, that was in my car, and then he just started staring at the wall, he was just like dazed or something, I don't know what was wrong with him. And then he goes something about like I tried to abduct 3 girls and they're trying to get me for that too. Now I couldn't catch it all because he was slurring, but he did say something about 3 girls and that they were trying to get him for that too, or something like that. And I says, I asked him what, and he kinda just shook his head and said nothing, you know, and didn't say anything again. Well Rose is standing out in the hall, the door was opened, and she said she heard it, because I walked over there and I says did you hear what he told me and she says yeah, and I says I wonder why he said that. She says, aah,

A: (female) He said too… A tear in his seat.

A: (male) Yeah, or something about a tear in his seat that he'd mentioned, it was just kind of, I don't know whether he'd been drinking the night before or what, but he was pretty well bombed and I couldn't get really a lot of understanding out of what he said, but the few things he did say was something like that he did abduct 3 girls, and he was, they were trying to get me for it, I think is what he said, and then something about a rip in his back seat, and I repeated myself again, you know, I asked him what, and he says well and just kind of shook his head, just kinda said nothing.

• • •

Q: did he say anything about why he hadn't changed the rip in his back seat or did you mention anything about it to him?

A: Well, he, I asked him what he was doing to his car, and, I mean it looked really fishy to me, all of a sudden Ted was selling his car when it was the only thing he had, and it was a good little car, it was economical and everything. He went and redone the whole body on it, took the offender off, the front fender, said he wasn't gonna put another one on it, took all the rust spots out of it, and I don't know if he did anything inside or not.

Q: When did he do this? Was this after he said he'd been arrested for these burglary tools?

A: Yeah, yeah it was right after that, right after he started working on his car.

A: (female) You didn't, you didn't paint his car before that?

A: (male) No, uh uh, that's what looked suspicious to me, you know, after he told me he'd been arrested he started working on his car. But see he's done things like, at parties and things that he's been at with, with us people across the hall there, he's sat and talked about how he likes homosexuals, and how he liked to be around them at the bar, I don't remember what bar he said, son lounge or something like that. He's just done odd things with 1 of the girls that was up there one night, he pulled, he tried to pull something with her, I don't know exactly what, but I know Barbara and she wouldn't be the type to come in and tell yeah, you know, you got weird friends if he didn't do something pretty strange, from what I've heard, I could say but I don't like to say it, you know, out loud.

. . .

Q: Well, let me say this, Chuck, what is, you can't believe the importance, if you can recall or anyone in this room of his comments about how he like to be around homosexuals or the weird things he did with girls. We need to know, if you can really, what these weird things are. I mean it's one hell of an important thing in this investigation.

A: Well, he had some, only these are more or less things that I've probably, you'd have noticed if you'd seen them too. I've heard something about the guy that supposedly had raped all these girls, had painted them up or something, had done something, drawn lipstick on them and so forth; well, (when I was moving him out of his apartment, I ran into some magazines that had a bunch of weird pictures like that in them.)

Q: Do you know what kind of magazines they were?

A: I'd mentioned Cosmopolitan today, but Rose said no that's a girl's magazine, so I was wrong. I was just thinking, you know, off the top of my head, I knew it wasn't a Playboy, or a Penthouse. It had to be some other off brand or something, I don't know where you'd buy them. It was a pretty strange magazine, I just, you know, piled them up and threw them in the car.

Q: It wasn't more or less just pornography, I mean it was an unusual type, was it, to you?

A: Oh yeah, yeah, their faces were like makeup, you know, or made up like rock singers or something like that.

Q: I see, did he have a lot of these or just 2 or 3?

A: There were about 3 or 4 magazines there. I didn't look

at them all, I just saw a couple of them and I saw the names on the edge of the binding, so I knew they were all the same or, you know, more or less like each other.

Q: What was his comment about these homosexuals in these bars? Why did he like to be around them? Can you tell me anymore about that.

A: He said they were fun people. He said they were fun to be with. They were real happy people, and I, I told him, I says well I don't want to hear about things like that, Ted, I says you know I got my own beliefs and I says I don't care too much for 'em, and he says well I like to go to the son lounge and I like to be around them kind of people. Now I mean he didn't say whether or not if he involved himself with any type of relations with them, but as far as it sounded to me he had, you know, I mean the way he was expressing himself. I don't know, he's just done some really weird things around there, and like I talked to a few people downstairs, and the thing he did with this girl is he walked up and pinched her in the privates. Now I told the guy downstairs about this, and the guy downstairs says well maybe he was horny, and I says well, down, I says you know, I mean you've been that way and I've been that way and I says I ain't never done that and I don't think you have either.

Q: Was this at a party?

A: Yeah, it was right in my apartment.

A: (Female) Yeah, she was, Barbara was fallen asleep on the bed because she didn't feel good.

A: (Male) She was going, on the bed and he come in the

door, he never used Tanakh, never used to knock on my apartment, and I guess he walked up and pinched her.

Q: I see, and so he just walks in and pinches her and that was it?

A: Yeah, I guess, because she ran in there.

Q: Who was this girl?

A: BARBARA BALLEJO

Q: Has she ever gone out with him? Do you know?

A: Uh uh, no never. She didn't even know him.

Q: And she just got up and made that comment. Were there any comments by him, did she say?

A: No. He just kind of smirked and made a funny look and come in and sat down by me again.

Q: And she told you about it?

A: Yeah, well she told Darwin what happened. And her and Darwin used to be boyfriend and girlfriend, and then he told me, so I guess she was kinda embarrassed to tell me. But I don't know, like that night Ted made, Ted kept some pretty weird hours that night, he left about 1 o'clock and we were still partying at about 3:30 or 4 in the morning and he come walking in my door again and Rose was in bed, just walks right through the bedroom, just walks through the door, and he had both his hands in his pockets playing with himself when he walked in the door, I mean just things like this that

Ted done that I kept to myself, you know, and all my friends had sat right there and seen it themselves, but we never did say much about it, we just tried to keep it in our, you know, back of our minds. And the thing that bugged me about it was the fact that he'd never partied with any of these other people that were in the apartment building, and me and he had also gotten drunk with me and said a few things that I thought were awfully suspicious, due to the fact of like the 3 girls. So, whether the 3 girls came up in the conversation I don't know.

Q: Did he ever mention any kind of names, places, or anything about the 3 girls?

A: Uh uh.

Q: Just the 3 girls?

A: Yeah, he just said something about 3 girls. He didn't say nothing about, he just said there's 3 girls that I tried to abduct and they're trying to get me for, just slurred it out, you know. And he just acted like he was in the days when he said it, like I wasn't even there, or something. Then I think he caught himself and when he said "oh nothing" when I asked him what, you know, asked him to repeat himself.

Q: Did he ever make any comments about that he was never going to get caught or anything about the law or did he ever mention my name?

A: No, he never mentioned your name, but he said that day that he wasn't worried about getting busted for it, and I asked him why and he says well I'm innocent, you know, I'm innocent, that's what he told everybody in the whole apartment building. But the thing that bothered me is… (Rest of page is cut off and illegible)

(picking up statement on the next page.)

… Told people downstairs different stories than what he told me. He told them that he got pulled over for traffic tickets, and then he told me a different story, you know, so.

Q: How close was him and Margaret?

A: I don't know, that's strange, they were pretty close, but I don't know what kind of relationship it was, you know.

A: (Female) She's told me what kind of a relationship it was.

Q: Can you tell me about it, I won't tell her. Let me tell you this right now, I'm not going to tell anyone else who I get my information from. I have talked to her and she has been very evasive with me, but I can read between the lines. Can you tell me anything that's striking to you about it?

A: Well, she told me about a year ago when Ted barely moved in that they were lovers, I don't know what she meant by that. She just came out and told me they were lovers, you know, she goes and then off and on he'd come downstairs and maybe spend the night with me. And I go oh, okay, you know, people usually tell me stuff about their self and I don't even ask them.

Q: Did she ever mention anything about a book that he had called The Joys of Sex and that they, there was ever anything discussed about this book?

A: Uh uh, she never told me anything about it.

• • •

Q: Did you ever see that book or any comment that he'd made to you about it?

A: (Male) No, but he probably had the magazine in that group of magazines I did see.

Q: No, he doesn't.

A: I have no idea, but, he coulda had something like that in there. I didn't film through them, you know, it was his personal business.

A: (Female) You know, oh, I've got something to tell you that I had told him before, one day he was at work, I didn't want to tell you because I thought you'd get mad, one day he was at work and I went over there to get the vacuum, because he's the manager you know, so I went over there to get the vacuum, and I knocked on the door and I heard him, I heard the floor squeak, you know, I heard him walk up to the door, and there's a peek hole where you can look through and see who's out there, you know, and he stood there for a few minutes and then he opened the door and he had some boxers on, long shorts, and he stood there for a minute and then he goes oh excuse me, and I know he looked out that peek hole before he opened the door, and then he backs behind the door like that. He's weird though, he seen me standing there and yet he gets in front of the door like and then he goes oh excuse me, after he was standing there.

Q: Has he ever made any sexual advances to any of you, comments, or weird comments.

A: No.

A: (Male) He knew better than that with me around.

A: (Female) He didn't comment with me, but he looked like he could see right through me whenever I said hi.

A: (Male) There is one thing, there's 2 things I know that he's said, and that also bothered me very much, because Sherry stuck up for him a lot after he got arrested. We were, um,

Q: Who's Sherry?

A: The girl that lives downstairs with Dan. Dan Lish. Sherry, um, I don't know her last name, they're just roomies. But um, I was inside with Sherry one day, talking to her, he was visiting, Rose was upstairs, and I think Dan was at work that day, and Ted had come over for some reason, you know, he was mowing the lawn after he had already moved out. I couldn't figure out why, but I guess maybe he was making some extra money or something, I have no idea. And um, he come over to the window and started singing this nasty song about a girl that was 16, and Sherry just looked out the window really funny, and I go why didn't you, you know, tell me about, because I was in the bathroom and she told me about it, and I says why didn't you come in there and tell me, I'da went out there and told him to knock it off, you know, and she says well I didn't think anything of it. And then one other time when I was sitting on the front porch, Margaret was in talking on her phone and you could see it in through the window you know, the curtains, and her cat was also sitting on a windowsill, so he thought he'd, he'd play a joke or whatever, he says well look at that proceed in the window, you know, and then he says that Kitty cat. He just always did weird things like that, you know. But he knew better to do anything like that with these girls.

Q: Was he quite foulmouthed to be around?

A: Um, I don't know, it just depends… Yeah, he had a,

he was just schizophrenic, man, he had the weirdest personality of anybody I've ever met. I've caught him, he'd get high with me during the week, like I told you, we'd drink and everything else, like that day I told you on the porch, and then he'd go to church on Sunday, and I couldn't really figure the cat out total schizophrenic as far as I'm concerned.

Q: Did any of you ever have a conversation or talk to any of the girls that he had actually gone out with?

A: (Female) Margaret's the only one I know.

Q: Margaret is the only one you know?

A: There's one girl that I told you before that I've seen him maybe twice out of the whole time he lived here, she had a little girl, I seen him

Q: Long blonde hair?

A: Yeah.

Q: She was going to buy his car.

A: Well Margaret told me that he was just getting married to some lady with a kid or something.

A: (Male) Now I heard that he was going with that girl or something, but I seen him kissing her goodbye one time, I didn't see her since then. I thought maybe she was leaving town or something.

Q: Was he out a lot at night, you say, and kept weird hours?

A: Yeah. Well, a couple of times, see,

A: (Female) Can I tell you something, these kids are telling me things, see I've been out of town tonight.

Q: You bet. Let me tell you right now.

A: ...I worry about my daughter's safety. You know what I mean. I was the one that told him to tell you what he told you, that he tried, he was drinking one night and told him, related to him, I guess he thought in comments, you know, that he had tried to kidnap these 3 girls, and that admits the guilt right there, you better tell them what he said. I mean it's not right they turn him loose and have him do it again, you know.

Q: Okay, well,

A: Now wait a minute, this is not what I'm going to tell you, I just want to tell you, they were having a party the same night this thing happened, you know, when he went and pinched this girl. Anyway, she was, he was, the kids had so many people over there sometimes, you know, there's 7, maybe 10, maybe as much as 12, don't you, at one time?

A: (Male) Very seldom, but yeah, sometimes.

A: (Female) And there really wasn't that much seating in there, so I guess he'd been sitting on a sore, I mean the floor, pardon me, and he kinda leaned over like this, and later on he just laid right down on the floor and he was drunk and Margaret went to the bathroom.

A: (Female) Yeah, they stayed there really late, you know, and me and Darwin and Margaret and Ted were all there, but Ted passed out on the floor. He was like this, and then everybody left me in the room by myself and he was laying on the floor. So, I had the feeling someone was watching, so I just sat there and was looking out the window, and I turned around, and he went like this back down.

A: (female) He was looking at her, in other words she was looking like this, and he saw her looking at him and he turned back around. He must've really liked some girls!

A: (Male) Yeah, he's sat and stared at Rose all the time.

Q: Did he ever mention anything about your hair, he liked long hair, or anything in that line, do you know?

A: When your hair was curled one time, I remember him telling you that you looked nice, when we'd come out to go out, but you know, he always, I just thought that normally as a compliment.

A: (Female) He told you he liked dark hair.

Q: He liked dark hair?

A: Yeah.

Q: That it was pretty. Did he say anything else about the way it was calm, long or short?

A: No.

Q: Did he ever mention anything about his past, what he'd done?

A: (Male) All he did one time was told me that he used to work for a, help the police in Seattle or something, he said he helped get a purse snatcher. I read that in the paper, I think too, I'm not sure if I did or not.

• • •

Q: Yeah, it's very possible.

A: See that's why it all, I mean I just, me myself I just sort of put 2 and 2 together after what he told me, and then after him getting arrested and his Volkswagen, now I don't know what this trip in the backseat has to do with it, and I don't know what the 3 girls has to do with it, after the fact, other than him, there's been 3 girls missing, but I don't know why he ever even brought it out, you know, because it wasn't even.

Q: He said he attempted to abduct them or he did abduct them.

A: He goes, well I abducted 3 girls and they're trying to get me for it, and he slurred as he said it. So, I said what did you say Ted, and he says nothing, nothing, he was just like in a daze, he was just staring at the wall when he said it, and I asked him to repeat himself because right after that I ran over to Rose and I says

(rest of phrase cut off by bottom of page)

... No, and I didn't think nothing of it, and then he got arrested, so it kinda,

A: (Female) He told you this is what they come up to arrest him on?

A: (Male) Oh yeah, they'd been bothering him, you know, and questioning him, this was before he sold his car.

Q: Did you comment to him when he was repairing his car, why are you fixing it up or what's the deal?

A: Yeah.

Q: What did he say?

A: Yeah, I went over one day in the driveway, me and Dan did, and he says "I'm in debt, I gotta sell", and I didn't pry into his personal business and ask him why, but come to find out from what I heard is that he got a lawyer or something when he got arrested one time and he had to pay off that debt, that's what he told, or not him, Margaret. I think it was told me.

Q: Did he make any comment that he didn't want you tell anyone where he was moving or anything like that?

A: Yeah, he told me, you know, if anybody comes around just say well you don't know where he went.

Q: Does Margaret still live there, do you know?

A: Um, probably.

Q: Is she still good friends of his?

A: I wouldn't have no idea.

A: (Female) He asked me what I thought about the whole thing, and she goes isn't that dumb the way they're treating Ted. She goes you can tell he's intelligent…

A: (Male) They're the ones that have the brains to get away with it a little bit, you know.

A: (Female) Have you seen that big meat block he's got in his house?

Q: Yes, I have. Has he ever commented to you about it?

A: (Male) Yeah, it was really strange to me.

A: (Female) …'cuz I've never seen him buy a whole lot of meat before, all he buys is cookies and stuff like, "well how come you bought that thing", "well, oh, it's an antique thing, I like it" he goes…

A: (Male) But the thing is, see, I don't know Ted didn't cook meat much at all, because he had to come over and ask me and Rose how to cook a chicken, so I knew for a fact that he didn't use the meat block much for that, I mean you know, for all I know it coulda just, like you said, been antique, could just piece there, I like 'em myself, I wouldn't mind having one in my kitchen, I think they're sharp looking. But um, you know, I don't know what he, what his purpose was for it, and he had all the knives and the cleaver and the works you know. I'd just gotten off of work and I don't think Ted knew I was home yet, but he come to my door and I was sitting back away from the door on the couch, me and Mark was, and he says "well can I crawl through your window to get in my apartment", well Rose said yeah, sure, you know because she knew I was there then and she didn't mind, and then when he come walking in the door, he looked at me and he got, I noticed that he got a funny look on his face and then he didn't say another word about it, didn't even ask if he could go through the window, and then he goes "well I guess I'll see you later, Margaret's probably got the stuff I needed". Now I don't know if he meant to try to do anything with these guys or you know what the problem is. But he seen me and Mark and he totally changed his mind.

END OF INTERVIEW & STATEMENT.

TWO

Suspect Summary

THEODORE ROBERT BUNDY

This is a summary of a suspect developed in the killing of the girls in the Salt Lake area, and possibly into surrounding states, being compiled by Detective Jerry Thompson of the Salt Lake County Sheriff's Office, Homicide Division.

The suspect is a THEODORE ROBERT BUNDY, DOB 11-24-46, white male, 170 pounds, brown eyes. Salt Lake County Sheriff's Office arrest number is 78058.

The subject first basically really came to light in my eyes on 8-16-75 when he was arrested by a Highway Patrol trooper in the early morning hours driving around a subdivision, and in his vehicle, he had a satchel full of numerous items--handcuffs, pantyhose, a ski mask, strips of rope, a crowbar, and an ice pick. His explanation for these items was very poor.

On 8-21-7 this detective picked the subject up from the

Salt Lake County Jail and took him to his apartment at First Avenue where he signed a consent form to search his apartment. A thorough search was made of the apartment by this detective. Basically, we came up with only three results?-- a Colorado map, a brochure from Colorado on the ski resorts in the state, and a recreational type brochure from a Bountiful recreation center. Also, one book named the Joys of Sex. Before finding these particular items, subject was asked by this officer if he had ever been to the state of Colorado, he had ever been over there skiing. His comment was, "No, that state I have never been in." He was asked if he had ever been in the city? Of Bountiful, just north of Salt Lake, and he stated, "Not to my knowledge; passed through." In finding these items, he was asked by core? he had them. He had another explanation for everything, that and, he couldn't remember who, left them in his apartment, he didn't they were in there. The subject was then asked for his permission to look through his car and also to take photographs. Photos were taken of his Volkswagen vehicle, which at this time was bearing Utah license LJE 3795 on a 68 Volkswagen, registered to the •subject. The color was either an off-white or a light brown or light beige. Observed in the vehicle at this time is that it did not have a front bumper nor a front license plate, and that in the back window the back seat on the top had a large tear across the top; also, there was a different paint coloration on the right door and towards the fender. The subject never at any time asked why or what we wanted any pictures for or anything else. He was asked to come into the office the next day and talk to myself and Capt. Hayward, to Which he stated he would be more than willing to, again never asking what for. The very next morning we received a call from his attorney, John O., who stated that his client would not come in, he had advised him not to come in and talk to us, and he wanted to know what we wanted to talk to Bundy about, we sure didn't think that he had killed all these girls. He was informed negative, we just wanted to talk to him.

From this point on, a more thorough investigation went into the individual by myself; Mike F. from the District Attorney's Office in Aspen, Colorado; Sgt. Baldridge from the Pitkin County Sheriff's office in Colorado; Milo V. from the Mesa County Sheriff's office in Grand Junction, Colorado; and Lieut. Ballantine from the Bountiful city Police Department and the rest of his staff; and Robert K. from the King County Sheriff's office in Seattle, Washington, and his staff. It was then learned from Mike F. from Colorado, where he obtained some charge receipt invoices from Chevron oil, after having been given Bundy's credit card number by the detective, and came up with the first six months of 1975's charge cards. For (illegible) it was observed at this time, however, of particular notice that on 1-12-75 the subject bought gasoline in Glenwood Springs, Colorado, two times on this date. This is the date in question when CARYN CAMPBELL turned up missing and was killed out of Aspen, Colorado. Glenwood Springs is just a short distance from Aspen. Again of particular notice, on 3-15-75 the subject was observed buying gas in Golden, Colorado; also, on the same date in Silverthorne, Colorado; and the same date in Dillon, Colorado. This is the date when JULIE CUNNINGHAM turned up missing from Vail, Colorado, and has never been seen or heard from since. These towns are all within a very short distance of the ski resort. Again, in April 1975, on the fourth, it was observed that the subject bought gas in Golden, Colorado; in the fifth in Silverthorne, Colorado; on the sixth in Grand Junction, Colorado. This is the date when DENISE OLIVERSON from Grand Junction, Colorado, turned up missing and has never been heard from or seen since. Her bicycle was recovered along a street.

Bundy's whereabouts other than that are not known, other than that he was living in the Salt Lake area during October and November, the last time that our girls were missing, and that he was living in Seattle, Washington, in the early part of 1974, when the seven or nine girls were missing up there.

In an attempt to learn more about this individual, a subpoena was served on Mountain Bell by this detective, and I obtained telephone receipts of his long-distance phone calls. Once a particular notice went to a Dr. HIRST in Ogden, Utah and ELIZABETH K., who lives in Seattle, Washington. Several others were noted and are on record, but these two are of significant value. In checking out the call to Dr. Hirst in Ogden, it was learned that this subject is the father of Bundy's girlfriend, Elizabeth K., and that he was familiar with the subject. An interview was made with the doctor by this detective and Lt. Ballantine. From this interview it was determined that it would be of great value to interview his daughter in Seattle; Washington.

On 9-17-75 this detective, Detective Beal from Bountiful Police Department, and Detective Couch from the Salt Lake County Sheriff's Office went to Seattle and talked to Elizabeth K. It was of particular interest to this officer that his girlfriend had numerous doubts about him, going back to when the girls turned up missing in the Seattle area and had at that time contacted the King County Sheriff's office with her suspicions. Her suspicions first started approximately June or July 1974 when Seattle put out a composite which resembled 10 very much, according to her, and also that the subject's name was Ted. From then on, she claims that she found numerous items in her apartment which were unexplained, like plaster of Paris, elastic bandages, which the subject so-called used up in the Seattle area, which Bundy could not explain to her. She also found a meat cleaver, and ax, and a large knife in her apartment, which he could not explain to her. Her lug wrench from her Volkswagen was taken out of the trunk and it was about halfway up and put in the front seat of her vehicle. He told her that that was in case she ever needed it. He was observed on other numerous occasions of going out during the middle of the night most of the time, and one particular time he hid an object in his pocket, which later found out to be surgical gloves. She claimed that he napped a lot during the day and was out during the night; that he followed her and her girlfriends and seemed to like to jump out or come out from behind the bushes and grab them just to scare them. Things from here had just built up, and in Liz's opinion, she is still very fearful of the individual and believes that he is the one involved. She has known him for six years, and just this last year his sex habits have changed considerably, which is on another report.

Another girl friend in the Seattle area was confronted about him, MARY C. She more or less substantiates the same feelings as Liz does about Ted. Between the two of them it was found that his family background goes as follows: his father is a cook at Ft. Lewis in Washington; his mother is a secretary at Puget Sound University; they do not have a lot of money; there are five or six brothers and sisters in the family; they are originally from Vermont or Pennsylvania; they apparently came to Seattle in 1969. The subject was told by a cousin that he was an illegitimate child and that his parents have never really told him that; they claim that has had quite a bearing on his life. They claim that the subject is a petty thief and he has stolen televisions and numerous items up there; that he is an individual that has a champagne diet and a beer income, he does not have money. In fact, at the present time he needs money badly for his tuition. He asked his girl Friend for $700.00 to help pay attorneys This subject does have a college degree from the University of Washington, a B.S. degree in Psychology. He is presently attending the University of Utah in Law School . He has been quite prominent in the Republican Committee in the Seattle area and the Governor Evans' campaign in 1972. He appears to be definitely a loner, according to everyone we have contacted. We have been unable to come up with any close friends at this time, other than Elizabeth, his girlfriend. They claim he has tremendous personality when he first meets people, but shortly after you can see through him and the fact that he likes to use you. They all described him as very educated, a very handsome individual, and the tremendous personality.

An around-the-clock surveillance has been put on the subject by our office and Bountiful Police Department in an attempt to locate or come up with friends or associates. We have been unable to come up with this, even during our surveillance. We did come up with the information that he joined the Mormon Church a month or so ago and went to one of their overnight outings at Sweetwater in Bear Lake, Utah. He appeared to stay for the most part alone up there. He does not appear to have any close friends that we have been able to come up with up _ there either. We have com: up with one possible girlfriend, a Margarith Maughan, who lives in the same apartment complex on First Avenue. She was observed with this individual on two or three occasions. It should also be noted that she does have an arrest record with our office for Possession of Narcotics and a shoplifting charge.

That basically is all we know about the subject at this time.

Jerry Thompson, DP 141/ D
September 23, 1975

Summary of THEODORE BUNDY

(NOTE: This information should be inserted in the middle of page 2)

On 11-8-74 a CAROL DaRonch was abducted from the area of the Fashion Place Mall this evening in a Volkswagen she describes as an older model light in color, with a large tear in the back seat across the top. Also, there was a discoloration or some type of marking on the right door and fender. The subject attempted to handcuff her and got both handcuffs on one wrist. He also produced a small caliber weapon, unknown on the caliber, and at one time produced what she describes as an 8-sided lug wrench) or something to that effect. Since that time, this detective showed this victim numerous pictures, approximately 40, with the suspect Bundy. She pulled out Bundy's picture, giving all the rest back, stating she had not seen the -individual in there. When questioned about the one in her hand, she stated "I don't know why I pulled it out, I guess it's because he looks like him." She was then shown the photos that I took of the subject's car. She stated that in her opinion it was the same color, the same type of tear in the back window, and the only thing she could tell was that looked like the that she was in. Since that time, Police Department officers showed her a group of driver's license pictures, along with the subject, and she pulled out the suspect's picture, stating , "I believe that's the man, but I cannot be positive." She was then taken up in an attempt to eyeball the vehicle in person. At this time Subject had put in a new back seat or else had the back seat repaired, there is no tear in the back of it. He has put on the front bumper and the license plate. The hubcaps are changed from what originally photographed by this detective, and it appears that the vehicle has been painted a darker brown color than originally painted. Also, the Bountiful Police

Department took both photos of the subject and showed them to their witnesses at the Bountiful High School, who saw the so-called suspicious person on the night of the DEBBIE KENT disappearance. They pulled a driver's license and mug shot photo from a group of others out and stated, "If you would put a mustache on the man, I would say that that was him."

It should also be noted that the subject's attorney, John O., called Bob K., King County Sheriff's Office in Seattle, Washington, and made the comment to him that the police in Salt Lake were harassing or bothering his client and that he wanted to know basically if they thought he was involved in the killing of the girls in that area, that his client definitely was not and that his client would be more than willing to come in there and talk to them about this if this is what they were looking at him for. They informed him that he could come in and talk with them anytime and they would be more than happy to talk to him about anything. What the Salt Lake authorities were doing here, they did not know and they suggested that he talk to the Salt Lake police. They stated it appeared that- he was more. or less fishing wanting some information about what we knew about his client.

Also, it should be noted that a Detective Denning from Clear Creek County Sheriff's Office in Golden, Colorado, contacted this officer and stated that they had found a nude female down in a mine shaft late in August and it was determined that she turned up missing around July 1 or July 2 of this year. He was inquiring if we had any information that this subject was in that town at this time. I do not have July records from the Chevron Oil Company to see if he was over there in July. They are in the process of obtaining them now. He was in the Golden, Colorado, area however on two occasions, one in March and one in April. A copy of his report is being sent over in regards to his case.

. . .

74-59463

STATEMENT OF MAUGHAN

An interview was conducted on 1-9-76 on First Ave, at the apartment belonging to a MARGARITH MAUGHAN

Present during this interview was Detective Jerry Thompson of the Salt Lake County Sheriff's office, Lt. Ballantine from the Bountiful Police Department and Dave Y. from the Salt Lake County Attorney's office.

Margarith stated that she moved into this apartment in September 1974. Approximately two weeks after she moved in, Ted Bundy moved upstairs. That is the first time she got acquainted with you. She stated to her knowledge at that time there was a DENNA and GLENN B., who supposedly are the owners of the apartment and were living there. A SCOTT N., who she claims has now moved to Toronto, Canada, was a very close friend of Ted, and that if anyone knew anything it would be this individual. A CARL W. was living upstairs, goes by the name of (name redacted on original document) and new Ted was a fair friend of his also She stated the first time she had gone out with Ted was when the first ballgame in 1974 at the University of Utah was. She doesn't recall the exact date. She stated that she did not go with him heavily there at first. She had gone to Park city with him one night just to ride around and see things. She was asked for information about the car. She stated that when he arrived there, he did have this light-colored brown Volkswagen. She remembered that the front seat was not anchored or something, because she would slide back and forth in it and commented to him several times that she might fall out. She (rest of line missing) tear in the upper part of the back seat of the Volkswagen, as the stuffing was coming out of it. She was asked personal questions in regards to her sex life with Mr. Bundy. She stated that she truly had only had sex with him three times during the time that she knew him; that the first time was sometime in October 1974, which she classified that as a normal, enjoyable sex act. She stated that the other two occurred sometime either later in October or into November. She believes the last time was in late November, but is not sure. She stated the only thing she could tell about the second one is that it was not like the first time, there seemed to be something wrong or something cold. The third time, it seemed like he did not really want to at all, that she was more or less the aggressor. She didn't know how to explain this but it was definitely one that she did not feel was enjoyable to him. She stated there was nothing out of the ordinary with them. There was no bondage type thing, there was no sodomy type thing, there was no anal intercourse it was just that he seemed extremely cold and she thought there was something wrong with her. She had made comments to him about this at a later time, and she states she doesn't know exactly what he said, he just kind of shrugged it off and said something about that he was tired, busy with his studies or something and was not involved. So, she stated that she never did have intercourse with him from that time on, however, she was a friend of his. She stated that she recalled one time when they were up in his apartment, and she recalls this date exactly as it was in November 1974 and it was three days after the DEBBIE KENT girl was missing, because it was on the news that night and there were a lot of comments about it. She was in his apartment, she believes it was on

Monday night, and she made the comment to Ted at this time she was worried for such a guy like that running around and that why would a girl let something like that happen to her; she stated, "I would kill him first." She states (rest of phrase illegible) big, and he says, "you would kill him?" And she said. "Yes, I would kill him." He says, "well, you don't have to worry about that." She stated she didn't ask him any further questions and didn't pay much more attention to that comment, but she distinctly now remembers him stating, "well you don't have to worry about that." She states that she recalls also one time that when he told her he got arrested by the Highway Patrol, he only told her that he had a crowbar, a pair of gloves at a short length of rope in his car and they thought those were burglar tools. She was not aware of the handcuffs, pantyhose, etc., but Ted did tell her after this minor arrest that she should not tell her dad about this because someday before this was over her dad may be hearing this as an appeal in the Supreme Court. She thought that was unusual at the time for such a misdemeanor to be appealed to her dad's Supreme Court. She states she recalls one thing after Christmas of 1974, She stated that on numerous times she heard Ted, one time in particular, that in January, February, and March, Ted seemed to have gone somewhere almost every single weekend. She didn't know just exactly what all he was saying about them, but she did hear him comment many times how rotten women really were. She stated that she has formed an opinion and did at that time that he was possibly involved homosexually with Scott N.; that she got the opinion that he was possibly along this line. She stated that at one time during the summer the city had a lot of rapes going on in the avenues. Ted commented to her about it, stating that he thought he knew who did it; that one night he got her and said it's a guy down the street on a corner here, he's kind of weird, "come on and I'll show him to you." She stated that they walked down there and it just so happened that a guy happened to come out on his porch, so they walked on by. Ted then commented to her, "you go on and walk by, see what he'll do." She stated, "I was extremely frightened and didn't want to, but he stated, "go on, go on and walk by, I'm a voyeur (?) and I want to watch anyway." She stated she thought that was highly unusual.

He recalls numerous times that sometimes Ted would be hiding in front of her car and all of a sudden he would jump up and scare her and he knew this scared her extremely; that he would sneak along the side of her apartment and al l of a sudden be peering in the window, and she stated this also scared her very much so that he went into the apartment at night or during the day and he could creep up on you so quietly you didn't know he was there and you would turn around and he would be standing there. She stated, "this also frightened me and he seemed to delight on my fear whenever he could frighten me." She stated that he made another couple of weird comments right out of the clear blue sky and she can't remember when that he told her that he really liked virgins, and that he said something to the effect that, "I can have them anytime I want." She stated something about that they were kind of hard to find or something, and she said she doesn't know what he said, that she wasn't in a very good mood at the time, so she doesn't recall too much about it. She stated that it was definitely his idea not to have sex anymore, that he just didn't seem to want it, and this was after November 1974. She also stated that she recalled that Ted came home and told her that when he was pulled over by the Highway Patrol that he let them search his car. She asked him, "well why did you let them do that, they have to have a search warrant," and he said, "no, I led them, I got nothing to hide, they're too dumb to find anything anyway." She stated that he never mentioned anything to her about

Colorado whatsoever, other than when he first moved into the apartment, he made the comment that he had been over to Colorado skiing and that would have been before the fall of 1974. He had made comments to her and asked her if she had ever driven over Lamb's Canyon, that it was a beautiful drive and he had been over there in the fall of 1974 just before the snow fell and that she should go up there sometime. She stated that he made numerous indications and talked about that it made no difference between right and wrong, that he couldn't see any difference between the two of them; that he never did talk about joining the Mormon church and she couldn't really believe that he did. She stated that he did drink beer, that he smoked on occasions, and they were usually Salem's, but whoever he could bomb them from he would do that. She stated on January 25, 1976, after she had a talk with Lt. Ballantine, Ted came to her home. She stated that he seemed extremely different and she felt that he was sent over there by John O. to get some information from her. He didn't say this but she stated that she knew he was grasping for conversation and was more or less afraid to ask her, trying to feel her out to see which side she was really on, and she thinks that he got the opinion that she wasn't on his side any longer that she was very fearful of him at this time. She stated that she remembers another thing — that a guy by the name of JIM D., who lives next door in the apartments just west of them was also a close friend of Ted. She doesn't know if he would be very willing to talk to us or not. She stated she got the information also somewhere that Ted had been married before and that he had an illegitimate child, but she wasn't sure if this was true or not and wanted to know if we knew. This is basically all that I can remember of the conversation from my notes, as Margarith did not want me to tape the conversation. She was willing to go along and talk to us and relay what she could remember from memory, but she was very fearful and did not want to use a recorder so one was not used.

This statement is made by this detective (Detective Jerry Thompson) from the notes that I took that night while in her apartment.

Jerry Thompson
1 41/ D

THREE

Supplementary Police Report

SUPPLEMENTARY REPORT
Bountiful Police Department

Type of Crime or Complaint: ATTEMPT TO LOCATE
Day of Week: SATURDAY
Date of This Report: OCT. 4, 1975
Case No. 9340-74
COMPLAINANT: DEAN KENT
VICTIM: DEBRA KENT
POSSIBLE SUSPECT: THEODORE ROBERT BUNDY

Reporting officer attended a formal line-up at approximately 10:30 AM hours on Thursday, October 2, 1975. At this lineup was two witnesses from the Viewmont high school incident, Raylene S. and Tami T. along with Carol DaRonch, the victim of the Fashion Place Mall abduction or kidnapping on November 8, 1974.

Present were eight individuals in the line-up. After the line-up was completed, all three witnesses wrote their choice on the card and handed it to Dave Y. of the Salt Lake County Attorney's Office. Upon checking the cards, it was found that all three witnesses pick party #7 which was in fact one Theodore Robert Bundy.

Shortly thereafter a complaint and a warrant were signed by Sgt. Forbes of the Murray city Police Department against Mr. Bundy for the charges of aggravated kidnapping and attempted criminal homicide. Mr. Bundy was placed under arrest and booked into the Salt Lake County jail under a $100,000 bond.

At that time Mr. Bundy as well as his attorney refused to speak with officers in regards to any cases involving any of the girls.

Sgt. Forbes then returned to the County Attorney's Office and obtained a search warrant for Mr. Bundy's apartment which was served by Sgt. Forbes and Detective Jerry Thompson of the Salt Lake County Sheriff's Office. Reporting officer spoke with Deputy Thompson who indicated that they did not locate any evidence in the apartment. He also mentioned that several of the items which were in his apartment a few weeks ago when he went through the apartment with Mr. Bundy on a consent search were not there at this time. Some of these items were several pairs of patent leather shoes and several sports jackets.

Also, Detective Thompson indicated that he was at that time preparing to seize Mr. Bundy's vehicle which had since been sold to another party in pursuant to a seizure warrant and that this vehicle would be locked up and stored to subsequent preparation for processing.

Detective Thompson also indicated that he had received several calls from friends and acquaintances of Mr. Bundy and was at the present time setting up appointments for interviews as soon as possible. Reporting officer will re-contact Detective Thompson and assist in any way possible.

Typed by BUSCHKE

Copies to Officers Assigned & Writing Report FILES/INVESTIGATORS

Follow up Assigned to DETECTIVE BEALE

Case Is ACTIVE

Docket No.

FOUR

Jerry Thompson's Investigation

Detective Jerry Thompson's Investigation
(Extracted from "The 1976 Psychological Assessment of Ted Bundy" by Al Carlisle.)

I interviewed Detective Jerry Thompson of the Salt Lake Sheriff's Department to get his opinion about Ted when he was doing his investigation of him. This interview took place after Ted had been sent to prison. I didn't have this information when I wrote my report on Ted for the court. I'm including my interview with Detective Thompson here to give you a perception of how he was viewed by the Salt Lake Sheriff's Department.

Al Carlisle

Q: What was Ted like when you first began investigating him?

A: He is the exception to anything I've worked on, let's put it that way. He's the exception to the rule. He was very nice. He was very polite. He was educated. He thought things out. He thought he was better than everybody else and I think that was his downfall.

Q: What did you see in him when you were doing the investigation?

A: Well, I guess just his action, the way he talked. You got the impression that [he thought] he knew more than you. I guess the thing that disturbed me was the very first night that I met him when I brought him up from the jail, I had never seen him. I didn't know anything about him. We took him to his apartment. I had never had a guy apologize to me —and haven't yet—for him making me work so hard. Not apologizing for his actions at all because he [said he was] totally innocent. He [believed he was] a victim of his circumstances. He was very, very neat like I say. He liked to talk and that was part of his downfall too. He talked too much. He was an individual you had to watch. We took him into his front room. I had another deputy with me. He sat down on the couch and I started looking around. He offered me the world. I didn't like that at all.

Q: How do you mean?

A: Oh, whatever you want, sure. Can I help you here? Do you want to go through here? Just do this. That's not just a con because they don't act like that. That's not John Q Citizen who is innocent because they are very upset that you're tearing their house apart. That disturbed me. I would watch him when he wasn't looking at me. I remember I was on my hands and knees looking in his bedroom and I'd kind of look over to the side at him like this [demonstrates]. He watched me like a hawk. I could see his eyes and the minute

I'd turn towards him he would turn his head away. He was studying me. He was watching me very close. I could observe that he was getting nervous. I'm sure he was wondering: What's he looking for? What's he going to find? From that night on, I said, there's something radically wrong here. This is a different personality than I have dealt with in my life and I really don't like it.

Q: In what other ways did you see him as being different?

A: Well, you know, the guy was pleasant. He called me. How do you get a guy to call you? A hundred times! This guy calls you on the phone! He totally calls you on the phone! I can still hear that sneering laugh of his today. I'd like to strangle him. Laugh and, "Hi Jerry. How're you doing?" You know, like he's my friend.

Q: What would he talk about?

A: Oh whatever. If he'd think you might have found out something, "I know you're busy on me. I really hate to bother you. After all, you get paid for it. It's a job and stuff. I don't know why you're working so hard on me because I'm not the guy you think I am." And I'd ask him, "Who do you think I think you are?" "Well," he'd say, "you tell me," and he'd laugh. And I said, "No, I'm waiting for you to tell me." As it went on, later on, he turned around and said, "You think I'm the individual involved in these killings and stuff." But then he'd ask me, "Why are you following me, Jerry?" I'd say, "I'm not following you." "Oh yes you were. I saw you at the University up there. "Yeah, I saw you up at the

University too but I wasn't following you. I'm doing my job. Yeah, I'm working on you but I wasn't following you.

• • •

Q: Did he seem to be calling you to find out what you knew?

A: Oh, sure! He's trying to find out what I knew. Yeah. And he'd say, "Yeah you are Jerry. Your car was parked around in back. Most guys park out in front unless you're hiding." I said, "Did that bother you why I was parked around there?" He said, "Well, no." I said, "I'll give you a big secret if it will make you feel better, Ted." I said, "The parking lot is full. It's hard to get a parking spot." I said, "You go around in back where the faculty parks and you can drive right up and walk in." I said, "I'm a lazy individual." But I said, "If that bugs you, no I'm not following you but I saw you up there sneaking from door to door.'

When we had surveillance on him, I knew that he was watching us. He'd wave. I believe it built his ego. I'm smarter than them dumb cops, you know. Even when he washed his car and tore it apart, everything in it, we took photos. He knew that. It built his ego.

Q: He called me from Colorado after he escaped and got caught.

A: Oh yeah, he called me so much from Colorado I wanted to strangle him.

Q: Why did he keep calling you?

A: He kept calling on his murder case over there before it went to court. "Well, you know, I'm my own attorney and I need this or I need that, I need this report." I'd just laugh at him. He said, "You know, I have a right to this," and I said, "You know Ted, you don't have a right to nothing as far as I'm concerned," "Well, you're not listening to me." I said, "No, I hear you well." I said, "I'll give you anything you want. Just tell me one thing. Where's Debbie [Kent]?" He'd sigh and he'd laugh, "Who is Debbie?" I said, "You play your silly games. I'll play mine." We'd do that time and time again. He'd say, "I can't do that Jerry." "What do you mean you can't do that?" He'd say, "I'm not going to help you. I'm not going to make you look good. I'm not going to make you look like a hero." I said, "I ain't a hero. I ain't nothing." I said, "I don't care if you tell me or who you tell. There's a million ways [to tell someone where her body is]. Just let her be found."

I'd try to play on him. I said, "You know, I don't know if you've got any feelings inside you or not. You claim you do. If you do, if you've got a daughter, wouldn't you want to know where she was at?" I said, "Show me if you've got anything inside you." I said, "But don't tell me. Don't incriminate yourself. I could care less [how you do it]. There's a million ways." "Oh no," he said, "You've got so many ways of finding out things." He'd go on talking and you knew right then that he's telling you everything but that he did it. "You know, I can't do that," he'd say. If he'd go any further than that he'd catch himself or he'd know that you'd caught him on that and he'd back right off.

I was criticized when I first started working on him.

"How can you get involved? This kid's a graduate from college. He's going to law school. He's a sharp dresser. He's been involved with campaigns." I said, "The guy's a total phony." [The way he acted] totally disturbed my mind, Because of his apartment?

Oh yeah. The way he was. The way he talked. I don't know if you'll ever find another like that.

Q: What was his apartment like?

A: Immaculate. He even had his shoes lined up.

• • •

Q: Clothes lined up?

A: Yep. Everything. In fact, I asked him, "Have you ever been in the military? He said, "No, why do you ask?" "The only place I have ever seen in my life, hangers, in the military they are two fingers apart." His closet was like that. I said, "I have never seen that before in my life. You must have been in the military." "Oh no, that's just the way I hang them up.

Q: Did you see any deterioration in him as the investigation continued?

A: He got more nervous. Totally more nervous. I don't know how to describe it. His eyes told the story. Rather than being the happy-go-lucky individual, more and more that look changed. His look, I don't know if it was fear or if it was hate in his eyes. That became more and more as things wore on. He loved attention too. He loved attention. He wanted everybody in the world to think that he was the neatest thing in the world.

Q: How did he react when you finally arrested him for attempted kidnapping?

A: I think he was overwhelmed and yet I think he had a sigh of relief because the arrest was not for murder. I think he was really looking for Murder One and when we charged him with the kidnapping, at first he was as white as a ghost. He was trembling and rather than me telling him, I handed him the paper. He read it and said, "Oh God, is that all?" I said, "You were waiting for the Murder One weren't you, Ted." I said, "That's next." Like I said, he was really uptight.

FIVE

Initial Court Assessment for Judge Hansen

DIAGNOSTIC STUDY REPORT
STATE OF UTAH
DIVISION OF CORRECTIONS
SALT LAKE CITY, UTAH

Date Referred: March 22, 1976
Date Due: June 22, 1976
JUDGE Stewart M. Hanson, Jr
Third District COURT
Salt Lake (City)
Salt Lake County, Utah
OFFENSE: Aggravated Kidnapping - First Degree Felony
PROSECUTING ATTORNEY: David Yocom
DEFENSE ATTORNEY: John O'Connell

NAME: BUNDY, Theodore Robert
ADDRESS: B Street

Salt Lake City, Utah
BIRTHDATE: November 24, 1946
BIRTHPLACE: Burlington, Vermont
COURT CASE NUMBER: 28629

COMPLAINT:

That on or about the 8th day of November, 1974, in Salt Lake County, State of Utah, the said Theodore Robert Bundy, did intentionally or knowingly by force, threat or deceit, detain or restrain Carol DaRonch against her will with the intent to: (a) Facilitate the commission or attempted commission of a felony, to-wit: criminal homicide or aggravated assault; or, (b) Inflict bodily injury on or to terrorize Carol DaRonch.

PRESENT OFFENSE:

The following information represents this investigator's personal interview with Sgt. Robert A. Hayward, Utah Highway Patrol. Sgt. Hayward in the early morning hours of August 16, 1975, (approximately 2:30 a.m.) was seated in his automobile in front of his own residence. Sgt. Hayward observed a gray appearing Volkswagen going by him at a relatively high rate of speed. At this point, the officer called for assistance on his radio and began pursuing the suspect vehicle. Sgt. Hayward recounts that he pursued the defendant's Volkswagen through the winding residential community, almost losing site of the suspect vehicle inasmuch as the Volkswagen was able to out-corner and · out-maneuver the rather large, cumbersome police vehicle. Sgt. Hayward recalls that he ran stop signs at Brock Street and LeMay and again at the entrance of 35th South off of Brock Street.

Throughout the pursuit, Sgt. Hayward had his red spotlight on the fleeing vehicle during the chase. At the corner of 27th West and 35th South, the pursuit ended as Mr. Bundy pulled over to the side of the road. At that point in time, Sgt. Hayward asked the defendant for his driver license which was immediately produced and surrendered to the officer. The subject stated to the Highway Patrol Officer that he was lost in the subdivision and was trying to find his way out. Sgt. Hayward questioned Mr. Bundy as to his reasons for being in the community at 2:30 a.m., and the defendant replied that he had just returned from viewing a movie, the Towering Inferno, which had been playing at a local drive-in theatre. Apparently, a check revealed that the Towering Inferno had not been playing that particular evening; and when confronted with this fact, the subject then changed his story to say that he was lost in the subdivision and was simply trying to find his way out.

Sgt. Hayward, after having stopped Mr. Bundy's vehicle, made a consensual search of the automobile and found a number of tools and items that subsequently led to a charge of Possession of Burglary Tools, that charge being formally brought on August 21, 1975. In the defendant's car were found a set of handcuffs, a pair of nylon pantyhose which had a mouth hole and eyes cut out, a ski mask, several lengths of sheet material torn into strips in addition to lengths of rope. Also found in the automobile was an ice pick and other tools scattered about the vehicle.

On August 16, 1975, the subject was arrested and charged with Attempting to Evade a Police Officer.

As a direct result of Mr. Bundy's arrest on August 16, 1975, came the defendant's arrest of October 2, 1975, when he was charged with the offense currently before the Court for sentencing, that being Aggravated Kidnapping, a Felony of the First Degree. This offense, for which the subject was convicted by trial on March 1, 1976, was the result of Mr.

Bundy's abortive attempt to kidnap Ms. Carol DaRonch, on November 8, 1974. It should be noted that this agent makes reference to the defendant as the person being responsible for the abduction of Ms. DaRonch, this reference is made from the standpoint that the subject had previously been adjudicated guilty of the offense. At any rate, the circumstances surrounding the abduction of Ms. Carol DaRonch are presented by this investigator in a summarized version inasmuch as the initial report submitted by the Murray City Police Department is voluminous. and consumes a considerable amount of space.

Officer Cummings, Murray City Police Department, on November 8, 1974, investigated the abduction of Ms. Carol DaRonch from the parking lot of the Fashion Place Mall in Murray, Utah. The victim, Carol DaRonch, stated that at approximately 7:00 p.m. on November 8, 1974, she parked her vehicle in the parking lot west of Sears at the Fashion Place Mall and proceeded inside the store. Ms. DaRonch proceeded into the Mall through Sears and walked towards Castleton s and down towards Auerbach's. While in the Mall, she encountered some cousins and stopped to talk for a few moments. Following her conversation with her cousins, she proceeded back toward the Sears store and was approached by an individual near Walden's Book Store. Carol suspects that she had been in the Mall approximately ten to fifteen minutes at this point in time.

The suspect was described as being a male, white, American, 25-30 years of age, brown hair, medium length, approximately six feet, thin to medium build, with a neatly trimmed mustache. The suspect was wearing green pants and a sport jacket, the color of which was unknown. In addition, Carol's abductor was wearing shiny, black patent leather shoes. The victim's would-be abductor. gave his name as Officer Rosland.

The suspect asked Ms. DaRonch if she had a car in the parking lot to the west of the Sears store. The victim replied in the affirmative, and he then asked her for the license number. Carol relates that she gave him her plate number. It was at this point that her would-be abductor identified himself as a police officer and related that he had caught a suspect breaking into Ms. DaRonch's automobile with a pry wire, and he wanted her to accompany him back to the vehicle in order to ascertain whether or not anything was missing and also to see if she could identify the suspect.

Carol and her would-be abductor proceeded through the Mall into the Sears store and out the doors to the parking lot; at this time, the victim checked her vehicle, looked inside and could not see anything out of place. At this point in time, the suspect asked her to open up the passenger side, that he wanted to check inside. The victim told him no, it would not be necessary as she could see that everything was in place.

At this point in time, the suspect stated that he would like Ms. DaRonch to accompany him to the other side of the Mall where he indicated that the car prowl suspect would be located. Carol was led to believe that she would be instrumental in identifying the person and sign a complaint.

The suspect and the victim proceeded back through Sears and out into the east parking lot. The suspect looked around and stated that the car prowl suspect must have been taken to the Murray Police Substation. Her would-be abductor asked that Ms. DaRonch accompany him to the substation. They then doubled back through the parking lot, went back into the Mall, and exited on the north side by the entrance to Farrell's Ice Cream Parlor. They walked across the parking lot, crossed 6100 South and arrived at a laundromat. At this point, the suspect told the victim that this was the Murray Police Substation, and he believed the auto prowl suspect would be located within, and Carol could sign a c6mplaint. The suspect tried the door which appeared to be the entrance to a maintenance room; the door was locked. Ms. DaRonch's would-be abductor indicated that they would have to go to the Main Murray Police Department and would she accompany him to his vehicle which was parked on the north side of 6100 South near the east of the Lockhart Company; the victim complied and entered her abductor's vehicle.

While enroute to the supposed police substation, Carol asked her abductor for some identification and was shown a "miniature size badge" which appeared to be gold in color. Once inside her abductor's Volkswagen, he made certain that she locked her door. He made a U-turn and proceeded up 6100 South to 300 East where he made a left turn and proceeded north on 300 East to the area of approximately 5800 South on 300 East, the McMillan School.

At this point, Ms. DaRonch's abductor pulled the vehicle over to the side of the road and the assault began. The victim recalled that she tried to get out of the car, and the suspect reached over and grabbed her, her abductor produced a pair of handcuffs, grabbed her by the right wrist and put the handcuffs on the right wrist. Carol began resisting vigorously. Her abductor was attempting to handcuff both hands, however, he only ended up putting both handcuffs on the right wrist. At this point in time, the suspect reached into his coat pocket and produced a pistol, pointed the pistol at Carol and told her if she did not quit struggling, he would shoot her. To Ms. DaRonch's credit, she began struggling all the harder. She managed to open the door and got outside, the abductor also exited the vehicle and approached her. At this point in time, the suspect had what Ms. DaRonch believed was a crowbar in his left hand and lifted it over his head as though to strike her. Carol grabbed the bar and started pushing and shoving her abductor. Finally, Ms.

DaRonch broke free and began running out into the roadway where she flagged down Mr. and Mrs. Walch. They admitted her to their vehicle and took her to the Murray City Police Department where she recounted her harrowing experience, and the investigation was launched for her abductor. Some eleven months later, on October 2, 1975, the defendant was charged with the Aggravated Kidnapping of Ms. Carol DaRonch and was subsequently convicted by trial on March 1, 1976.

DEFENDANT'S STATEMENT:

This investigator requested and received a typewritten statement from Mr. Bundy on June 10, 1976, and the following information is presented verbatim:

"Activity and whereabouts on the evening of November 8, 1974, and the morning of August 16, 1975.

"A statement by Theodore Bundy:

"Incidents occurring on November 8, 1974 and August 16, 1975 have, it appears, shaped my destiny for all time. On November 8, 1974, a young woman was abducted from a shopping mall and shortly thereafter she escaped unharmed from her abductor. On August 16, 1975, I was stopped by a State Patrolman in the early morning hours ostensibly because I failed to heed his signal to stop. Two incidents, on two days separated significantly in both time and circumstance, have become strangely and intimately interdependent.

"I was arrested, charged, tried, and found guilty of the kidnapping which occurred on November 8, 1974 following an investigation which grew out of the August 16, 1975, episode. During the kidnapping trial, I testified extensively concerning both my whereabouts on November 8 and my activities on August 15 and 16. My testimony was heard by Judge Stewart Hanson, Jr., who was also the trier of fact in the case because I chose to waive my rights to a jury trial. My testimony is a matter of record, and it is my understanding that the record has been reduced to writing in a transcript form. My testimony was made under oath, was a complete and accurate account of my recollection of events on November 8 and August 16, and remains to this day the most reliable statement pertaining to the occasions in question. Therefore, I recommend that those interested in my version first refer to the transcript of my testimony.

"Inevitably, even extensive examination and cross-examination leave questions unanswered which are in retrospect intriguing but which, because of the fallibility of counsel or the constraints of evidence law, are not asked. I would willingly respond to questions left unanswered by my testimony which are of interest to those with some legitimate Involvement in my case. Since I am not possessed of an intuition which would permit me to comprehend each and every specific question referring to matters associated with November 8, and August 16, I would prefer responding to precise inquiries rather than launching myself on a broad explanation, much of which would be redundant in light of my testimony.

"From my point of view, the most critical questions were asked and answered during my testimony. A summary of my recollection of November 8, 1974 follows:

"1. I was not at fashion Place mall on that evening.

"2. I vaguely recall being home for time, taking in a movie and going to a local tavern.

"3. At approximately 11:50 PM, (as est. by phone

records), I made a call to my fiancé in Seattle, and she recalls a discussion of the movie.

"4. My car had broken down late in the afternoon at was not in good working order.

"5. I was not, nor have I ever worn a mustache, green slacks, or patent leather shoes.

"6. I did not own a gun or a police badge on that day or at any other time.

"7. I did not own handcuffs on November 8.

"8. I was not driving a light blue Volkswagen, nor did my base Volkswagen have unnoticeable air in the backseat during the winter of 1974-75.

"9. I was not the man who abducted Carol DaRonch.

"If I cannot remember precisely what occurred on a date which is now 18 and one-half months old and which occurred 11 months prior to my arrest for kidnapping, it is because my memory does not improve with time. It is safe to say what I was not doing, however. I was not having heart surgery, nor was I taking ballet lessons, nor was I in Mexico, nor was I am adopting a complete stranger at gunpoint. There are just some things a person does not forget and just some things a person is not inclined to do under any circumstances.

"The point is that my version of my whereabouts and activities on November 8, although understandably vague, have not been refuted by any testimony or physical evidence other than the testimony of Carol DaRonch. The fact is that evidence tending to exculpate me was not successful1y challenged or refuted. The reality is that the entirety of the defense's case was disbelieved. ·

"Turning now to the night of August 15, 1975, and the early morning hours of August 16, 1975.

"No fact seems to have had more incriminating significance to the prosecution in the kidnapping case and, at the same time, no fact was more patently immaterial to the issue of guilt or innocence in that case than an incident which took place over nine months after the crime. The fact that I was stopped on August 16, 1975, and that handcuffs were found in my car was a dominating factor in the kidnapping trial. Undeniably, handcuffs, a crowbar, ski mask, pantyhose, strips of cloth, an ice pick were collected from various locations in my car.

"The fact is that I had never contemplated using these items for any unlawful purpose, nor can any such purpose be shown. The fact is that these items were a part of a vast array of tools and miscellanea carried in my car, some as 'strange' as the allegedly nefarious items seized. Not seized by the police was an Army shovel, plastic boat oars, flares, tire chains, VW repair manuals, hack saws, coveralls, a rubber hose, cans of oil, a length of heavy chain, and a complete tool box containing among other things, a rubber mallet.

"Admittedly, the circumstances were unusual. If my explanation involving the use of marijuana and my late working hours is not to be believed, then, I suppose some will turn to a plethora of clandestine hypotheses which lack only one thing: evidence to substantiate them. So, while I stand guilty of being strange on one occasion at the age of twenty-nine, I am perplexed by the imaginative insinuations which attempt to link the 'strangeness' with a ten-month old kidnapping.

"If Carol DaRonch had been abducted at 2 o'clock in the morning by a man dressed in dark clothing, wearing a ski mask, threatening her with an ice pick, and having the passenger seat removed from his car, there would be genuine cause to associate the two incidents. However, she was not.

"If during the search of my car on August 16, or any subsequent search, a police badge and a handgun had been found, there would be a relationship between the two incidents. However, they were not.

"If the handcuffs found in my car on August 16, were the same ones used on the kidnapped victim or bore some distinguishing similarity to those placed on the victim, there would be reason to associate the two events. However, they were not the same nor did they bear any unique similarity.

"If Miss DaRonch had testified that a weapon brandished by her attacker had definitely been a crowbar, there could be some remote association, although such tools are common and not commonly purchased as weapons. However, she testified that she did not see the weapon but only felt a many-sided metal object which she assumed was a crowbar. (Interestingly enough, at an earlier hearing, she estimated the length of the weapon and later when she testified at trial, she stated she had not seen it.) Two blind men touching an elephant, one feeling the leg and the other the tail, described the beast respectively as a tree trunk and a snake. The metal object Ms. DaRonch felt became a crowbar but not just any crowbar. It became precisely the one found in my car ten months later. I find the logic quite implausible.

"Finally, I wish to discuss my statements made to officers at the scene on August 16, and other considerations which allegedly diminished my credibility.

"My statements to the police that I had been somewhere that evening where I had in fact not been was a regrettable subterfuge. I should not have told the police in untruth. I had the right to remain silent, even though I was never advised of that right, I should have exercised it. Caught in a compromising situation, between telling the officers I had been smoking marijuana or proposing some less intimidating explanation, I chose the wrong compromise. There was really no need to compromise at all.

"The prosecution inferred that my lie to the police on

that evening and my failure to reveal my actual activity to my attorney made me a pathological liar and a discredited witness. The argument is totally unpersuasive. To begin with, I voluntarily took the stand and admitted my errors. I submit that making an erroneous statement to a group of belligerent police officers while standing alone on a deserted street corner at 2:00 in the morning does not suggest that I would lie while under oath in court of law about my non-involvement in a kidnapping. Nor is there any validity to the assumption that a person who lies, whether out of habit or necessity is the kind of a person who would abduct a teenage girl from a shopping mall. The prosecutory argument which asserts I was not a credible witness has no basis in logic or fact because it cannot be shown that I lied on the witness stand.

"My failure to inform my attorney of my true activities on August 16 reflects a difference in priorities as much as it does my own shortcomings. Mr. O'Connell was concerned about the prejudicial repercussions that testimony regarding August 16 would have on the kidnapping trial. On the other hand, I felt strongly then, as I do now, that August 16 was just a ploy advanced by a desperate prosecution and, with the exception of the seizure of the handcuffs, was a completely immaterial occurrence. I saw no reason to advertise my use of marijuana which I also felt was immaterial and itself potentially prejudicial.

Given the embarrassment my admission concerning marijuana caused me, it was to my credit that I revealed my use of it in public. I doubt that all members of the legal profession, who have smoked the substance, would be as candid.

"There was also the inference that a law student, who has completed a course in criminal law, has the knowledge to perceive the legal ramifications of any act he engages in or admission he makes. The rudimentary nature of introductory criminal law courses qualifies a person as an interpreter of appellate court decisions in such areas as cruel and unusual punishment and hybrid due process violations. I was not prepared to cope with the challenges to fundamental rights faced by a criminal suspect and defendant. It has been an education. I knew I did not want to be harassed as a suspected possessor end user of a controlled substance but I did not know the precise wording of applicable Utah statutes. Nor did I know that absent a Miranda warning, statements made by a suspect in custody and undergoing interrogation could be admitted against it. Nor was I aware that without probable cause, and a request for a consent search, a thorough search of an automobile could be conducted. Now I feel like I have finished a course in criminal law.

"Judge Hanson, when administering 'jury instructions' to himself, openly assured those present that only testimony and evidence probative to November 8, 1974, would guide his determination in the kidnapping trial. The conclusion, I believe, was that he would ignore the bad man inferences offered by the prosecution based on August 16, 1975. In the final analysis, the only remotely probative fact arising out of August 16, was my possession of handcuffs nine months after a kidnapping in which a different pair of handcuffs was used. The prosecutor's preoccupation with a motor vehicle violation unrelated in time and circumstance to the offense in question belied their desperation and the weakness of their case. Hopefully, the judge was able to dismiss the immaterial allegations associated with August 16, 1975.

"Such are my opinions and observations regarding November 8, 1974, and August 16, 1975. My testimony stands as my definitive statement about these occasions. Additional questions are welcome." Prepared June 8, 1976. /s/ Theodore Bundy.

. . .

JUVENILE AND ADULT CRIMINAL RECORD:

As near as can be ascertained by the records received by the Adult Probation and Parole Section, Theodore has never been arrested as a juvenile. According to the Utah Bureau of Criminal Identification, the United States Federal Bureau of Investigation and the Salt Lake County Sheriff's Office, the subject has the following adult arrests and disposition"

Department Date Charge: Disposition

So. Salt Lake City, Utah 8-16-75 Failure to Stop at the Command of a Police Officer: The defendant was convicted by jury trial. Sentencing set for 6-22-76 before the Honorable Gordon Hall.

So. Salt Lake City, Utah 8-21-75 Possession of Burglary Tools: Pending Defendant convicted of Aggravated Kidnapping by trial on 3-1-76. Subject committed to the custody of the Division of Corrections pursuant to U.C.A. 76-3-404, on 3-22-76, for the purpose of a 90-day Diagnostic Evaluation and Report.

So. Salt Lake City, Utah 10- 2-75 Aggravated Kidnapping and Attempted Criminal Homicide: Disposition Pending.

It should be noted that there is a pending offense which is not represented on the defendant's arrest record, that being the offense of Fraudulent Application for a Duplicate Automobile Title, a Felony of the Third Degree. According to the

County Attorney, Mr. David Yocom, this offense had not yet gone to preliminary hearing.

SOCIAL HISTORY:

General Background Information:

Theodore Robert Bundy was born in Burlington, Vermont, on November 24, 1946. Theodore relates that he was born illegitimately and never knew his natural father. Mr. Donald Hull, the Presentence Investigator, reported that his contacts with Mrs. Louise Bundy, the subject's mother, confirmed that the defendant was born illegitimately as the result of· a relationship between Mrs. Bundy and a young sailor who was stationed in the Burlington, Vermont area in 1946. According to Mr. Hull, records in the State of Vermont indicate that Mrs. Bundy spent approximately sixty-three days in the Elizabeth Lund Home For Unwed Mothers prior to her son's birth. The defendant was actually born Theodore Robert Cowell (the subject's mother's maiden name); it was not until the Spring of 1951 that Theodore's mother married her present husband, Mr. John C. Bundy, and the defendant was henceforth known as Theodore Robert Bundy.

Following the subject's birth, he and his mother resided in Burlington, Vermont, for "several months" when they moved to Philadelphia, Pennsylvania to the home of Mrs. Bundy's parents, Samuel and Elinore Cowell. Theodore relates that his grandparents resided in the rural community of Roxborough, a suburb of Philadelphia and regarded this portion of his life as being very pleasant. The defendant and his mother actually lived in his grandparents' residence for a four-year period of time. For some reason, not clearly understood by this investigator, Mrs. Bundy and the subject moved to Tacoma, Washington, where they resided in the residence of Mr. John R. Cowell, Theodore's maternal uncle, and they remained there less than one year while Mrs. Louise Bundy maintained employment in the secretarial field. The defendant recalls that he and his uncle were very close, and even though they have been unable to maintain a close physical proximity, through the years, the emotional closeness has remained. Mr. John R. Cowell is an accomplished composer and pianist and as a result of his talents had lived in areas outside of the United States, necessarily limiting his contact with the subject.

As previously indicated, the defendant's mother married Mr. John C. Bundy in the Spring of 1951; Theodore was five years of age when his mother married his stepfather. According to the subject, his stepfather is currently employed as a dietitian at the Madigan Army Hospital located on the military reservation at Fort Lewis, Washington. Mr. John C. Bundy has been so employed for as long as the defendant can recall. Theodore confides that he and his stepfather have had a close relationship, as a matter of fact, the subject found it difficult to refer to Mr. John C. Bundy as his stepfather as he has always regarded him as his "real father". It is this agent's understanding that the defendant's name was formally changed to Bundy when Theodore's stepfather adopted him after the marriage in 1951.

The subject indicates that his stepfather, while administering discipline, was more apt to rely upon physical force, and his mother used means other than corporal punishment. The defendant advises that his mother a tendency to intercede during his stepfather's attempts to discipline, however, Theodore states that his mother's interference was the exception rather than the rule. The subject confides that to the best of his knowledge, his mother and father have never been separated; and further, he has never heard them involved in a bitter argument. The defendant describes his parents as having a "stable relationship" and showing affection toward each other as well as their children. Theodore relates that his mother and step-father showed "deep affection" toward him and his brothers and sisters.

In 1952, the subject's mother gave birth to Linda Bundy; Glenn Bundy followed in 1953; Sandra Bundy arrived in 1956 and Richard in 1961. The constellation of the Bundy family then is as follows: John C. Bundy, adoptive father, age fifty-five; Louise Bundy, natural mother, age fifty-one; Theodore Bundy, age twenty-nine; Linda Bundy, sister, age twenty-three; Glenn Bundy, brother, age twenty-two; Sandra Johnson, a married sister, age nineteen; and Richard Bundy, brother, thirteen years of age.

The subject advises that his mother, following her marriage, remained in the home providing care for the children. Presently, Mrs. Louise Bundy is employed at the University of Puget Sound in the Department of Speech and Drama. Mrs. Bundy has been working in this capacity of a secretary for the past three or four years. The defendant stated that although her title was that of secretary, she was "more often than not" regarded as the "administrative assistant".

In a letter dated March 10, 1976, Mrs. Louise Bundy describes Theodore's life as essentially normal lacking any excessively traumatic influences. With regard to the subject's dating habits, Mrs. Bundy states, "I mentioned Ted's many friends, but did not mention girlfriends in particular. I feel that, in this case in particular, his attitude toward women, especially his peers, is important. Ted liked (likes) girls, very naturally. He had an assortment of girlfriends during late junior high and through high school. They surely liked him, because they were always calling· him. He didn't solo date a lot, but was invited to many parties, which he enjoyed. Until he got his driver's license, we performed a lot of taxi service for those events" According to the defendant, he first began dating, group dating, when he was in junior high school. Theodore advises that he discontinued dating throughout high school and when queried about this, the subject was unable to offer an explanation. The fact that the subject didn't date in high school is not necessarily all that unusual; however, what is unusual is his mother's statement that he dated throughout high school, and she was particularly aware of girlfriends who "surely liked him, because they were always calling him". During the period of late adolescence, Ted seemed to prefer a more solitary existence; it is important to note that from information available, there is no indication of abnormal, stressful events which occurred that might offer an explanation for the defendant's involvement in the present offense.

This investigator has spent a considerable amount of time personally interviewing Theodore, asking questions which have been asked and answered many times before. The subject, regardless of the questions asked, always seems to provide the appropriate answer. The defendant is obviously very bright; with his bachelor's degree in psychology, it is suspected that he has a fairly good comprehension of what the various interviewers are attempting to determine, that being any indication of pathology or lack thereof. Frequently, this agent left the interview with a preponderance of notes and "answers" to some very critical questions, however, the feeling tone which was pervasive upon leaving an interview with Theodore was that of not really knowing the subject at all. This feeling has been shared by a number of other individuals involved in the assessment of the defendant both during the 90-day evaluation and the presentence investigation. Theodore's lack of candor relative to various questions asked was best summarized by Dr. Al Carlisle when he stated, "Mr. Bundy is a private person who does not allow himself to become known very intimately by others. When one tries to understand him, he becomes evasive."

The subject remained in his mother and step-father's home until he was approximately nineteen years old. Following the defendant's graduation from high school, he enrolled at the University of Puget Sound and attended during the academic year of 1965 to 1966; Theodore was living at home while attending the University of Puget Sound. In the autumn of 1966, the subject moved to Seattle, Washington, and began attending the University of Washington at Seattle where he actually completed four quarters. The defendant was pursuing a Chinese language curriculum and desired, at that time, to gain a position of authority to improve relationships between the United States and China. Theodore received a grant which allowed him to attend Stanford University for one quarter during the summer. It was during his attendance at Stanford University that he felt he was not measuring up and found that his interest in China became "bit too alien" so he terminated this area of study. The subject returned to the University of Washington and attended his fourth quarter there and discontinued his schooling in January of 1968. The defendant left Seattle, Washington, and began traveling for approximately a one-year period of time. It is this investigator's impression: an impression which is shared by Dr. Carlisle, that it was during this period of time that Theodore was perhaps experiencing some emotional problems and left his schooling and home in an effort to "regroup". The subject traveled to San Francisco, then· to Denver and when he tired of skiing in Colorado, he then went to Philadelphia, Pennsylvania. The defendant left Philadelphia and traveled to see his uncle, Jack Cowell in

Arkansas. In September of 1968, the defendant returned to Seattle, Washington, and obtained employment in a shoe store. Theodore indicates that he was desirous of returning to college, however, he did not want to continue at the University of Washington as he had some bad memories. In January of 1969, the subject traveled to Philadelphia, Pennsylvania and enrolled for one semester at Temple University in Philadelphia majoring in art, science and political science. The defendant left Temple University as he found the environment "crowded, dirty, with no forest". In May of 1969, following Theodore's experience at Temple University, he traveled to San Francisco, California, stayed there for approximately two to three weeks with friends, then he moved to Tacoma, Washington, where he obtained employment in a lumber mill. In September of 1969, the subject "split" and moved to Seattle, Washington, obtained an apartment where he lived for the next five years and re-enrolled in the University of Washington in June of 1970. The defendant subsequently graduated in June of 1972 with a Bachelor of Science Degree in Psychology from the University of Washington.

On September 31, 1969, Theodore, while in a Seattle tavern, met Ms. Elizabeth Kloepfer. This began a very close relationship interspersed with several affairs with other women. Ms. Kloepfer, according to the subject, was raised in the Ogden, Utah, area and moved up to Seattle, Washington, following her divorce in order to remove herself from the effects of a bad marriage and to ostensibly start her own life. Ms. Kloepfer is the daughter of an Ogden physician, Dr. Russell Hirst. The defendant indicated that Elizabeth's parents had withdrawn their support from Ms. Kloepfer and Theodore upon his involvement in the present offense. The subject states-, "Dr. and Mrs. Hirst have been a source of some disappointment in that they have given so little support to Liz since this thing happened to me." At one point, the defendant and Ms. Kloepfer were to be married, and the date was set for Christmas of 1975.

Presently, Elizabeth Kloepfer is employed as a secretary for the University of Washington and is specifically employed by the Medical Instruments Facility where she has maintained this position for approximately seven years. Ms. Kloepfer possesses a degree in Home Economics from Utah State University.

While working on his undergraduate degree, Theodore obtained employment with the Attorneys Messenger and Process Service located in Seattle, Washington. The subject filled the position of file clerk and courier. The defendant maintained this employment until May of 1970 when he states that he was fired as he was absent from work taking care of Ms. Kloepfer's child, Molly Kloepfer. Upon Theodore's return to work the following day, his supervisor advised him that he had a week to find a new job. The subject obtained a part-time position working at the Pedline Supply Company and this position, supplemented with loan which he received, carried him through the remainder of his schooling. The defendant relates that he was well thought of at the Pedline Supply Company and only lost his job when they moved to another part of Seattle, and the distance was too great for Theodore to travel since he did not have adequate transportation.

The subject, after having completed his undergraduate degree, desired to pursue law school and made a number of applications prior to his graduation, however, he was not accepted. The defendant was finally accepted at the University of Puget Sound and began attending Law School at night, however, Theodore, relates that he did not enjoy it. The subject subsequently made application to the University of Utah Law School, was accepted and began attending in September of 1974. According to information received from the University of Utah, College of Law, the defendant, for his first academic year, received B's and C's and was viewed as a student with a slightly above standard grade point average. Theodore's first quarter's attendance was quite sparse; however, it is somewhat difficult to objectively confirm the attendance inasmuch as formal attendance records are not kept on the law students. During his second and third quarter, the subject's attendance appeared to improve and his grade point average was high enough to allow his return for the second year.

This agent's contact with Mr. Bruce Zimmer, Dean of the University of Utah, College of Law, revealed that Mr. Bundy, on his law school admission form, had failed to note that he had attended the University of Puget Sound Law School. Dean Zimmer instructed his Director of Admissions to check with the University of Puget Sound College of Law and attempt to ascertain whether or not the defendant had in fact attended. The Director of Admissions reported back to Dean Zimmer that the University of Puget Sound had no record of Theodore attending their College of Law. Dean Zimmer points out that he cannot assure the accuracy of the statement made by the records clerk at the University of Puget Sound. Further, Dean Zimmer indicated that should Mr. Bundy be placed on probation, his readmission to the University of Utah Law School would not necessarily be ruled out. Where an individual has been convicted of a felony, a review by the faculty for reacceptance would be necessary. ·

In the Fall of 1974, the defendant had developed an interest in the Latter-day Saints Church and was subsequently baptized a member of that organization. Theodore, at that time, was experiencing some disappointment in the way his life had been progressing to that point in time, and indicated that he desired a more disciplined approach, hence his involvement in the LOS Religion. Apparently, those habits which had caused the subject a considerable amount of consternation were continued following his baptism. Dr. Carlisle, in the body of his psychological evaluation, addresses what he feels to be pertinent questions concerning the defendant's character at that point in time.

Employment records of the University of Utah indicate that in June of 1975, Theodore was given a job through the University as a "night manager" in charge of the bailiff hall earning two dollars per hour. The subject terminated this employment at the conclusion of the school year. In July of 1975 to August of 1975, the defendant was employed as a security guard for the University of Utah earning $2.50 an hour. According to the personnel records, Theodore was terminated from this position due to a "budget cut". In September of 1975 to October 4, 1975, the subject was employed by the University of Utah as a part of the custodial staff in plant operations. The defendant was actually hired on September 15, 1975, and the records indicate that his last day of work was October l, 1975. Theodore was terminated from this position while being housed in the Salt Lake County Jail on the present offense.

Comments made by various supervisors describe the subject, while working for the University of Utah, as having a "super attitude," "a willingness to do excellent work in any area". Essentially, the defendant received excellent work ratings from his various superiors.

Essentially, Theodore maintains that he enjoyed a satisfactory childhood and adolescence. The fact that the subject was illegitimate has not caused him any unnecessary strain according to the defendant. The Adult Probation and Parole Section has received letters from Theodore's immediate family all indicating a tremendous amount of support for him. According to the subject, his girlfriend, Elizabeth

Kloepfer, continues to correspond with him and apparently believes in his innocence.

Intellectual Development and School Adjustment:

According to information received by the Adult Probation and Parole Section, the defendant attended the elementary school system in Tacoma, Washington. Theodore then matriculated to Hunt Junior High School in Tacoma and subsequently entered Wilson High School, again located in Tacoma, Washington. The subject apparently has a history of good attendance with fluctuations in the level of performance within the school curriculum. According to Mr. Donald Hull, the defendant was viewed as intelligent and did, on occasion, work at a high caliber level. The consistency of his work was, however, somewhat lacking.

Theodore apparently received above average grades, while attending Wilson High School and subsequently graduated in 1965. While enrolled at Wilson High School, he participated in athletic activities, particularly track and did relatively well in that sport. The subject also tried out for basketball; however, he was found to be too small and as a result, did not make the team.

As previously indicated, following the defendant's graduation from Wilson high school, he attended the University of Puget Sound during the academic year of 1965 to 1966. Theodore had attended several universities off and on and subsequently graduated from the University of Washington in June 1972 with a bachelor of science in psychology.

The subject applied for and was accepted to the University of Utah College of Law during the summer of 1974. The defendant moved to the Salt Lake City area in late August

1974 and began attending law school. Theodore completed one full academic year and was prepared to continue with his second year of training when he was arrested on the present offense.

On June 2, 1976, the results of a thorough psychological evaluation were compiled and submitted by Dr. Al Carlisle, Ph.D., Clinical Psychologist. The results of Carlisle's psychological evaluation are attached to the Diagnostic Study for the Court's review. Additionally, it should be noted that Dr. Van O. Austin, MD, Prison Psychiatrist, also conducted a thorough and complete psychiatric evaluation in which skull x-rays, electroencephalograms, a computerized thermographic brain scan and multiple interviews were utilized. The results of Dr. Austin's psychiatric examination are also attached to the body of this report. ·

RESPONSE TO PRESENT DIAGNOSTIC AND EVALUATION EFFORT:

The subject, since his commitment to the custody of the Division of Corrections on March 22, 1976, has spent the entire study period housed at the Utah State Prison. The Diagnostic Staffing Committee on June 15, 1976, reviewed all pertinent information regarding the defendant, and it was respectfully recommended on that date that Theodore be committed to the Utah State Prison for the indeterminate term as proscribed by law.

The subject's adjustment while housed at the Diagnostic Unit in Medium Security has been satisfactory. To the best of this agent's knowledge, the defendant has not violated any rules or regulations of the institution. Theodore related on one occasion that certain inmates have made derogatory remarks toward him, however, the subject has been able to maintain a positive· attitude and outlook it should be noted that Mr. Bundy was recommended to be moved to the minimum-security facility, however, the prison administration blocked his transfer. This situation has caused the defendant to somewhat strongly suggest that he has not been evaluated fairly. Apparently, Theodore has filed a "petition" with the Court and this matter will be heard on the subject's date of sentencing.

It could be safely stated that the various members of the diagnostic staffing committee feel that Mr. Bundy has been less than candid in revealing certain pertinent items about his personality. This has somewhat frustrated the professionals involved in making an accurate assessment. For example, Dr. Carlisle states: "I feel Mr. Bundy has not allowed me to get to know him, and I believe there are many significant things about him that remain hidden." Dr. Van Austin relates, "I feel that Mr. Bundy is either a man who has no problems or is smart enough and clever enough to appear close to the edge of single of 'normal'. I do not feel that he is a candidate for treatment at this time. Since it has been determined by the Court that he is not telling the truth regarding his present crime, I seriously question if he can be expected to tell the truth regarding participation in any program or probation agreement. It is my feeling that there is much more to his personality structure than either the psychologist or I have been able to determine. However, as long as he compartmentalizes, rationalizes, and debates every facet of his life, I do not feel that I adequately know him, and until I do, I cannot predict his future behavior."

SUMMARY OF POSITIVE AND NEGATIVE INDICATORS

. . .

GAINED FROM THE SOCIAL STUDY:

Positives

1. The defendant has a high intelligence.

2. It would appear from the social history that the defendant was not subject to severely traumatizing influences in his childhood or adolescence.

3. Few or no distortions existed in the subject's relationship with his mother and step-father.

4. From the information available, the developmental history shows no serious defects in physical development, habits, school adjustment, emotional maturation or sexual development.

5. From the available information, the defendant has adequate-? interests, hobbies and recreational pursuits.

6. From the available information, the defendant's habitual environmental pressures and responsibilities are average.

7. From the available information, it would appear that the defendant has had no previous attacks of emotional illness.

8. From the available information, the defendant has never received psychotherapy or counseling in the past.

Negatives

1. The defendant has been convicted of a very serious charge where violence played a major role in the commission of the offense.

2. According to the psychological and psychiatric evaluations, when one attempts to understand Mr. Bundy, he becomes evasive.

3. Outwardly, the defendant appears confident and

reveals himself as a secure person; underneath this veneer are fairly strong feelings of insecurity.

4. The defendant is somewhat threatened by people unless he feels he can structure the outcome of the relationship.

5. A fairly strong conflict was evidenced in the testing profile, that being the subject's fairly strong dependency on women, yet his need to be independent. Mr. Bundy would like a close relationship with females but is fearful of being hurt by them.

6. There were indications of general anger and more particularly, well-masked anger toward women according to the psychological evaluation.

7. The defendant tends to remain emotionally distant from others probably as a defense against being hurt by them.

8. According to the psychological profile, the defendant has difficulty handling stress and has a strong tendency to run from his problems. His use of marijuana and the fact that he has been a heavy drinker at one time are indicators of difficulty in dealing with stress.

9. Passive/aggressive features were also evident. There was hostility observed on the subject part which is directed toward the diagnostic personnel even though Mr. Bundy would carefully point out that it was not aimed directly at those responsible for his evaluation.

10. The defendant has refused to acknowledge his guilt in the present offense. He maintains his innocence, therefore, making it impossible to consider a treatment program as Mr. Bundy indicates he has no problems to treat. In the psychiatric evaluation, Dr. Van Austin states, "the second fact is that he adamantly denies his guilt and in fact, denies that he has any personal problems of a magnitude that could lead to

such a crime. I do not feel that he is a candidate for treatment at this time."

This case involves a 29-year-old, white, male American who has previously been convicted by trial of the offense of Aggravated Kidnapping, a First-Degree Felony, on March 1, 1976.

On March 22, 1976, Theodore was committed to the custody of the Division of Corrections pursuant to Utah Code 76-3-404, for the purpose of a Diagnostic Evaluation and Report.

On June 15, 1976, the Diagnostic Staffing Committee reviewed all pertinent material regarding the subject's case, and it was the recommendation at that time that he be committed to the Utah State Prison for the indeterminate term as proscribed by law. The defendant, since his commitment to the Division of Corrections has remained at the Utah State Prison, housed in the Diagnostic Unit.

The offense for which Mr. Bundy was found guilty involved the abduction of Ms. Carol DaRonch on November 8, 1974, from the Sears parking lot west of the Fashion Place Mall. The subject approached Ms. DaRonch and purported to be a Murray City Police Officer and showed her a badge. Ms. DaRonch entered her abductor's automobile when she was told that her personal appearance was required at the Murray City Police Department in order to sign a complaint against a man who was supposedly trying to break into her automobile. The defendant allegedly transported Ms. DaRonch several blocks from the mall to an area near McMillan School and suddenly stopped his automobile and lunged at the victim. During the course of the struggle, handcuffs were produced and placed on Ms. DaRonch's wrists; she was able to exit the vehicle on the passenger side and her abductor followed after her across the seat At this point, a revolver was produced and her abductor also had a blunt instrument which was identified by the victim as having been or feeling like a crowbar. Ms. DaRonch's abductor made a gesture as to strike her on the head with that instrument. The victim was able to break away from her abductor and· ran down the street a short distance, stopped an automobile belonging to Wilbur and Mary Walch and entered their automobile. Mr. and Mrs. Walch took Ms. DaRonch to the Murray City Police Department where she gave a detailed statement.

With regard to prior arrests, Mr. Bundy does not have a record previous to August 16, 1975. The defendant was charged with the present offense on October 2, 1975. It should be noted that the subject was also charged with Failure to Stop at the Command of a Police Officer, and he was convicted by a jury trial and sentencing has been set for June 22, 1976, before the Honorable Gordon Hall. On August 21, 1975, Mr. Bundy was charged with Possession of Burglary Tools, and it is this investigator's understanding that this -charge has not had a preliminary hearing, therefore, it is still pending.

The defendant was born on November 24, 1946, in Burlington, Vermont. He was the product of an out-of-wedlock relationship between his mother, Mrs. Louise Bundy and a young man she hid met in the Burlington area. The subject and his mother resided for a short period of time in Burlington, Vermont, and then moved to Philadelphia, Pennsylvania, where they lived with Mrs. Bundy's parents. They remained there until Theodore was approximately four and one-half years of age and then moved to Browns Point, a suburb of Tacoma, Washington. In 1951, shortly after having moved to Tacoma, Washington, Mrs. Bundy met her first husband, John Bundy, and they were married. The defendant was formally adopted and his name was changed from Cowell to Bundy at that time. It is of interest to note that the subject was born Theodore Robert Cowell. According to Mr. Don Hull, Theodore's mother had his name legally changed in a Philadelphia Court from Cowell to Nelson on October 6,.1950. This agent discussed the defendant's name change from Cowell to Nelson with Mrs. Bundy. She indicated that at the time they were going to move to Tacoma, Washington, to live with Mr. John Cowell, and "on the advice of her friends" (Mrs. Bundy's), she decided to change the subject's name from Cowell to Nelson as she did not feel it was right to have Theodore going by the name of Cowell while living in his uncle's residence. Mrs. Bundy assured this investigator that she had not married anyone by the last name of Nelson and simply selected the name for the above stated reason

From all reports, the defendant appears to have done well in elementary school, Hunt Junior High School-and Tacoma, Washington, and also Wilson High School in Tacoma, Washington. The subject relates that he began dating sometime during junior high school, however, did not date during high school. Theodore's mother somewhat contradicts this statement when she indicates that the defendant frequently dated during high school.

The subject has the following family constellation: John C. Bundy, an adoptive father, currently age fifty-eight, who resides in Tacoma, Washington with Theodore's mother. He is currently employed as a dietitian for the · Madigan Hospital on the grounds of Fort Lewis, Washington. The defendant's mother is Mrs. Louise Bundy who is age fifty-one. She is employed full-time. as a secretary at the University of Puget Sound. The subject has four younger half-brothers and sisters who are as follows: Linda Bundy, a sister, age twenty-three; Glenn Bundy, a brother, age twenty-two who is in the Navy; Sandra Johnson, a married sister, age nineteen; and Richard Bundy, a brother, age fourteen. From all reports, the family is quite close knit.

Theodore has never married; however, he was engaged to be married to Ms. Elizabeth Kloepfer in December of 1975. Ms. Kloepfer appears to be "sticking by" the defendant and offers a considerable amount of support to him.

The subject does not have a drug abuse history, however, admits to the use of marijuana. With regard to alcohol abuse, Theodore relates that he has discontinued his drinking as it "made me sick". The defendant was raised as a Methodist but was baptized a Latter Day Saint in August of 1975. The subject did go on outings with the LDS members and attended some meetings but reportedly had a Word of Wisdom difficulty in that he did continue to smoke and drink alcoholic beverages.

Respectfully submitted,
DGM: dm

Part II: Additional Utah Information

Additional information on Ted Bundy gathered before, during, and after the 1976 assessment.

SIX

Dan Clark Interview

Dan Clark Interview
March 23, 2017

(Extraacted from "The 1976 Psychological Assessment of Ted Bundy" by Al Carlisle.)

Dan Clark was a police officer who was put in charge of searching for one of Ted Bundy's victims. The following are excerpts from an interview I had with him:

Dan: When I was working with the BYU [Brigham Young University] Police Department. A little gal came up missing who was there for a youth conference. The LDS Church sponsors these kids to come to BYU and they have a three to four day visit at the university, and they get involved with games and activities to help these kids grow, and then they have a dance, either Friday or Saturday depending on the schedule, but they have a formal dance and one of the little gals came up missing on Friday. She changed clothes and got ready and walked towards the dance on her own and she never arrived. She was wearing a long yellow formal and never showed up. I got the call when I was the investigator on duty, and we started looking for her.

We interviewed the kids that were there with her, her friends and associates from the group that had walked some distance with her, and nobody had any clue on where she had gone. In those first few hours, there was not a lot to go on. We didn't have pictures; we didn't have anything. The parents made contact with us the next day. I am a little ahead of myself… The friends had notified the parents and on Saturday morning, I got the call and we started looking for her.

We made contact with the bus stations and nobody had seen her there. We started looking around the foothills thinking that maybe she just wandered off. The parents indicated that they had some trouble with her earlier on but thought that everything had been resolved, so they didn't think that she just wandered off. We had no idea about Ted Bundy at the time.

Al: What was the date?

Dan: Oh gosh, I can't remember the dates now. I wouldn't even offer to guess. It has been 30 years, but Bundy had yet to be identified for anything. He was currently a student at the University of Utah Law School and this was before he picked up the one gal that escaped from him.

Al: Carol DaRonch.

• • •

Dan: Yeah, in Salt Lake. She was working at the Cottonwood Mall. He picked her up and she escaped. She got a really good description of his Volkswagen and maybe a plate number. I think it was Salt Lake PD that picked him up and served a search warrant. They found hair and he was sequentially charged. But that happened after this little gal, I guess we can use her name, Sue Curtis, had disappeared. So somewhere between the time that he was in law school and when he finally got arrested in Salt Lake is when Sue disappeared. I apologize that I don't have the dates. If you need them, I can dig them up.

Al: Was it spring or summer?

Dan: This would have been during the summer. That is when most of these youth conferences are. I think at the time Sue was a high school sophomore or junior from the Bountiful or Woods Cross area. She just vanished. We didn't have a clue what had happened to her. This went on for several years. That first year, the parents went to the University of Utah and listened to a lecture by a psychic. They hired him and also hired a private investigator.

The psychic told them that from what he could see she had been picked up by someone that she thought she knew and she was taken up a canyon with red rocks, past an old railroad trestle, and had been dumped. That was all he had given them. So, the parents called me and gave me that information and we started looking up the various canyons around Provo.

When you go far enough up Spanish Fork Canyon, there are some red rock cliffs up there and an old railroad trestle. So, we started searching. But it had been a couple of years and we thought that because of the deer hunters in the area, that if she had been dumped up in that canyon, she would have been found. The likelihood of her body being discovered the first couple of years is pretty good, so that trail went cold.

We had, over the course of the investigation, gotten pictures and distributed them. We got dental records in case we found something, and every time a female body was found, the medical examiner would pull up her dental records and see if it was her. An interesting thing about her, about Sue, when you look at Bundy's victims, their physical description, these girls could be sisters. Of the 30 or so pictures [of women] that they suspect that he was responsible for killing, long straight brown hair, parted in the middle, same facial characteristics, same height, same body build, he had a type that he was attracted to. You have seen the pictures and Sue Curtis's would fit right in the middle of them and there would be no question. During the time that this was going on he was driving his little VW bug and had been around this area. One of his victims was the Kent girl.

Al: Debbie Kent. From Bountiful. He got her out of a high school theater where they were having a play.

Dan: Her body has never been found, has it? Above Manti… no, Fairview…they found part of a body up there, years after, and they had an arm but it disappeared. They had it for years and never had DNA tested. Nobody knew about DNA back then. By the time they thought that he may have been involved with her the evidence had been lost.

So, your buddy Wally Barrus and Jim from BYU that flew these model aircraft with cameras in them would go out and film areas in the morning or late afternoon with the sun coming in at an oblique angle and look for places that had been disturbed, and so Jim went down and flew this area about Fairview where they thought that they had found this body, and there were a couple of sites that they went back in and excavated but they couldn't find anything. So, we thought about using Wally, but by the time we had an idea about Bundy or where we thought this gal might be, this body, or the parts of a body, were found above Fairview, and we didn't know if they were Sue C or Debbie Kent's remains. We just didn't know.

That petered out. Basically, it just dried up. It went totally cold until Bundy got bagged up in Florida for beating that girl with the piece of a tree branch, killing her in her sorority room. Those killings and those victims looked just like Sue. Over the course of these years, when we found out about Bundy, I started looking at the pictures of his victims from up in Washington/Oregon areas, where they figured he killed 20 or 30, and I went to my boss. I had those pictures, and I put Sue Curtis's photo in there. I said, is there any question in your mind where she went? Who got her? And he kind of poopooed the idea, but I figured that Bundy had taken her. But here he is in Florida; he has finally been arrested after he escaped from Colorado.

Al: He was in prison in Utah and we gave him up to Colorado because they were doing an investigation and he escaped.

Dan: Jumped out the courtroom window.

• • •

Al: Yes, jumped out the courtroom window, and he got caught and came back and he was there. He called me and we had about a 15-minute telephone conversation.

Dan: You interviewed him at the state prison?

Al: I did the psych evaluation on him. Then he escaped the second time and went up Northeast and then down to Florida.

Dan: When all of these pictures started coming in and we figured out he was in the area, we thought why not? We thought that he would be good for it. I wanted to go to Florida and interview him. I had a boss that was all about pinching pennies and wouldn't let me go. He said, "I bet he is from Salt Lake County. My buddies will do that one." Nobody went down to interview him.

So, the clock is running on his execution, the stays are exhausted and a Salt Lake County Deputy went down and interviewed him at length, at least several hours, to talk about Debbie Kent and these other gals, but I am not sure what they found out. My boss would not let me go down and I will always hold it against him because the family needs some closure. They had her declared legally dead and had a memorial service and everything else.

Over the course of all these years the family moved from Bountiful and they ended up in a little town called Wellington out by Price. Mr. Curtis was running a sporting goods store out there, and they lived on a hill outside of Wellington in a nice neighborhood and it had a view to the south and to the west and even to the east for miles out on the highway. We maintained contact over the years and any time anything would happen I would call them or they would call me. Good people, just solid people.

So here comes Bundy's execution and in the elevator going to the execution chamber the assistant warden asked him if there is anybody else. He had already talked to the Salt Lake County detective for a couple of hours, but he didn't care about our case, he cared about his own.

I wanted to go down there, even make a phone call, if I had been allowed to call him on the phone and ask him about our case, because Bundy freely gave it up in the elevator. Bundy said to the assistant warden, "Yes there was a little gal that I picked up from BYU on campus."

"And where is her body?"

And he said, "I drove out towards Price." He actually told him a little more than that but that was all that was legally given to the press.

This was big news. Bundy was a big deal in Utah, and so when this happened the media in Salt Lake said Bundy confessed to picking up this little gal from BYU and so it was that day, the same day, the phone starts ringing off the hook at the department and the TV channels, Channel 5 and Channel 2 and Channel 4, they all wanted interviews because Bundy had confessed to taking this gal and they heard it the same time we heard it. Big news flash on the TV.

So, they came down and interviewed me at the police department, and they said, "What are you going to do?" and I said, "Well, based on what he said and based on what his statements were, we have an idea of where he may have taken her and we are going to go out tomorrow and initiate a search. I made contact with the Carbon County Sheriff and he lined up his sheriff's posse and search and rescue and we will be out there in the morning."

So that morning, some detectives and I head out to Price and we meet the Sheriff. The Sheriff is not in a position to go out there so I said, "Let me take over, sheriff. Look, here is the deal. This is what we are looking for: Bundy said he went through town, within five or six miles of town, and he dumped her. That is all we got. I would have thought by now that a rabbit hunter or deer hunter or somebody would have found the body, so I am not too hopeful, but the media is here and they want to show us searching out through the boonies, so that is what we are going to do."

So, we load up the cars, we get the maps out, and we decide where we are going to go. It isn't where I wanted to go. It isn't where Bundy told us where he dumped her. I didn't want them out there stomping around and destroying evidence. So, we go somewhere else that is a noxious place out in the sagebrush, because those things typically become a circus.

You got these deputies and civilians roaming around. We go out in the sagebrush and we divide up into a grid and they start walking and they got metal detectors, and they are finding all sorts of bullets from rabbit hunters and plinkers. They march off on these grids and they are back and forth, back and forth, and I am standing there with the detective that I took and we were just kind of grinning because we know that it is not the place we want to look.

All of a sudden off in the distance from the northeast, a helicopter came flying straight at us and he sits down. There was about six inches of snow on the ground when we were out there in the sagebrush. It was a beautiful day, clear blue sky, and this helicopter sits down and out climbs a camera guy with his tripod and his monster video camera and a CBS reporter from San Francisco that had flown into Denver and chartered a helicopter that cost CBS some money.

So, they split up and interview me standing out there in the sagebrush and I end up on the CBS Evening News with

Dan Rather. This clip plays every now and again on some cable show about Bundy. It is still out there.

So, all of that hoopla goes away and the KSL guy, who was a nice guy, was still there. He had been there the whole time and he had seen the interaction with the other detective, and he looked at me and he said, "This is nowhere near where Bundy told you that he dumped her, is it?"

I said, "No it is not."

And he said, "When you go search that area if you find anything would you call me and give us an exclusive?"

And I said, "Yes, and I appreciate you keeping this under your hat." He was a smart guy.

When that is all over with, we bundle up our car, we go back, and I get maps out. Some of the other investigators, maybe from the Northwest, said Bundy had a habit of driving and making a left turn and another left turn. I don't know where that came from but this was kind of his MO as he would dump his bodies. He didn't bury them, he just covered them up a little bit with whatever he could find; and so, based on his comments and based on the maps and the road layout, we had a pretty good idea of where he would go.

He said that he drove out of town 10 miles, made a left on a road, and then made another quick left out in this open area. Well, the best spot we could find was kind of a place where people dump stuff, a local dump site, and what better spot to put a body because people are going to go out there and smell something. They would also dump their dead dog or cat or cow or whatever. Think about it, it was the perfect place for him to dispose of the body.

Remember she is wearing a long yellow formal dress, so we are thinking a 20-inch zipper on the back of this dress may have survived, and she had a full set of dental appliances. So, we are hoping that maybe the skull or jaw may be found, and we have the metal detector and we are digging and digging, and I find a chuck of zipper with some fabric and sent it up to the crime lab but they couldn't distinguish it, because it was so bleached out that they had no idea of the color, and we couldn't find hide nor hair of the skull.

There were all kinds of critters out there that made nests, and coyotes are out there, so who knows? We spent three days out there on our hands and knees, digging through this stuff.

This was probably a week later; it had warmed up and the snow was gone. So, we are pretty much at the end of our rope. And I am standing there…

Let me back up. When the media frenzy was over and they had bugged me and they wanted to know where the mom and dad were living, I wouldn't tell them. I didn't give them phone numbers, I didn't give them anything, because they had moved several times from Bountiful. After that media frenzy day, I called them and they had heard it on the media, on the news, and I said that I was not going to give them their names and numbers, if you want to call them, you can call them, but I am not going to.

We had an idea of where we were going to search. It's out here, and the wife said something very interesting, she said, "You know, when we moved out here four or five years ago, I just had this feeling that she was close."

So, after that second day or third day crawling on our hands and knees, I am standing there, it is done, we have finished, and I am looking back over towards Wellington, and I can almost see the family home where the parents were living. It was really kind of eerie because mom and dad had this feeling that she was close, and I think she was, based on what Bundy had said, how far he said that he drove. If I had been back there, I would have a set of maps and he would have pinpointed the area. So, it was really kind of interesting.

And even after that, any time a body was found I would

perk up if I heard female body, human remains anywhere up that direction. I would perk up and wonder, but with decomposition out in the area and the critters, I don't think a body would last very long.

After I left the department, one of my detectives would pull that case file out every couple of years and make a phone call to the mom and dad and say that the file is still here, we haven't forgotten about it, and that we keep looking.

SEVEN

Phone Call from Colorado

(Extracted from "The 1976 Psychological Assessment of Ted Bundy" by Al Carlisle.)

On October 3, 1977, a colleague of mine, Dr. Allan Roe, and I went into Salt Lake City for lunch. When we got back to the prison there was a message waiting for me to call an operator in Salt Lake. I called her back and she said Ted Bundy had called from Colorado and he wanted me to return his call. He had escaped from jail and had been caught. Now he was back in jail and he was calling *me*?

I was intrigued as to why this serial killer would want to talk to me. During the call, I learned that he had called twice previously but had been unable to get in touch with me. He wanted to make sure we connected this time. I had not talked with Ted since my session with him just before he went to Colorado. What was so important to make three attempts to get hold of me?

I called the operator in Salt Lake who connected me with

the jail in Colorado and then the connection went to Ted's cell. He had his own credit card to pay for the call.

Ted asked how I was doing. I answered,

I'm doing all right, Ted. How are you doing?

Well, I'm hanging in there. I just got the bug last week and just wanted to chat with you briefly because obviously I've been away for a long time.

How are things going for you over there?

Well, quite well, frankly, I was just talking to someone the other day and the experience of coming over here is one of those, you know, good things, bad things experiences. If I hadn't come over here, I probably wouldn't be looking at a new trial in the Carol DaRonch case and a number of things have opened up and I suppose that if I had to spend several years behind bars, I might as well spend a little here, a little there. (laughs)

Ted was in Colorado because he was being investigated for a homicide, which was bad for him. On the other hand, he was saying that had he not come to Colorado he wouldn't have obtained information that might allow him to have a new trial on the DaRonch case, which was good as he saw it. As with previous conversations I had had with him he was attempting to tell me he wasn't guilty of that crime. He sounded optimistic. Why was it so important for him to bring up the DaRonch case?

Are they treating you pretty good?

Well, yeah, sure they are. They've developed this paranoia about me. They have this unrealistic fear that I'm going to escape or something.

In essence, he was saying: It's silly that they would believe that I might be thinking about escaping again. These guys are paranoid. They are overreacting.

I can't imagine where they're getting that from. (both laugh)

Yeah, exactly (laughs). Al, I just wanted to call you up, mainly…there are a lot of things that've been happening. My escape venture, which has caused a great furor of activity around here and I guess some complicity over there, and now we're looking at what looks like a 95% chance of a new trial in the Carol DaRonch case. And this case over here gets curiouser and curiouser because they've added a couple of additional Utah transactions, alleged transactions, in an attempt to gain a conviction in the Colorado case.

I don't know... I've been so overwhelmed by work recently, that uh… You know, there's just a lot to do. You know, way back when, I guess it was back in April, when I decided to represent myself in this case, I could just… (laughs) I was thinking to myself, I could hear Al Carlisle saying, "Yeah, I knew you'd try something like that." (laughs)

Yeah, I assumed you would. (laughs)

Why did he bring this up? He almost told me why he called, but before he could say just what it was, he mentioned the Carol DaRonch case again and reiterated that it was almost certain that he would get a new trial. Was he really trying to convince me he was innocent? If so, why was this so important? He had been telling everyone that he had never hurt anyone, and many people seemed convinced that he could not have committed the DaRonch crime. I, on the other hand, had submitted a report to the court saying I thought he was violent. Was he trying to say I was wrong? Perhaps.

I remember one time you commented… I can't remember if it was something… I think it was something I read in one your reports, quite frankly. Ah, how did you say it? That I can't delegate responsibility or something to that effect, I don't know. I don't think that's exactly the way you put it, but something more or less that I like to do things myself and I have a hard time entrusting things to others.

Uh huh.

I was wondering, I know you are really at arm's length on this thing and we haven't really talked personally obviously since the latter part of January. But I've been wondering if you've had any impression about all that you've been hearing about me and ah… and ah…

How do you mean?

Well, like the escape and everything. I wonder what your impression of that was, again just from a party who knows me but didn't have an opportunity to speak to me after that happened.

The call reminded me of a boy who called his father wanting to know what he thought of the ball game on TV the night before. Did he want my approval, or forgiveness? Did he want to know if I was angry at him? I was puzzled about what he wanted from me. I decided that rather than answering the question I would take this opportunity to learn more about why he escaped. He was caught attempting to make a false ID when he was in prison so it wasn't surprising that he jumped at the opportunity to escape from jail in Colorado.

I had mixed impressions. I was wondering if you were really getting uptight and the pressure looked like it was on. I was wondering if it was getting to look like, in your mind, you were going to be convicted, so when the opportunity was there you just took it. In your own mind, what was happening?

You know, I'd given it a great deal of thought. I'd been moved from Aspen… I'd been in the Pitkin County Jail, which is in Aspen, from January 31st until April the 11th, which is 73 days. I have all this memorized. In Aspen, it was an open affair. It's seven cells and all the doors are open all the time. The place had been built in 1887. Here was where I could come out and relate and talk to other prisoners going in their cell. Something like the State Prison [in Utah], not like Max [Maximum Security Facility in Utah]. And then they moved me down here—this is part of the escape because I was a security risk. They put me in a six by twelve by eight-foot-high cell and ordered no one to speak to me. Quite frankly, that's why I decided to represent myself. Concrete, solid steel doors with [a] small window. This is worse than the hole. Honest Al, this was worse than the hole in Max, because there you could at least talk to people and see people. This [tension] was building up and building up and building up, and over the months I'd noticed a number of opportunities to just walk right out, walk right out of the court house, but I didn't know how to put it all together. I was very concerned about what people would think. People say, weren't you afraid that somebody would shoot you or something?

No, it was one of the lower fears in my hierarchy of fears.

But I don't know, that day I came there and I thought a great deal about escape and I didn't know if I had the guts to do it, quite frankly. The guard went outside for a smoke and there was not one person in the whole courtroom. You'd have to see the courthouse in Aspen to understand. The windows were open and the fresh air was blowing through and the sky was blue and I said, I'm ready to go, and I walked to the window and I jumped out. (laughs) And I started chugging.

I had no plan. I had nobody helping me. I had no money and no nothing. I just ran right up into the mountains.

But anyway, you know when I was recaptured and they brought me back in, I spoke very freely about my adventures during those six days. It was something I couldn't deny. But one of the investigators working on my case came into the room after I had been there some time and said, Well, would you like to talk about the Campbell case? Would you like to tell me all about it now, Ted? Would you like to confess and all this stuff? I could see the twinkle in his eye. He thought that I had panicked and the gig was up and I was ready to bust open. And I told him, Mike, listen, I just went out the window because I wanted to be free.

It wasn't a fear of conviction because I believed then and I believe more firmly now that I'll be acquitted. And not only that I'll get a new trial on DaRonch. The irony of it all, Al, is that probably the only solid conviction they will have on me will be the escape. Honest to God, I just got sick and tired of being locked up.

I kept saying to myself, Ted, in the event that you're acquitted here in Colorado and you go back to Utah and let's say you got a new trial on DaRonch, which I estimate would take three years, because even if we won at the trial court level with a new trial the state would appeal, and unless the Supreme Court overturns we'll have to go to Federal Court. The Federal Court takes years and years, and even if I got a new trial on DaRonch three years from now there's a chance I could be convicted just basically on just the publicity of the whole thing. I mean I'm pretty notorious. And if I was acquitted three or four years from now on the DaRonch case, what would I have left?

Maybe unrealistically, but I asked myself could you go to law school? Could you go back to Liz? Would your friends be able to look you in the eye? Could you be Ted Bundy again? I figured, whether you're free tomorrow or you're free four years from now you're still going to have to make an entirely new life and really hide from the old life, whether legitimately or illegitimately. So those are the priorities.

Is it possible that he was telling me that he would make another attempt to escape if he got the chance? Ted was a very perceptive person and likely memorized everything he could about the jail he was in, including the routines of the staff. His ploy was to be friends with everyone so they would begin to trust him. Then he would strike. This was the same approach he used with his victims. Ted continued,

I wasn't up against a wall. Maybe it was something I could have done then, something I could wait to do but I was honestly just fed way up above my chin with being locked up. And, it was just one of those things. I still have the scars and blisters on my feet. I'm sitting here barefooted… (laughs) Running around in the mountains.

It was an extraordinary experience because I thought I was… I'm a pretty strong-willed person. But, believe it or not, it was the body that was strong but the mind that was weak. The morning after…. Well, I ran up, you know, like 4,000 feet of very steep hill. Actually, Aspen mountain, and over the other side. They didn't know where in the world I was, and I was feeling really good that evening, and I started hiking up; and if I could have kept hiking I would have been long gone. But a very cold, sleet rainstorm hit me. I got very cold and I went into a state of shock. And I managed to find my way back to the cabin. There was no way to get into it and here I was shivering and hungry and cold and it was raining and blowing. And early the next morning, about 7:00 in the morning, I was just sitting there seriously considering giving myself up. It was just a complete mind blow for me to have longed for freedom for so long and now, like I was living my ultimate dream. All of a sudden, I was willing to throw it away because I was cold and hungry.

I got in the cabin and recuperated, believe it or not, and had a second chance at it. And then I made a wrong turn and then I hurt my knee. Three or four days of high altitude and cold got to me and again my mind got weak. That night I walked back into Aspen. No one knew me. People saw me, no one could recognize me. I was totally disoriented. It's something I've never known before. I just laid down like an animal ready to die. It was just an incredible experience. I was disoriented and quite frankly I foolishly just hopped in a car and drove. I knew I would get caught. I mean, I didn't want to get caught but I knew it would happen. I was just so tired and I said, well, let's see what will happen. It was a fluke, actually. They stopped me. When I got captured, I just stood there. Anyway, that was one of the more profound experiences of being over here. It certainly did cause a furor.

Ted and I talked for a couple more minutes. I asked him about my coming out to Colorado and talking more about this and other aspects of his history. Ted was amenable to this, but before I could get over there, he escaped again.

The impression I got from that call was that Ted was lonely and he had a need to talk. In my work at the prison, I had a number of guys who seemed to have a need to talk, and often it was about their crimes. They seemed to want someone to understand them. If they were only trying to convince me that they were not guilty I wouldn't have continued talking to them. But it was interesting to me that so many hardened criminals would open up and talk about very personal events in their lives, including violent crimes they had committed that they had never been arrested for.

I learned that psychopaths could seem to feel regret for their crimes.

EIGHT

Anonymous Letter To Ted

Oct. 26th "76"

Dear "Ted",

You don't know me, but I'm one of the few thousands that have been reading up on you in the papers as well as a few different magazines & I should say you are a very interesting person to read about.

First of all, I would like to say you are a very nice looking and attractive man & from what I understand, quite intelligent! I know me for one, wouldn't have turned you down for a date if I was ever asked, but you see, anymore you cannot trust anybody.

This is not all I have to say. I can't understand why you had to force girls to go places with you, because it seems with your background & all, you didn't have to!! I'm sure a few of them would have gone with you willingly.

Actually the reason I am writing is because me and a lot of people, as well as (mothers & fathers) would like to learn a lot more about you, etc. etc. Like I say, you would be more interesting to read about if you would only talk a little bit more & admit a few wrong things that you have apparently done. Things couldn't go any worse for you than they already are.

(no signature)

cc: Al Carlisle
Van Austin
John O'Connell

Judge Hanson, Jr.
Don Morgan

June 7, 1976
Monday

Theodore Bundy

Willy Diddens
Ninety-Day Program
Diagnostic Unit
Utah State Prison

Dear Mr. Diddens:

I understand that my staffing is to take place tomorrow, Tuesday, June 8, 1976. There will be persons on the committee, which is to make a recommendation in my case, with whom I have not spoken or met. There are also those on the committee who know me only by way of brief introduction. I believe these people must have an opportunity to see me and hear me speak briefly about my case and myself. I am requesting that I be allowed to make a brief five minute address to the Diagnostic Committee and cover:

1. my case (and the nature of the crime)
2. my background
3. and my future.

Just five minutes. I hope you will approve this request. Please take this matter up with the committee.

Respectfully, Theodore Bundy

Willy Diddens
Tom Stroud
May 12, 1976
Page 2

I wrote Mr. Don Morgan of Adult Probation and Parole, requesting a meeting with him. There has been no response whatsoever to that letter.

I do not believe that the apparent bias displayed toward me has had its origins within the Diagnostic Unit itself. Publicity, official and political pressures, and personal prejudices are as much to blame for this situation as anything. Whatever the cause, I think you should know that I am skeptical of the Diagnostic Staff's ability to develop a sound, well-reasoned recommendation in my case.

Respectfully,

TB

Theodore Bundy

cc: Sam Smith
Leon Hatch
Dr. Al Carlisle ✓
Dr. Van Austin
John D. O'Connell
Don Morgan
Judge Hanson, Jr.

P.S. I have recently discovered that Deputy Warden Bell has also opposed my move to the farm. The entire burden, it seems, does not rest with Leon Hatch. I would like to know just <u>who</u> is responsible.

Sorry about the other day. We must get together again soon.

Part III: The Assessments

NINE

Dr. Van Austin Assessment

STATE OF UTAH - DEPARTMENT OF SOCIAL SERVICES

CALVIN L. RAMPTON
Governor

PAUL S. ROSE
Executive Director

DIVISION OF CORRECTIONS
UTAH STATE PRISON
PO Box 250
Draper, UT 84020

BOARD OF CORRECTIONS
7 June 1976

. . .

Honorable Stewart M. Hanson, Jr, Judge Third District Court

240 East 400 South
Salt Lake City, Utah

Dear Judge Hanson:

RE:BUNDY, Theodore R. Case #28629

I have completed my evaluation of Mr. Bundy whom you committed to the Division of Corrections for a ninety-day presentence evaluation. My evaluation has consisted of multiple interviews, skull x-rays, electroencephalograms, a computerized thermographic brain scan, review of collateral information, review of current psychological test data, and discussions of the case with Drs. Howell and Carlisle. This report is only intended to assist the court during the sentencing process.

The skull x-ray showed a small osteoma of the left frontal sinus. Otherwise, the skull x-rays, electroencephalograms, and brain scan were completely unremarkable. Because of these negative findings and an unremarkable medical history, I did not feel that further testing and neurological evaluation were indicated.

I do not feel that Mr. Bundy is psychotic. There is no evidence of a major thinking, mood; or behavior disorder at this time. Although his mood is dominated by some ambivalence, a somewhat flat emotional responsiveness and lack of empathy for others, I do not feel they are present to the degree seen in a psychosis. His thought processes show good contact with reality, good concept formation, and no evidence of delusions or hallucinations. If he had been psychotic in the past, I would expect to see certain personality features at this time which are not present.

I can find no evidence of organic brain disease (problems associated with impairment of brain tissue function). He is fully oriented and has excellent recent and past memory. There is no evidence of impairment of any of his intellectual functions, impairment of his ability to use good judgement or impairment of his ability to show appropriate affect.

There is no evidence of a neurotic disorder. He displays none of the anxiety or subjective discomfort seen in this diagnostic category. It is possible to propose that the current crime was product or a hysterical neurosis of the dissociative type.

This is not consistent with my current observations of his personality or psychological test data. A second neurotic condition which must be considered is an obsessive-compulsive neurosis.

This disorder is characterized by persistent intrusion of unwanted thoughts, urges, and/or actions which the individual is unable to stop without developing considerable anxiety. I can only find minimal support for this diagnosis during my interviews and in the psychological test data.

A fourth diagnostic category which must be considered is the personality disorders (character disorders). These disorders are characterized by deeply ingrained, life-long, maladaptive behavior patterns. There is considerable evidence of past successful adaptive behavior in Mr. Bundy. He does have some features of the antisocial personality such as lack of guilt feelings, callousness, and a very pronounced tendency to compartmentalize and methodically rationalize his behavior. I feel that he has also used this compartmentalization and rationalization in a passive and obstructive manner during my interviews. It is my impression that this is due to the deep-seated hostility which is evident on the psychological tests. At times he has lived a lonely, somewhat withdrawn, seclusive existence which is consistent with, but not diagnostic of, a schizoid personality.

I have reviewed his pattern of alcohol and drug abuse and do not feel that these are dominant features in his personality.

I have been unable to find data to support a diagnosis of sexual deviation.

His denial of memory for the crime is not consistent with amnesia due to a hysterical reaction, alcohol or drug intoxication, or temporal lobe epilepsy. This amnesia seems too circumscriptive and convenient to be real.

At this point, diagnostically I can only conclude that Mr. Bundy has no mental illness, but does have a personality structure which is dominated by passive aggressive features.

The question of treatment and disposition in this case poses some serious problems. The first consideration is that he has been found guilty. The second fact is that he adamantly denies his guilt and in fact denies that he has any personal problems of a magnitude that could lead to such a crime. I do not feel that he is candidate for treatment at this time

In conclusion, I feel that Mr. Bundy is either a man who has no problems or is smart enough and clever enough to appear close to the edge of "normal." I do not feel that he is a candidate for treatment at this time. Since it has been determined by the court. that he is not telling the truth regarding his present crime, I seriously question if he can be expected to tell the truth regarding participation in any program or probation agreement.

It is my feeling that there is much more to his personality structure than either the psychologist or I have been able to determine. However, as long as he compartmentalizes, rationalizes, and debates every facet of his life, I do not feel that I adequately know him, and until I do, I cannot predict his future behavior.

Sincerely,

Van Austin, M. D., Prison Psychiatrist
cc: Diagnostic Unit

TEN

Dr. Robert Howell Assessment

PSYCHOLOGICAL EVALUATION

NAME: BUNDY, Theodore
USP: 0522
DATE OF BIRTH: November 24, 1946
AGE: 29 – '75
DATE OF ASSESSMENT: March 25, & April 1, 1976
REFERRAL SOURCE: 90-Day Evaluation

ASSESSMENT PROCEDURES

INTELLECTUAL ASSESSMENT

PERSONALITY ASSESSMENT

. . .

Mr. Theodore Bundy is a 29-year-old single Caucasian male who is 5' 11 1/2" tall, weighs 170 pounds and has dark brown hair and blue eyes. He is here at the Diagnostic Unit for a 90-day evaluation prior to his sentencing after having been found guilty of kidnapping.

Mr. Bundy comes from Tacoma, Washington. His family consists of a step-father who is now 55 years of age and is a dietitian and cook at a hospital. His mother, age 48, is a secretary at the University of Puget Sound. His mother became pregnant with him prior to marriage and reared him until he was about 4 ½ years of age when she married. He has ½-sister D Linda who is 22 years of age and a housewife. She and her husband have two children. He has a younger brother Glenn who is 21 and is in the Navy. He has a younger sister, Sandra, 19 years of age, who is married and is currently expecting a baby and finally ½-brother Richard who is 13 years of age, just in junior high school.

He describes his family as being a busy family, but a family that did many things together. He said that when he was young, they were very much a home-oriented family and a church-oriented family. He was reared as a Methodist and though he lost interest in the Methodist church, his parents are very active today. His parents neither smoke nor drink. Mr. Bundy described himself as a very religious individual until he became a teenager and then he felt dissatisfaction and divorced himself from it until about 1974 he indicated he is now a priest in the Mormon church.

Mr. Bundy indicates that with his facing the charges that he has and the trial that he has gone through, that his family has become much closer and he has felt a good deal of support from his family. In reflecting upon his early life, he made a point of saying that he felt very close to his youngest brother Richard. However, when I commented that he omitted his other half brothers and sisters, Linda, Glen and

Sandra, he said that he was always the disciplinarian in the family being some years older than the rest and it wasn't until recent years that he felt closer to Linda, Glen and Sandra.

Mr. Bundy attended school in the Tacoma area and after graduating from high school, he first went to the University in the area near his home. Then he went to the University of Washington and Seattle and it was from here that he graduated with his bachelor's degree. He was accepted for law school at the University of Utah and started law school in the fall of 1974. He said that he found the law school very challenging for him and that he had to study much harder than he had done previously

Mr. Bundy describes his drinking habits as having a beer with his meals and drinking beer with the law students quite frequently. He said he would get "rip-roaring drunk" about once every two months but he said this has become less over the years because marijuana has become a substitute for the alcohol. He described marijuana as a social thing and indicated that he has never used other drugs such as speed, LSD, cocaine. He indicated that he has taken marijuana about three times a month but after he joined the Mormon Church, that he reduced the amount of marijuana use, how ever, he said that he did not quit his alcohol or drug use after joining the church. He said he would have a beer or a joint of marijuana about once or twice a month after joining the church.

THEODORE BUNDY, #0522

Mr. Bundy described his interest in girls is dating back to the sixth grade. He said that in high school he started dating them and said that his first heterosexual experience was in

1968 when he was in his early 20s. He said that he was drunk at this time and that he was working on a political campaign and he became involved with a woman at whose house he stopped because he was so inebriated. He said after this he would have intercourse about once every six months until he met a girl named Ms. in 1969. He said he became very close to her and has maintained this close relationship with her. He indicated that at times "we were on opposite cycles. When she wanted to get married, I didn't want to, and when I wanted to, she was out of the mood."

While Mr. Bundy was in Salt Lake, she maintained a close telephone relationship with him about three times a week, but became annoyed with him because he was getting himself involved with other girls in Salt Lake City. He said he would tell her about going out with this girl or that girl and also tell her about having affairs with them. He talked about meeting a schoolteacher here in Salt Lake and that he had an affair with her in July and August 1974.

Mr. Bundy indicated that he pretty much put himself through the University of Washing ton with summer jobs, part-time work and loans. As is known, Mr. Bundy has been found guilty of kidnapping Carol DaRonch. He indicated that this event was supposed to have taken place on November 8, 1974. He told me that he was actually arrested on October 2 of 1975. Mr. Bundy denies any knowledge of this crime. Reference is made to the police report and presentence investigation in terms of the crime.

Regarding the behavior during this interview, I was impressed with Mr. Bundy's extreme guardedness throughout the interview. He picked his words very carefully. He was defensive, evasive, and noncommittal. I was impressed with the incongruity between his joining the LDS church in August 1975 and yet indicating that he maintains his smoking, his drinking, his using marijuana and his sexual activities at the same time. When I pointed this seeming incongruity out to him, he agreed that it did seem a bit unusual, however, he told me that things like the word of wisdom were not the important things in the Mormon church and so he did not feel as though he was being inconsistent.

I felt like there was a good deal availed hostility expressed toward me. He would carefully point out that he was not referring to be directly, however, he had to see many psychologists and other mental health people and did not feel like there was anything he could gain from them and felt as though the evaluations would be of little value. This passive-aggressive characteristic of Mr. Bundy was reflected in his description of the police, the judicial system and the victim Carol DaRonch. He specifically asked me if he could talk about his feelings here and so when I invited him to, he again said very little except that he had always had a good deal of trust for the establishment (illegible handwriting) "I have always had a deep respect for the system and I feel bad because she has suffered so much and was deeply hurt. I don't like to be."

ROBERT HOWELL, PhD, Consulting Psychologist

ELEVEN

Dr. Al Carlisle Assessment

PSYCHOLOGICAL EVALUATION

NAME: BUNDY, Theodore Robert
USP#: 0522
DATE OF BIRTH: November 24, 1946
AGE: 29
OFFENSE: Aggravated Kidnapping June 2, 1976
DATE OF ASSESSMENT: June 14, 1976

REFERRAL SOURCE: 90-Day Evaluation

BACKGROUND INFORMATION

Ted was born in Vermont but lived in Philadelphia until he was four years of age. This seemed to have been a fairly happy time in his life. However, at the age of four his mother moved to Tacoma, Washington. When asked why, he said both his mother and grandfather were strong-minded people. In Tacoma, they lived with her brother who was a professor in music at Puget Sound. He had a cousin, John, with whom he seemed to have had a competitive relationship. He found his initial life in Tacoma a period of readjustment and indicated "Life was not as sweet but not a nightmare." He felt there was not the completeness that he had found in Philadelphia. His mother married and they moved to the country. He found this a moderately lonely life, but indicated the loneliness was not pervasive.

He moved back to Tacoma and lived in an Italian, Catholic neighborhood for the kindergarten, first and second grades. He was less lonely because he lived in a larger house and found life a little more adventurous. His early years in school were moderately enjoyable. He did have a second-grade teacher who "put the fear of God in you." After the second grade, he moved to a new area in Tacoma where he lived until he graduated from high school. In the fourth grade he had a desire to be in the "inner circle" in reading but he said his ability level was not such to place him there. He said he felt somewhat humiliated by this. He described his fourth-grade teacher as a "voluptuous disciplinarian," but said she treated him well.

Ted began playing football in the fifth and sixth grades. In junior high he became active in track and football. He ran the hurdles and took third place, but indicated he was not the greatest runner. He tried out for the basketball team but was not successful in getting on it. He also ran for Student Body Vice-President but lost. This possibly initiated a change in his personality during these junior high years because he began being "less dependent" on his friends. Mr. Bundy said that he "didn't adapt to the broader social schemes and he

!!restricted myself to the friends in my neighborhood." He felt he was left as his friends began going out in other directions. When asked why he didn't broaden his social activities as his friends were doing, he indicated he "had apprehension toward establishing new relationships," and that he was "just as secure with the academic life." Although he did not date, he did go to parties and had a girlfriend. He engaged in kissing and some petting activities and said that he enjoyed them. However, for some reason he became less involved with girls and did not date any more until at least his senior year of high school. When asked about this, he was unable to give any explanation for the change in his personality.

Ted was fairly resourceful during his high school years. For example, he had a "lawn cutting company" in which he was involved with three other boys. He did discontinue sports but then while in the 12th grade began getting involved in campaigns. He indicated that while in the 12th grade, his "social deficits were cured," he had ''neutral feelings about girls," and he indicated he had no inhibitions or fears but just a lack of motivation toward dating. He worked during the summer after his graduation at a lucrative job and then bought a 1933 Plymouth Coupe.

Ted indicated that although he did not do many things of a social nature with friends, he was consistently involved with a skiing group who went to the resorts on weekends. They put together a "fogery ring" where they made their own tickets. This was done by bleaching the letters off the old tickets and through using a rubber stamp and different colored stamp pads, they could recreate new tickets. Ted said he saved a lot of money this way.

Following his graduation from high school, Ted entered the University of Puget Sound because it was close to home. Ted talked about a relationship with only one girl while at this university. He did say he may have been somewhat hurt by her but could not remember her name nor many details about the event. About this period of his life, he said he "had a longing for the beautiful coed," but he felt, "I didn't have the skill or social acumen to cope with it." He remained there for a year then went to the University of Washington to major in ancient studies. He indicated he was somewhat of an opinionated person who enjoyed supporting the under? dog. His goal was to obtain a degree and work for the State Department in an academic position, such as in trade on Mainland China. He wanted to gain a position of authority to improve the relationships between the United States and China. Following this year at the University of Washington, he went to Stanford University for the summer but felt he was not measuring up and that it was "a bit too alien," so he terminated this area of study. While at the University of Washington, he engaged in a fraternity rush for four days but then moved to a dorm. On one hand, he indicated he wasn't interested in "parties, clothes and appearances" but also indicated he was living off his own finances and couldn't afford it.

Mr. Bundy met a girl while at the University of Washington. He said this was his "first real involvement," and indicated it was a "very intense" relationship. He later said, however, there was no deep love between them. This was a sometimes good and sometimes stormy relationship. She "Diane" came from a wealthy family and was further along in college than he. Ted had no savings and was often broke. He, therefore, felt quite insecure about their relationship. He felt their relationship was "strained over petty matters" and in many ways they were "worlds apart." He appeared to show a sense of resentment as he talked about her. Ted returned to the University of Washington to major in architecture and urban planning. However, after the first quarter of 1967, he had several incompletes and seemed to be going through some emotional problems so he decided it was time to "regroup." He left school and went to San Francisco, then to Denver (Aspen or Vail) and when he got tired to skiing, he went to Philadelphia. After leaving there, he traveled to see his Uncle Jack in Arkansas and then again came out west. About this time, he became involved in politics. He became very out-going and self-confident through his campaign work. While doing campaign work for Art Fletcher, he was able to critique his speeches and his polices, and he felt this life was more meaningful.

In September, 1968, he went back to Seattle and worked in a shoe store. He made the decision to return to school and wanted to major in the area of law. He indicated he was not ready for the University of Washington because of the memories of the failure experiences he had while there. In January of 1969, he went to Temple University in Philadelphia majoring in general art, science and political science. Mr. Bundy said he left there because he was unaware of what to expect in the East before going there and he found it "crowded, dirty, with no forests." He said it was not as stimulating as the University of Washington and he didn't find what he wanted in the curriculum. In the spring of 1969, he left school and returned to San Francisco and then to Washington where he got a job in a lumber mill. In June, 1970, he re-entered the University of Washington and two years later graduated with a degree in Psychology. In the summer of 1972, Ted worked at the Harbor View Mental Health Center in Seattle. Although he was very much in love with a girl named Liz Kloepfer (his present girlfriend) he began going with another girl who worked at the clinic which caused considerable problems between he and Liz. He worked at this clinic for a short period of time but became disconcerted with his inability to work with some of the clients. Because of his lack of success there, he left. He then became•: involved in the campaign of Washington's Governor Evans as a volunteer worker. He also obtained a consultant contract for three months' study on misdemeanant behavior but never finished this study. He also worked for a few months as an assistant to the director of the crime commission. While he was there, he studied white collar crime and rape prevention. He found that the pay was small and that the commission was an advisory board with no power. He worked for the State Republican Party and was able to suggest new ideas for reconstructing the party and improving campaign services with the use of computers. In December of 1974, Ted became engaged to Diane while still going with Liz. As soon as the engagement was made, Ted decided he really didn't want to marry Diane, so he did not remain in touch with her. Diane did not know she was not engaged to be married to Ted until she called him up a few months later to ask him why he had not called nor written to her. About this event, Mr. Bundy said he was "trying to demonstrate to myself I could have married her." Ted continued his education by going to night school at the University of Puget Sound during the winter and spring. He then withdrew from there without taking the finals. There was dis? agreement over a paper he wrote and he felt he was going to lose credit on it. He also indicated he may have had test anxiety that kept him from taking the finals. Ted then applied at the Un1versity of Utah but when he began in the Fall, he found difficulty adjusting and attended only a few classes during that semester. In spite of this, his grades were fairly good. In the fall of 1974, he joined the L.D.S. Church.

Ted said he was getting tired of his own failures and he wanted to adapt a more disciplined approach. He was drinking alcohol, using some marijuana and was having sex with girls, both before and after he joined the L.D.S. Church. He felt that joining this church would help him gain the strength over these habits. In the summer of 1975, he became a part-time security guard at the University of Utah.

He was arrested on August 6, 1975. He indicated he was restless and about 12:30 a.m. began driving around. He said he wanted to go to Kennecott because he knew they were open all night. He missed the location and so he started back. According to him, he had smoked one marijuana cigarette and had pulled over to the side of the road to smoke another one. About 2:00 a.m. he said he saw a car "coming fast around a corner and I panicked." He knew he wanted to get out of there so he threw the marijuana out of the car and ran through a stop sign. Ted justified his not having his lights on by indicating at times he would start out a night without his lights on and may have done it on this night. The car was a police car which proceeded to pursue Ted. He tried to explain his fleeing by saying that he was somewhat confused because this car had the red light on the side and not on the top, as he had been used to police having in Washington. He indicated the police searched his car illegally and found an old pair of handcuffs. He said he obtained them just before getting the security job position and he felt he might need them. They also found strips of cloth which he said was used for cleaning the Volkswagen seat runner. An ice pick was also found but he said this was also to clean the runners because his screw driver would not fit. Two other items were ski mask and an insert of a ski mask made out of pantyhose. Ted said the ski mask was fun? comfortable and he did not want to pay $10 for the insert and the pantyhose were much cheaper. A crow bar was also found which he said was used to help get the seat out of his car. Other items were hack saw, a tube for siphoning gas, coveralls, flares, etc.

Because of the handcuffs, he was linked to Carol

DaRonch who had earlier reported an attempted kidnap using handcuffs.

TEST BEHAVIOR

Mr. Bundy was moderately cooperative throughout the assessment. He was given several tests and was interviewed for over 20 hours over a six-week period. He took each of the tests but often questioned their usefulness stating he felt they were too open to subjective interpretation.

At times he seemed happy and outgoing. At other times he was angry and depressed. There were also times of rapid mood changes. Overall, he was extremely guarded throughout the interview. He picked his words very carefully. He was defensive, evasive and noncommittal.

Although he showed general control in his voice and through his facial expression, he demonstrated some anxiety through deep sighing when approaching the projective tests and perspired fairly heavily at certain points during the interview, indicating the presence of anxiety.

Test and interview material were evaluated by the psychology staff at the Utah State Prison.

INTELLECTUAL ASSESSMENT

On the intelligence test, Mr. Bundy obtained an I.Q. score of 122 which places him in the category of Superior intelligence. He scored high in most areas on the Education Performance Test and also scored high in most areas of the GATB. In general, his intellectual abilities are very good, as is also evidenced by his general college success. There were no indications of cerebral dysfunction found in the testing.

PERSONALITY ASSESSMENT

There were no indications of psychotic thinking or ideation found in the testing nor in the interview. He is reality oriented and can respond to the demands of most situations in an appropriate manner.

The Psychological Testing consisted of both objective, paper-and-pencil tests and projective tests. In the former, the person basically tells how he sees him? self. Mr. Bundy appeared in a very favorable light in these tests, giving an impression of a very well-adjusted person with no significant problems, anxieties or other negative emotions. Mr. Bundy sees himself as a fairly open person. This contrasted with the strong defensiveness shown throughout all the interviews. He also viewed himself as a person who experiences almost no anxiety, yet he showed definite indications of anxiety at times during the interviews. In general, the scores of the objective tests portray the picture of a person who is happy, confident and very well adjusted. These results contrasted with the 'results found' in the projective tests and in the interview. Even the turmoil he is experiencing because of his present situation did not show up on the objective tests. An intelligent person can answer the questions to place himself in a favorable light, which would help explain the conflicting results. Because of the discrepancy between the two types of tests, further testing and extended interview time was undertaken.

The following personality picture was obtained from testing and the interview data. Mr. Bundy is an intelligent person with a good verbal ability. He can present himself well and makes a good initial impression on most persons. Thus, he tends to win friends easily. He has a strong desire for achievement and has good perseverance in working toward his occupational goals. He has often withdrawn from his educational pursuits which has shown a definite pattern of instability but he does show determination in his desire to eventually reach his goal.

Mr. Bundy is a "private" person who does not allow himself to become known very intimately by others. When one tries to understand him, he becomes evasive. Outwardly he appears confident and reveals himself as a secure person. Underneath this veneer are fairly strong feelings of insecurity. He has a strong need for structure and control, such as in interpersonal relationships and in control of his own emotions. In the California Life Goals Evaluation Schedules, he scored very high in the area of Security (to have freedom from want), and high in the areas of Power (to control the actions of others), Leadership (to guide others with their consent), Interesting Experiences (to desire the avoidance of boredom), Self Expression (to desire self-fulfillment), and Independence (to live one's life in one's own way). He becomes somewhat threatened by people unless he feels he can structure the outcome of the relationship. The testing revealed an over responsiveness to his emotions which would indicate his defenses are not always adequate.

The constant theme running throughout the testing was a view of women being more competent than men. There were also indications of a fairly strong dependency on women, and yet he also has a strong need to be independent. I feel this creates a fairly strong conflict in that he would like a close relationship with females but is fearful of being hurt by them. There were indications of general anger and more particularly, well masked anger toward women. His attempt to remain emotionally distant from others is probably a defense against being hurt by them. There were indications of a fear of being put down and of humiliation which relates to this. He has difficulty handling stress and has a strong tendency to run from his problems. That his defenses break down under stress is shown by his general instability, both in the past and with his inability in adjusting during his first quarter at the University of Utah. His use of marijuana and the fact that he was a heavy drinker at one time are also indicators of difficulty with handling stress. These correlate with the evidence of anxiety, loneliness, and depression found in the testing.

There were signs of incongruity and dishonesty found in the assessment. In the Fall of 1975 Mr. Bundy joined the L.D.S. Church, yet contrary to church law he maintained his smoking, drinking, smoking of marijuana and his sexual habits.

This shows incongruity between his professed beliefs and his behavior, and indicates he must have been untruthful during his pre-baptism interview.

Passive-aggressive features were also evident. I felt there was a good deal of hostility directed toward me and other personnel even though he would carefully point out that it was not aimed directly at us personally.

The above personality profile is consistent with the possibility of violence and is consistent with the nature of the crime for which he is convicted. A prediction cannot be made as to whether or not Mr. Bundy will show violence in the future as the best predictor is past behavior, and he disclaims any violent acts in the past, including his present charge. However, I feel Mr. Bundy has not allowed me to get to know him and I believe there are many significant things about him that remain hidden. Therefore, I cannot comfortably say he would be a good risk if placed on-_probation.

. . .

A. L. Carlisle, Ph.D, Clinical Psychologist
ALC/tas

ASSESSMENT PROCEDURES

Rorschach, Otis Quick-Scoring Mental Ability Test, Make A Picture Story, Thematic Apperception Test, Bender-Gestalt, Sentence Completion Test, GATB, Education , Performance Test, Descriptive Words Inventory, California Life Goals Evaluation Schedules, Bipolar Psychological Inventory, and Interview.

Part IV: Ted Bundy in Florida

These are part of Dr. Carlisle's research on Ted Bundy and were shared with him at the time. Many of these are now public record.

TWELVE

Kenneth Misner (Bundy) Interview

WEDNESDAY
February 15, 1979

Today's date is February 15, 1979, the time is 4:25 AM. I am Detective Chapman of the Pensacola Police Department, also present is officer Lee of the Pensacola Police Department. This statement is being taken in the interrogation room, of 40 S. Alcaniz Street, in reference to grand larceny, possession of stolen property, and other charges that will be entered in later, complaint number is, city complaint number 7S-05257, 7S-05257. This incident occurred on this date, February 15, 1978, at approximately 1:34 AM

Q. Would you state your full name, please.

A. Kenneth Raymond Misner.

Q. Where do you live, Mr. Misner?

A. Presently I live in Tallahassee.

Q. Do you have a street address in Tallahassee?

A. Yes sir, 982 W. Brevard.

Q. Okay, how old are you, Mr. Misner?

A. Twenty-nine.

Q. How much education do you have?

A. I have a Bachelor of Science degree in education.

Q. Okay, I would like to talk to you in reference to this incident, but first as I have in the past it is my duty to advise you of your rights in regards to making a statement. You have the right to remain silent, you understand this?

A. Yes sir.

Q. Anything you say can be used against you in court, do you understand this?

A. Yes sir.

Q. If you cannot afford a lawyer, one will be appointed for you before any questioning, if you so wish, do you understand this?

A. Yes sir.

Q. If you decide to answer questions now without a lawyer present, you will still have the right to stop answering at any time until you talk to a lawyer, do you understand this?

A. Yes sir

Q. Okay, having these rights in mind, are you still willing to talk to us in reference to these, this incident that occurred this morning?

A. Yes, I am.

Q. Okay, is this your signature on this waiver of rights sheet?

A. Yes, it is my signature.

Q. Okay, this was a waiver of rights, witnessed by officer Lee and myself. Okay, Mr. Misner, when you were arrested this morning, you were in possession of a stolen vehicle, is this correct?

A. Yes, that's correct.

Q. Okay, where did you take the vehicle from?

A. Tallahassee.

Q. Okay, and do you know approximately where in Tallahassee the vehicle was stolen from?

A. Well, let's see, can't really tell you the street, oh boy! Okay, about two or three miles from campus, I guess.

Q. Okay, you also had another tag that was on the automobile, did you steal that tag also?

A. Yes sir.

Q. Okay, and do you know what that tag came off of?

A. A Volkswagen.

Q. It came off of another Volkswagen?

A. Yes.

Q. Okay, you also had in your possession some identification cards and a number of credit cards. Would you tell us where you received this identification?

A. Oh, they were in the pocketbook, decided to take the purses.

Q. Okay, where did you take these purses from?

A. Well, I didn't take the purses, they were pocketbooks (inaudible).

Q. All right, yeah, okay.

A. Took the small stuff, from, they were in taverns, well, the, the purses were in taverns, you know, in Tallahassee area that I thought, you know, that I just take the pocketbooks out.

Q. Was there any specific tavern that you took them from?

A. (Inaudible) No, no specific tavern.

Q. Okay, okay, would you tell us what occurred this morning in relationship to your being arrested?

A. Starting exactly when? From the time I was stopped?

Q. From the time you first observe the police officer behind you?

A. Well, the police officer followed me for some time and then turned on his lights and pulled up beside me and I stopped and he, I, I got out of my car and he got out of his car and he pulled his weapon and he said that, stand still and whatever and I put my hand, and I put my hands on top of the car and, I guess he made some radio call and, then asked me to lay down on the pavement in front of his car.

Q. Okay.

A. In which I did and he put the handcuffs on one rest and then I pushed him out of the way and he fell down and I…

Q. Okay, when you pushed officer Lee out of the way he fell to the pavement himself?

A. Well, when he fell, I guess he, he ended up on the pavement, I guess, I… I wouldn't know exactly what happened 'cause I just started running away from him. Okay, and, down the street and around the corner and he, I heard some shots fired and I assumed that he was shooting at me.

Q. Okay, but you did provoke the attack?

A. Well, if that's what you'd call it, I didn't, you know, if I had wanted to attack him I would've hit him, I, all I did was push him out of the way, 'cause I wanted to get away not because I wanted to hurt the man.

Q. Right, okay, is there anything else that you'd like to tell us at this time concerning this?

A. There's really nothing else to say about it really that I can think of right now.

Q. Okay, is this a true and correct statement to the best of your knowledge?

A. Yes. Well, let me see, I just want to make it clear you know I guess technically under the law it's assaulting a police officer, and/but I just like it to be known that I, I, the intent was not to hurt the police officer.

Q. Your intent was just to get him…

A. And I didn't hurt the police officer, I hope.

Q. Okay.

A. I, all I did was run away.

Q. Uh huh, your intent was to escape. Okay, there's one other thing I'd like to ask you about, there is a television in the back of your car, where did this television come from?

A. It came out of another car. I took it out several weeks ago.

Q. All right.

A. In Tallahassee.

Q. Okay, but you don't know which car it was in…

A. I don't know.

Q. But you did steal the television in Tallahassee?

A. Uh-huh.

Q. Okay, do you have any questions you'd like to ask, officer Lee? How about in relation to the credit cards?

Q. Okay, you have a number of credit cards here. Where did these cards come from?

A. Well, they were in the pocketbooks that I'd taken from persons, they were just part of (inaudible)

Q. Okay, is there anything else?

This is the end of this statement, the same date, the time is 4:33 AM.

THIRTEEN

Ted Letter to Chris

P.S. - You might let Carole read this, but only on the condition that she not scratch your eyes out, since it isn't that kind of letter. However, she would be well-advised if she sent me a perfumed letter pronto, before I begin thinking she's only in this, to give her hack exposure for reasons known-only to herself.

Tuesday, August 8, 1978

Dear Chris,

Your last letter (Aug. 3) has me looking over my shoulder every now and then. I don't think I've smelled-anything so fragrant since my mother pampered my baby's bottom with talcum powder. There are just some scents which can take you back to places you've been before. Sensory Deja vu. Like that-oldie on the radio that reminds you - happily or painfully - of a certain someone. Not that the per? fume of your stationary brings back any 11 someone" in particular.

It arouses the presence of something, as if someone were in the room with me, someone felt, someone known vaguely, but not seen vividly. 'I'm a sentimental sort, whose sentimentality is rather easily brought to life. I live in an environment that is stripped of all that is comforting, familiar and pleasure-giving. It's An environment where the only odor of any consequence is the stale smell of- cigarette smoke. My starved sense of smell is easily intoxicated by fragrances that I took for granted in happier times. I have this intoxicating, Deja vu-like sensation on the rare occasions when I am allowed to breathe lungs-full of fresh a\r. Last Spring, I remember being taken outside and taking a whiff of that awakening, fertile Mother Earth essence, and for an instant I was somewhere else; I was in a dozen places at once in that cool morning air, under a clear sky: in the Quadrangle with its cherry blossoms, the Arboretum, bobbing down the Yakima in a raft, lying in bed with the breeze rustling the curtains, in Stanley Park, in Berkley, in •••• So when I a least expecting it, this fresh, familiar fragrance reaches me like a flash, and I'll turn around to see who's there, and then I'll remember your letter.

Well, I am not such a nostalgic dwarf that I Drag through each day dredging up sugar-coated memories of the way things used to be. Reflection for me is an entertainment and not a morbid occupation. I broke that umbilical cord with the past long ago I'd be crippled otherwise. But there is no denying that the way-things used-to-be is a figurative womb that I run not ashamed of wanting to return to.

I've enjoyed your letters and deeply appreciate your words of encouragement. Even though Carole is the ultimate Bundy fan and defender - I mean to say, that she even keeps me on the straight and narrow when my spirits crash - and even though she is an amazingly forceful and convincing person - the amazing thing is that she can be influential without being pushy, but she can be damn pushy too –

I think you are a gutsy broad (I will be thoroughly thrashed for using that word) for writing to me. I can imagine that many young women

consider me to be the personification of their deepest fears and most horrifying nightmares. On the one hand, for me to recognize this view of me is painful. But I also realize that what is feared is not me, but the image created by others of me, and, ultimately, that the person or persons, whose monumental brutality has aroused those fears in the first place, is not me. Still, overcoming such fear and repulsion requires an enormous amount of self-control. Even the act of someone, like yourself, writing to me is a considerable accomplishment. One that bridge is built, though, I think there is a basis for understanding me as a real person, devoid of all the horror tales. If you can get by the image, the stripped-down version of Ted Bundy is far from frightening. I am not capable of the violent behavior which has been attributed to me, which is why those who know me are steadfast in their beliefs in my innocence. Forgive me for pleading my case. I don1t mean to sound defensive, I'm trying to make a point. The point is that I'm "okay" (you're okay?), no soap. But to know this, you have to know me, and to know me, well...that's not the easiest thing under the circumstances, but by writing You've taken a first step, you l1ave an open mind.

"Do I look like I write", you asked in a recent letter? You write very well. (By the way, Carole sent me an article you wrote for the Daily about the fortunes of a soccer player. Very authentic, informative, sporty style, Chris. Now if they'll only have the decency to let you into the locker room •••) And besides writing well, and looking better than well, your self-awareness is very disarming, which is to say that your capacity to be open about yourself puts me at ease.

Those of us who have limped past 30 have a tendency to think we've "mellowed out. Actually, we're just tired. So we'll lean back and wistfully sip our sophisticated liqueur, on the rocks naturally - we sip this stuff because we can't handle the other stuff in the quantities that left us burned-out wrecks. And there we'll sit and-nod knowingly as we discuss the trials and disasters of our early twenties. Christ, we can't believe we did those things, but we sure are wiser now. That the wisdom may have been achieved too late to be of any value, and that all the fun of being 30 was getting there, doesn't deflate our smugness or stop us from giving that tumbler full of Drambuie a knowing swirl. How disgusting. On that note, let me tell you a bundle of foolish things about being 21.

#1. I wish I was 21 again, with or without what I know now.

You don't. have to be a masochist to want to go through it twice. Of course, if I had your talent and your good looks, there's no doubt that I volunteer. Sure, I like knowing what I know, and I'm not terribly disappointed with how those years left me. But there , is no substitute for the confusion, the mystery if you will. The bloom is on the rose, so to speak, and its color is deeper on you than it is on us. Everything is more intense: success, failure, adventure, learning, new friends, sex, everything.

#2. BUT, on the ever-present other hand, I am no longer fond of roller coaster rides, and the years between 20 and 25 can give you one hell of a ride. There was a time or two when I was sure that I'd fallen off. Fact is, I don't know anyone who didn't feel derailed during those years. A time when all our best laid plans, our most erotic love affairs, took on all the appeal of very old underwear.

Days, weeks, even months, when we'd wander about like shell-shocked somnambulists. You'll wonder why, I mean REALLY wonder why you went to Washington, D.C., instead of pursuing broadcasting, or why you pursue broadcasting, instead of going to Washington, or did one or both of the above, instead of opting for the lucrative life of an executive Almond Roca salesperson. And maybe you won't become diseased with a general loss of purpose. (It's easy to detect the symptoms of this disease. Imagine how it would feel if you drank a fifth of bourbon, and then climbed into one of the dryers down at the laundromat for an hour's spin.) Maybe you're totally together – and I have no reason to doubt that you are not and every reason to hope that you are - and if you are, sit down with us old folks and have a shot of this expensive stuff we're sipping.

#3. "S0 how about it? Am I a normal 21-year-old going through the same process that we all do'?" On the score of love affairs and the battle of the sexes, my hide is already nailed prominently to the side of the barn. Good grief, Lucy, Boone knows a lot more about this stuff than this one. If I were to give you any advice concerning matters/of the heart, I should be forced to mainline Drano. I don't mind you bringing it, IT, up - in fact I am a mite flattered - but this requires some serious thought, and some even more serious drinking. Let me get a glass of water.

This requires a history lesson, which is more for my benefit as it is for anyone else's. Alright, s0 she had a Mustang with California plates. (It was 1967, the Spring before the Summer of Love in Haight-Ashbury. California was still what was happening.

All seems like ancient history now, like the Vietnam War.) And so what if she may have been the most beautiful woman I had ever seen, or have seen since: tall, dark.... haired, smooth, and oh-so sophisticated. She moved like something out of Vogue and anything she wore looked like a million dollars. I, on the other hand, possessed the innocence of a missionary, the worldliness of a farm boy, and a taste in clothing: that had just graduated from shinny wingtips. At the time I first saw her, she was into football jocks, and I was into waddling around the UW campus mumbling phrases in Chinese. My idea of a hot night was dinner at Tia Tung followed by a Samurai movie at the Japanese theater around the corner. She and I had about as much in common as Sears and Roebuck does with Saks. But we did have one thing in common.

I never considered D with any more romantic interest than

I considered some elegant creature on the fashion page. It was not that I felt out-classed, which I was, b11t I was simply disinterested. What could be more satisfying than a night watching a bunch of grunting Samurai? Tell me I wasn't naive? Virginal. bliss. There was one thing that could arouse me more than warring samurais; it was skiing. When it came to me and the ski slopes, nothing: would stand in my way. I was absolutely without fear, precocious beyond reason. It being Spring and near the end of the season, and I, having devoted myself like a monk to Chinese, had not been skiing at all that season. There was no time for formalities, even if I had known at the time what those formalities were. She had a car, and I assumed she skied since she had come to the U by way of Boulder.

So we had something in common: her car. I walked up to her and

told her we should-go skiing. Points for audacity should be awarded

Page 4.

for such a tactless performance. And she accepted, but I

found out much later, not without considerable, but well disguised, bewilderment.

Spring skiing at Snoqualmie Pass is an experience akin to water skiing. Wet and very warm, but to a fanatic like myself, there could be no bad days as long as I could slide downhill.

She and I didn't ski together; I was never much for waiting for someone to catch up when I skied. But we did ride home together, it being her car. And it was on the ride back to Seattle, with the skiing out of my system, and the beautiful D at the wheel of her Mustang, that it began to occur to me, imperceptibly at· first, that she offered something vaguely more satisfying than a night of subtitles and samurai swords. How to explain? I'll let Thomas Hardy do it for me:

"... It is scarcely an exaggeration to say that till this moment Jude had never looked at a woman to consider her as such, but had vaguely regarded the sex as beings outside his life and purposes. He gazed. from her mouth, thence to her bosom, and to her full round naked arms, wet, mottled with the chill of the water, and firm as marble.

"He had just inhaled a single breath from a new atmosphere, which had evidently been hanging round him everywhere he went, for he knew not how long, but had somehow been divided from his actual breathing as by a sheet of glass. The intentions as to reading, working, and learning, which he had so precisely formulated only a few minutes earlier, were suffering a curious collapse into a corner, he knew not how."

In spite of my insensitivity, my indiscrete innocence, and. finally, my clumsy infatuation, or perhaps because of them, the divine Miss D took to spending more and more of her time with me, and I with her. The order of my well-constructed routine became chaos, my devotion to Chinese hung by a slender thread. It was at once sublime and overpowering. The first touch of hands, the first kiss, the first night together. Weekends in Vancouver and at my uncle's cabin on the Peninsula. It was wild and dazzling all I could do just to hold onto the saddle.

During that summer I went to Stanford to study Chinese. It is extremely distracting to study a language like Chinese in a place where the days are forever filled with sunshine, where tennis courts are everywhere to lure the weak-willed and where the nights are always warm and sweet. It didn't take long before it dawned on me that the desire to pack my head full of Chinese characters was very ill. It was not my cup of tea.

Chinese is a lifetime study, like the study of English is likewise one requiring a lifetime, and I couldn't see myself doing that for a lifetime. It didn't seem relevant - the course of events has proven me wrong on this score. This realization didn't so much dawn on me as it collapsed about me as if from an earthquake.

So I played tennis, a lot of tennis, because I couldn't find anything else to do. Tough life, what? Well, it was traumatic, and as my resolve to study Chinese withered on sun drenched tennis courts, so did my fundamental and heretofore unquestioned self-assurance. (All this time I should remind you of that feeling you'd get after drinking a fifth of bourbon and taking a ride in a clothes dryer.) So Chinese became the major casualty of that Summer, and the secondary casualty was the thing between D and I.

For the next six years, D and I would meet under the most tentative of circumstances; in Vancouver, where she was living and working, for a day of skiing; in San Francisco for a few days, in Berkley for a weekend. I'd get it in my head to see her and I'd go see her. Always a very gracious person, D never complained of these intrusions, but neither did she seem to understand their purpose1 and neither did I. Then three years past and I had no desire to see or write to her, nor she to me. Then in 1973, I went to Sacramento and then to S.F. to do some research on telephone survey techniques for the Republicans. (You are such a squared-away kind of person, so well-adjusted and all that, that it came as a surprise when I found out that you were active in the Democrat party. Of course, these days, I can't imagine myself active in the RP. But what's a nice girl like you …) When in S.F. I looked D up, took her flowers, we had dinner and I ended up staying at her place for a week.

I'm trying to make this long story short. There's a moral here somewhere and I hope you'll be patient until I can find it.

A month later, she carne to Seattle and we spent a few days at Alpental. She flew in for the Christmas holidays, and bythe time New Year's Day rolled around we found ourselves at the breakfast table in a friend's apartment, in Magnolia talking serious marriage business. That's-what it sounded like: a business arrangement. And throughout the discussion I kept asking myself: what am I doing here with this woman? We knew each other but we were strangers. She was everything that I wanted and I did not want her at all. The years had made us different, irreconcilably different people, people pretty much set in our ways, and our ways were living in separate worlds. We were both proud people but the similarities ended there. She, in the image of her very successful and strong-willed father, had grown rigid, business-like even in her private dealings; she needed order and predictability in a form that w2.s alien to me. I was not a slave of order or much of an authority figure. My lack of organization was alien to her.

So why didn't I squelch this suicidal talk about marriage? Where was my honesty? Why was I saying "no" in my mind and doing nothing to discourage the bloodless planning? It was not my finest hour.

It was not my finest hour for several reasons, the most important of these reasons being L. L was why I was saying "no" in my head to D that morning. L was the reason I hadn't seen D for three years. It was LI was betraying, being unfaithful to in the extreme. It was the look on L's face that I knew would be there if she ever found out I was discussing marriage with another woman that kept appearing before me on that New Year's Morning. So I mumbled my assent to the idea that May would be a good time/to get married, packed Doff to the airport, and. breathed a deep sigh of relief when she was up and away. I had reached a new moral low. Or an unethical high.

I wasn't judging my behavior on an honesty scale at the time. I was ecstatic because I had made the most remarkable choice of my life without any misgivings, no matter that it was veiled in deceit. I drove like a crazy man to L's apartment, burst through her apartment door and caught her in the act of serenely cleaning the oven of all things. She looked at me with a trusting, glad-to-see-you gaze, and, while I should have felt like a slug, I was never happier to see anyone in my life. Seeing her was like waking up after a bad dream, grease-stained gloves, soot-smudged nose and all. L was beautiful in a way D could never be to me, although L was plain in appearance. L was meek and somewhat adverse to social gatherings and politics, whereas D and. I milked social gatherings like a couple of veteran doubles partners. L was immensely intelligent, although she never could exhibit it with the aggressive flare that D could. L did not have D's wealth or taste in clothes. On any objective scale, D would have made a far more attractive spouse for a young attorney/politician. But who's objective about such affairs? You see, to my amazement, I loved L in a manner and degree that simply overshadowed D's quality package. I never realized the strength of that love until New Year's day; I had never been presented a choice of abandoning it for more mercenary objectives. It was an awakening.

But, as I have said, it is not to be viewed without its less noble aspects.

I'll end the story at this point. I never saw D again.

And L and I... That's a different story.

Looking back on it, I can see the lessons which were there to be learned, lessons clearer to me now than then. The exquisite torment of a first infatuation. The way two people grow apart and become set in their approaches to life. How a would-be companion, who possesses all the requisites of an abstracted ideal mate, may not prove compatible in real life. The unparalleled feeling of being loved and loving. Then there's the one about guilt I have never, even to this day, been so miserable as the morning I sat at the breakfast table with D. Being faced with the prospect of selling out I was truly frightening.

I learned more than a little bit about sex too, and it about time. The difference between sex with D and sex with L was, the difference between ethyl alcohol and a fine, dry burgundy; It was the difference between listening to a chimpanzee play Chopin, and Arthur Rubenstein playing it. The difference was loving the person. It sounds like a cliche, but there is nothing more startling than discovering its truth for yourself. Given the inflated value of sex as a factor defining the intimacy of two people, it was pleasant to discover that sex was a function of love and not vice-versa. That without love, all that naked grappling takes on all the excitement of watching Washington play San Jose State in the cold rain of Husky Stadium. I just rather be doing something else, thank you.

When you made a few comments about your love life in

a recent letter, I'm sure that you didn't expect all this shit back, did you? While I've indulged myself with these confessions, I've done so not with the intention of offering advice. I'm not sure any can be offered as a substitute for trial and error. A successful love life is a complex formula of luck, good karma, genetics, common sense, honesty, timing, maturity, intuition, fearlessness, caution and a thousand other things besides.

Unless you are neuter or a hermaphrodite, it is a basic need and reality of living. Unless you are a genius or a magician, it involves one person at a time, although I am well aware of the fact different people offer different loving qualities and that it is easy, sometimes too easy, to be in love with more than one person at the same time.

And while our mothers tell us there are many fish in the sea, they sometimes forget to mention that among them are species of shark and octopus, and that there are some who enjoy fishing for the sake of fishing, and some of us who'd rather enjoy the catch and stay on shore. The point of this well-worn metaphor is that you are at a time of life when you are meeting many new and exciting people, you like fishing, but you're not ready to do any catching. And that's smart, anyone who gets married under the age of 25 should have his or her head examined. But somewhere along the line you are going to take a chance on someone, if you haven't already. At some time, the desire to indulge yourself in an in vivos experiment is going to be strong enough for you to be willing to take some risks. Then you'll start learning the things no one can teach you, except that you can teach yourself.

It was my turn to run off at the typewriter. But before ending, I'll answer your question. Are you a normal 21-year-old? Sounds like you're above normal. You have the advantage of being analytical and self-critical, although I'11 wager you'll be less so when Mr. Right sends you a dozen yellow roses. Then it's time for radar and watching out for the hidden shoals. However, in all fairness, I must reserve an opinion on your love life until I've had a chance to review a sample thereof submitted, postage prepaid, on 16 mm film. Expect a report within ten days.

Keep an eye on Carole. Now there's a woman who has taught me a lot about myself. She's fearless, loving, open. There's no repressing or concealing with Carole; there's no desire to, and just in case there is, she gives me an occasional stern lecture which much appreciated. She's outrageous, outspoken and occasionally, out of her mind; all of which tends to keep a person on his toes. I adore Carole for, among other reasons, being able and willing to discuss anything without embarrassment, and without treating the subject matter superficially or casually. Of course, that's not to say that she won't pinch you on the ass and call you a shithead if you're toying around with something either. I've told her to watch her step with you. Being liberated and somewhat libertine, I initially thought she might lead you astray, and let you fall into the hands of some of those craven men whose company she keeps. I'm less fearful of that now. I'm confident that you can hold your own with those perverse, unscrupulous hedonists.

Love, Ted

FOURTEEN

Florida Letter from Ted 1

(Extracted from "The 1976 Psychological Assessment of Ted Bundy" by Al Carlisle.)

I recently received a copy of a letter that Ted wrote to me in 1976 when he was still in the diagnostic program at the prison. The letter – well, actually letters—were evidently in the possession of one of Ted's lawyers before he became his own attorney, and was acquired by a documentary filmmaker who interviewed me and showed me the letters. It is unclear why the letters never surfaced before now. I'm very pleased that I was able to get copies of them.

It appears that Ted started a letter but wasn't satisfied with it so he rewrote it. The letter was addressed to me and it is in Ted's handwriting. It's a fascinating letter but I wonder why Ted wrote it. And why didn't I receive it at that time? As far as I know, he didn't write a similar letter to other members of the evaluation team. Here is his first attempt at the letter, exactly as written.

May 11, 1976
Theodore Bundy (signature)

Dear Dr. Carlisle,
Recently a fellow inmate gave me a tattered, year-old issue of the National Geographic. One article entitled 'Six Months Alone in a Cave' attracted my attention. It was a scientific chronical which sought to describe the effects of confinement and isolation on mental and biological rhythms. The study intrigued me because I am so acutely aware of my own reactions to confinement of a different variety.
Michael Siffre, the subject of the experiment and the author of the article began with these words:
Overcome with lethargy and bitterness I sit on a rock and stare at my campsite in the bowels of midnight Cave, near Del Rio, Texas. Behind me lie a hundred days of solitude; ahead loom two and a half more lonely months. But I—a wildly displaced Frenchman —know none of this, for I am living "beyond time," divorced from calendars and clocks and from sun and moon, to help determine among other things, the natural rhythms of human life.
While I am not, like Mr. Siffre, confined to determine the natural rhythms of human life, I am very conscious of my own particular rhythms, my reactions to incarceration, and feel that I, too, am living "beyond time" divorced from the elements of my existence which have tuned the rhythms of my own life over the years. With the empathy that only experience brings, I read Siffre's entry after 77 day[s] in the Midnight Cave that "I am in excellent form. I notice, though, a fragility of memory. I recall nothing from yesterday. Even events of this morning are lost.

If I do not write things down immediately, I forget them."

Incarceration, like confinement in the cave, dulls the memory. Uneventful thoughtless days blend into one another. Living only in the moment, isolated from the schedule which wound my clock on the outside, I see days pass swiftly and unintelligibly by. There is a negative reinforcement in not thinking and remembering because by not doing so I am reminded of the cruel reality of prison. The time passes quickly.

This outcome would be nothing less than justice by default, satisfying some vague notion of punishment possessed by the community and subjecting me to the degrading and deteriorating environment of prison.

The prospects for a resolution of this quandary are not bright. I am sure you appreciate the difficulty encountered by your colleagues, and, perhaps, you might even concur with their predilection not to formulate any prognosis in my case. On the other hand, I would hope that your exposure to prison life about the modifying impact incarceration is reputed to have on a person.

[End of first letter]

May 14, 1976

Theodore Bundy

Dr. Al Carlisle
Diagnostic Unit
Utah State Prison

Dear Dr. Carlisle,

Recently a fellow inmate gave me a tattered, year-old issue of the National Geographic. One article entitled 'Six Months Alone in a Cave' attracted my attention. It was a scientific chronical which sought to describe the effects of confinement and isolation on mental and biological rhythms. The study intrigued me because I am so acutely aware of my own reactions to confinement of a different variety.

Michel Siffre, the subject of the experiment and the author of the article began with these words:

Overcome with lethargy and bitterness, I sit on a rock and stare at my campsite in the bowels of Midnight Cave, near Del Rio, Texas. Behind me lie a hundred days of solitude; ahead loom two and a half more lonely months. But I - a wildly displaced Frenchman - know none of this, for I am living "beyond time," divorced from calendars and clocks, and from sun and moon, to help determine

Bundy Letter One, Page 1

among other things, the natural rhythms of human life..."

While I am not, like Mr. Siffre, concerned to determine the natural rhythms of human life, I am very conscious of my own particular rhythms, my reactions to incarceration, and feel that I, too, am living "beyond time" divorced from the elements of my existence which have timed the rhythms of my own life over the years. With the empathy that only experience brings, I read Siffre's entry after 77 days in the Midnight Cave that "I am in excellent form. I notice, though, a fragility of memory. I recall nothing from yesterday. Even events of this morning are lost. If I do not write things down immediately, I forget them."

Incarceration, like confinement in the cave, dulls the memory. Uneventful, thoughtless days blend into one another. Living only in the moment, isolated from the schedule which wound my clock on the outside, I see days pass swiftly and unintelligibly by. There is a negative reinforcement in not thinking and remembering because by not doing so I am reminded of the cruel reality of prison. The time passes quickly.

Bundy Letter One, Page 2

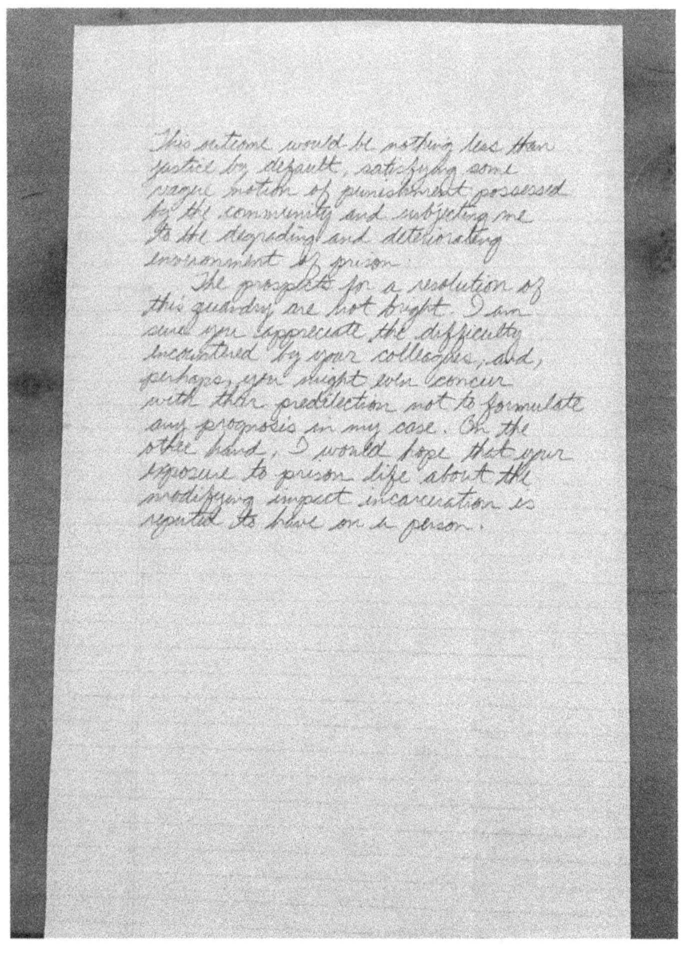

This outcome would be nothing less than justice by default, satisfying some vague notion of punishment possessed by the community and subjecting me to the degrading and deteriorating environment of prison.

The prospects for a resolution of this quandry are not bright. I am sure you appreciate the difficulty encountered by your colleagues, and, perhaps, you might even concur with their predilection not to formulate any prognosis in my case. On the other hand, I would hope that your exposure to prison life about the modifying impact incarceration is reputed to have on a person.

Bundy Letter One, Page 3

FIFTEEN

Florida Letter from Ted 2

(Extracted from "The 1976 Psychological Assessment of Ted Bundy" by Al Carlisle.)

Evidently, when Ted read through what he had written, he felt it wasn't strong enough. It's as if when he wrote the last paragraph, he became aware that he was specifically addressing me. A major difference between the two letters is that in the first attempt Ted is speaking in a general manner, while in the completed letter Ted is speaking directly to me, as if he was sitting across the desk from me pleading with me to see the error of my perception of him. Here's his final letter:

May 11, 1976

Theodore Bundy (signature)

. . .

Dr. Al Carlisle
Diagnostic Unit
Utah State Prison

Dear Dr. Carlisle,

Recently, a fellow inmate gave me a tattered year-old issue of the National Geographic. One article, entitled 'Six Months in a Cave', attracted my attention. It was a scientific chronical which sought to describe the effects of confinement and isolation on mental and biological rhythms. The study intrigued me because I am so acutely aware of my reactions to the isolation and confinement of prison.

Michel Siffre, the subject of the experiment and the author of the article began with these words:

"Overcome with lethargy and bitterness, I sit on a rock and stare at my campsite in the bowels of Midnight Cave, near Del Rio, Texas. … I am living "beyond time," divorced from calendars and clocks and from sun and moon, to help determine, among other things, the natural rhythms of human life …"

While I am not, like Mr. Siffre, confined to determine the natural rhythms of human life, I am very conscious of my particular rhythms, my reactions to incarceration. Imprisonment or experimental isolation, an experience common to both of these conditions is a sense of living "beyond time," and [is] a paralysis born by lethargy and bitterness.

Under conditions which induce emotional distress and deteriorated mental functioning, how can a psychologist, such as yourself, begin to distinguish traits distorted or produced by the deprivations of the prison environment from traits (characteristics/behaviors) displayed by an inmate when he is free to respond (in) a community environment? Are you, like Mr. Siffre, simply measuring reactions to stress, isolation, and confinement or can you naturally assess the real person, uncontaminated by imprisonment?

I ask these questions because I am concerned that a confounding variable may be interfering with the analysis made of an inmate. Hostility, anger, bitterness, neurosis, defensiveness, or antisocial attitudes may be a response to the pressures and realities of prison and not indices which truly reflect the character of the individual you are examining. Can you make the distinctions?

You have made some thoughtful judgments about me. You have indicated that I am hard to get to know, that I am angry, and that I am precise, objective and somewhat impersonal when discussing myself. These are accurate observations about Theodore Bundy the prisoner, but what about Theodore Bundy the person before he was subjected to months of intense stress and incarceration? Had we the opportunity to meet under different circumstances, socially and informally, what would your impression have been then?

The point I am trying to make involves normality versus abnormality versus adaptation. How would you react, how would any average citizen react, if you were taken from your familiar, everyday life and place[d] in the bizarre atmosphere of prison? Would you be angry, suspicious of authority, protective and defensive? Your adaptation may be reasonable when the circumstances are considered, but abnormal when compared to some abstract, normative scale.

Prison has had its effect on me. Lethargy, bitterness, depression, antisocial attitudes, and disorganized thought processes have *all* been reactions apparent to me. But I resist the destruction of my personality and myself and I will not be lured into the common weaknesses which prison breeds. I become objective about my situation because it raises me above the chaos and corruption of the moment. Defensive? Perhaps. I like myself, too much, to allow prison to make me a cruel, insensitive, violent and anti-establishment convict just to survive.

Beneath the reactions to confinement there remains the essential ingredients of my personality. I have not concealed them from you. Still, you seem uncomfortable. Why? What are you looking for? Is it some intuitive feeling which says you do not know me? Unfortunately, our relationship is artificial and forced by the pressures of time. You cannot know me and I cannot know you in such a short time.

[End of letter]

May 11, 1976

Theodore Bundy

Dr. Al Carlisle
Diagnostic Unit
Utah State Prison

Dear Dr. Carlisle,

Recently, a fellow inmate gave me a tattered, year old issue of the National Geographic. One article, entitled 'Six Months in a Cave', attracted my attention. It was a scientific chronical which sought to describe the effects of confinement and isolation on mental and biological rhythms. The study intrigued me because I am so acutely aware of my reactions to the isolation and confinement of prison.

Michel Siffre, the subject of the experiment and the author of the article began with these words:

"Overcome with lethargy and bitterness, I sit on a rock and stare at my campsite in the bowels of Midnight Cave, near Del Rio, Texas. . . . I am living "beyond time", divorced from calendars and clocks, and from sun and moon, to help determine, among other things, the natural rhythms of human life . . ."

Bundy Letter Two, Page 1

(2)

While I am not, like Mr. Siffre, confined to determine the natural rhythms of human life, I am very conscious of my particular rhythms, my reactions to incarceration. Imprisonment is experimental isolation; an experience common to both of these conditions is a sense of living "beyond time", and a paralysis born by lethargy and bitterness.

Under conditions which induce emotional distress and deteriorated mental functioning, how can a psychologist, such as yourself, begin to distinguish traits distorted or produced by the deprivations of the prison environment from traits (characteristics/behaviors) displayed by an inmate when he is free to respond a community environment? Are you, like Mr. Siffre, simply measuring reactions to stress, isolation, and confinement or can you actually assess the real person, uncontaminated by imprisonment.

I ask these questions because I am concerned that a confounding variable may be interfering with the analysis made of an inmate. Hostility, anger, bitterness, neurosis, defensiveness, or anti social attitudes may be a response to the pressures and realities of prison and not

Bundy Letter Two, Page 2

(4)

Prison has had its effect on me. Lethargy, bitterness, depression, anti-social attitudes, and disorganized thought processes have all been reactions apparent to me. But I resist the destruction of my personality and myself and I will not be lured into the common weaknesses which prison breeds. I become objective about my situation because it raises me above the chaos and corruption of the moment. Defensive? Perhaps. I like myself, too much, to allow prison to make me a cruel, insensitive, violent and anti establishment convict just to survive.

Beneath the reactions to confinement there remains the essential ingredients of my personality. I have not concealed them from you. Still you seem uncomfortable. Why? What are you looking for? Is it some intuitive feeling which says you do not know me? Unfortunately, our relationship is artificial and forced by the pressures of time; you cannot know me and I cannot know you in such a short time.

Bundy Letter Two, Page 3

SIXTEEN

Florida Court Document

IN THE CIRCUIT COURT OF THE SECOND JUDICIAL CIRCUIT OF FLORIDA, IN AND FOR LEON COUNTY.

CASE NO. 78-670-CF

STATE OF FLORIDA: Plaintiff,

vs.

THEODORE ROBERT BUNDY: Defendant

DEPOSITION OF: JAMES STEVEN BODIFORD

TAKEN AT THE INSISTENCE OF: THE DEFENDANT

DATE: FEBRUARY 27, 1979

TIME: 2:00 PM

LOCATION: LEON COUNTY COURTHOUSE TALLAHASSEE, FLORIDA

REPORTED BY: JADA D.

REGISTERED PROFESSIONAL REPORTER

OFFICIAL COURT REPORTER

303A LEON COUNTY COURTHOUSE

TALLAHASSEE, FLORIDA

...And he would say, "well, you know, I —" and this, that and the other.

And this was the feeling among us. The whole tone of conversation was that the "problem" was that something had developed in him that caused him to kill people. And I don't think there's any doubt that he understood what we were asking him.

Q: Can you recall as well as you can — well, let me strike that. Let me ask you a little better.

What specifically, to the best of your recollection would have given both you and him the impression that what you were talking about was killing people?

A: Well, we were talking — Obviously, he knew that Investigator Patchen and I were investigating the murders at the sorority in Tallahassee. We talked with him about his charge in Colorado and his conviction in Utah. We talked with him about the allegations in Seattle.

And it was perfectly clear that we were talking about a speech defect or a hearing problem when we referred to his "problem". The whole conversation was pointed at talking about murders, that he had been accused of or was at least suspected of.

Q: And when you asked him about when did his problem start, what did he tell you?

A: There again, in one conversation he said — I don't think it was this night. I think it was another night.

Q: Well, these may get mixed up a little bit, but, all right, go ahead. I would rather have the substance of what he said.

A: He said to me when I was talking to him, or I think

that I had to ask him something along the lines of when did it start and how did it start. He said, "Guys, remember this. It may be important later." He said, "One day I was going home." I think he said he was riding his bicycle, or walking, but he wasn't in a car.

He said, "I passed a girl on the street"; and he said, "I had a feeling I had never had." He said, "I wanted to possess her," and he used the word "possess," "by whatever means was necessary." He said, "I just had to have that girl."

And he said, "I followed her home, and she went inside and I never saw her again." But he said, "that's the first time that I remember really having a problem." You know, words to that effect. "It's the first time I ever remember," you know, and that had been when he was still in Seattle and still in school in Seattle. To give you an exact age, I can't, but it was in Seattle when he was still there.

Now he made a point of telling us to remember that, that it could be important. I don't know what the significance of it is right now but I remember him saying — and I forgotten your question.

Q: The question was where did it start.

A: Okay, that's the only thing that I can remember him actually saying, you know, "this is the first time that I had any feelings or problems." I don't know if this was before or after the voyeurism. I don't know if this was before or after he was cruising in his car at night. But this is what he told us that we should remember as a key point.

Q: Did he tell you about other instances in which he had experienced this problem?

A: Not like that. Not that I remember. Not any like that, that he would talk about, you know, actually pinpoint down one situation and one female.

Q: Did he ever talk about harming people or having the capability of harming people, in those words or similar words?

A: Here again, Mr. Minerva, it's difficult to explain to you because we didn't talk in terms of "have you ever hit anybody in the head?"

Q: Okay, that's what I wanted to find out first.

A: We talked one night, and this is back in Tallahassee, and I know I'm jumping from night tonight a lot but I'm trying to give you the context. I think that's what you're asking for.

Q: That's right.

A: We talked about one night, for example, his car. He said the front seat was either loose or out of it, the right front of his Volkswagen.

"Well, why?"

"Well, I can carry things easier that way."

"You mean you can carry bodies easier that way?"

And he said, "well, let's just say I can carry cargo better that way."

And he said, "sometimes it was damaged and sometimes it wasn't."

Now to me, you know, we're talking, and we might as well be speaking Spanish or Greek or something else, we're talking about human bodies and sometimes they are hurt and sometimes they aren't, you know. But that's the type of thing we're talking about context-wise.

You know, we didn't say, "did you ever — These bodies you were carrying around, where they hurt or were they well?" You know, we didn't say that. But we set it in so many words, and he understood what we were asking.

Q: Now eventually, you got to talking, did you not, about control, his abilities to control his problem? Do you recall that conversation?

A: I remember some conversation about that. I remember we talked that he felt like he had his problem under control.

(Transcript ends)

SEVENTEEN

Art Norman Tape 5

Ted Bundy, Tape 5: An Interview by Dr. Art Norman.

The purpose of the interview was to do a competency hearing for the court.

Ted spent a lot of time in his room or out walking during his early teen years. He walked all night.

"I was feeling increasingly isolated from my friends who were developing new friends outside the neighborhood in the bigger scheme of things in high school."

Consequently, they were often gone when he went over to their place to see them. He didn't make the junior varsity basketball team. But he wasn't an object of ridicule. He wasn't the nerd. He also wasn't totally out of touch with his friends. But the contact was largely in school. I just couldn't bring myself to take that step to really get into relationships outside of school like that. He wasn't sure what he did on weekends. He was spending more and more time by himself because the friends he had in the neighborhood were taking on other friends. No one tried to fix him up with a date. He was friends in school with those who were academically and socially adept and such. He wasn't a recluse in the traditional sense of the word. He wasn't totally withdrawn.

In his senior year Ted was a skiing fanatic . His relationship with girls was "totally nonexistent." He came from a middle-class home and his parents had very little money and Ted took up skiing. Ted earned his own money and bought his own stuff. He didn't steal his skis.

"When it comes to skiing, I was not the least bit bashful or shy. I was very assuming, very assertive and very much into skiing."

In skiing, he related with guys he wouldn't normally have related to in social settings but he had no reluctance to approaching them when it came to skiing. The class president and the head of the newspaper were all his close skiing buddies. He had close skiing buddies and they formed a car pool during his senior year. These were kids he hadn't had relationships with previously because they had their own cars and they were the socially elite.

"But when it came to skiing, I was right there with them. I wasn't doing it as a pretext to get involved. I did it out of the pure love for skiing. I just loved to ski. So, I lost all my inhibitions and all my reserve. Every week a different one of us drove up skiing and I scrapped together every cent I could on my own and I bought my own skis and boots and all those things. Every weekend all winter long in my junior and my senior year I skied. They had a great time in the car and lodge drinking hot chocolate. On the slopes and in the car going up and coming back, it was a very pleasant experience. We had a great time in the car and in the lodge."

When he got back home following a skiing trip, "I went back into the shell. I felt out of touch with them. It's odd how these things develop but that's how it developed. I just felt out of touch with what was happening. I just felt unequipped to socialize with these people. I'd do things with my friends on the ski slopes but when it got into the dating thing or the party thing or the after-school thing it just wasn't there. About the quality of his skiing: I never took lessons but I worked like a dog and read every book that I could get my hands on and so I imagine I progressed with a lot of youthful enthusiasm and blind courage. I felt I was as good as anybody. One of the fellows hit on a way of counterfeiting - it cost $5.00 a day plus gas money."

Warren Dodge had his own car. Ted rode to school with Warren for most of his high school years along with others who rode also. Five or six of them. He graduated from high school at the age of 18.

Regarding his interest in being a lawyer, it had a certain amount of prestige, importance and material well-being. His interest started when he was a child when saw a movie about a lawyer and he was "profoundly impressed." He didn't translate that into how to do it.

"However, my mind tended toward, to be interested during that period, toward political kinds of issues. I seemed to have a natural affinity as a student towards social studies, political science. I picked it up very quickly, was always listening to the news, would listen to talk shows which then were in their infancy. Ira Blue - Hungry Eye. I would stay up to 1:00 in the morning with a plug in my ear. I knew the names of political people and senators and governors and cabinet members naturally. It just seemed to come naturally."

He wasn't using it to impress others. He didn't tell others he was going to be a lawyer or in politics.

In the summer of 1965 (after graduating from high

school) he got involved in a congressional campaign for the United States Congress, the House of Representatives. Nobody in his family had been in politics. [The Yacht Club was 1966] He worked full time during that summer because he cut a guy's lawn who a supervisor at City Light in Tacoma. He got him a full-time job at excellent wages. He worked at that during the daytime and he started coming out of himself a little. He purchased a reconditioned 1933 Plymouth Coup. This was his first car.

He had to borrow the family car in high school - only one in the family. Ted said it was an impulsive action. He was coming out of himself a little. During the night he got involved with this campaign.

"I started to meet people and it felt really secure. Here was something I understood. Like skiing, there was a structured kind of setting around which social relationships could evolve. I felt comfortable with people. The same with politics and that began a kind of interest in politics."

However, he continued to have an interest in pornography, but he had graduated from the neighborhood library.

65-67 - After graduation from high school. He worked during the summer at a good job making good money and the summer after graduation he worked on a political campaign. He was also doing the library thing. He said he didn't feel inept or have a low self-worth. "A lot of that I did leave behind in high school." He said he was in a different setting than he had in high school, such as the pressure for dating, involvement on the school paper, etc. Still no women in his life.

He worked that summer and went to UPS. University of Puget Sound that fall. His parents moved from the old house to a lovely old warnl home. This house was a couple blocks away from UPS, small quiet street - a two story house. He had a scholarship of sorts and also a grant. So, his finances were taken care of. He lived at home. That was a difficult year though. He was living at home, and also like in high school "I was just going to classes. The whole social scene was impenetrable at UPS. UPS is a school where 80% of the students were part of fraternities and the fraternities themselves were part of student housing. Fraternities and sororities were part of student housing. They had very few. They had very, very few independent type students there." Ted went through rush and had the opportunity to join one of the houses but they required that he become involved full time and move into their housing and do all that stuff by the first of September. His job lasted until the latter part of that month so he decided not to join that fraternity. He couldn't afford to let his job go. "So, UPS became in its own way "an extension of the troubles I was having with the discontent I was experiencing in high school. Just a total lack of connection with the students outside the classroom. I would go to school and I'd come home." In high school he had a few close friends living in the neighborhood, but now he wasn't even living in the neighborhood any longer. He still skied but all his friends had gone off to college and he didn't even have a car pool. He sold his 1933

Plymouth and "Got into my beloved Volkswagen that winter. I struggled a little in some of the classes." But he had a 3.0 average.

For reasons not entirely clear to him he decided he wasn't going to go to UPS the next year. He had to get away from Tacoma. He decided to go to the University of Washington and major in Chinese. (This is the part he said that isn't entirely clear.) The only reason he can think of was that he was going to major in Chinese rather than accounting. He felt that there was a grave stupidity in the injustice towards

China so he was going to learn Chinese. It was a leap in terms of getting out on his own and in terms of sort of taking a shot in the dark. He was conservative and non-risk taking. He believes that there were some elements of disorganization in his thoughts, such as, he wasted a lot of time that year at UPS. He believes that he was less efficient to a degree in his cognitive processes at UPS than in high school. However, high school was more organized - he was in school all day long. He was less comfortable in UPS than at he had been in high school. He might have felt more incompetent. Ted said it might have been because he had fewer social contacts - significantly fewer social contacts than he did in high school. "So, I really didn't have anybody to talk to. I didn't know anybody."

Regarding his thinking during that time: Was there anything bothering you more specifically - such as fantasies, thoughts. Ted: "I'm trying to recall."

At UPS, Ted would walk home from school and shoot baskets for hours. He loved walking. "I just watched people and things."

For years and years and years he had a problem with acne. From the age of 25 he didn't have an acne problem but around 15-16 as he was starting high school it was, "One more burden. I was embarrassed by it.? However, he didn't want to give it more importance than it deserved. He has been asking himself, "What was going on in my life that made me pull back like that?

Was it just something so unconscious that I can't recall?"

When Norman read a thing to him on the body this memory of his acne came back. A point here is that Ted wasn't aware of what was controlling his life at that time. The same was true with others. "None that I knew of were aware of the direction they were taking in their life during their teens. I wasn't either.

It was the precipitating - the period that contained a lot of stuff of what became the low point of my life. I went off down there with all kinds of great expectations and high hopes and just feeling terrific about myself but I think my confidence was a mile wide and an inch deep. I don't know that I was ready to deal with all that I was going to have to deal with down there at Stanford. I flew down to Stanford in June of 1967 and it was a typical beautiful Palo Alto June, just beautiful sky, dry air and palm trees and it was a whole new environment and Stanford itself was just gorgeous."

He made a junket or two to San Francisco. He registered and met the people who were in the Chinese Language program, were in a dorm. "It was a neat place. The environment could not have been more conducive to doing well in studying. We had the best instructors in the business down there." They were assigned to classes.

"I don't know quite how to explain how things started to unfold. But, to begin with, I just couldn't apply myself to class. I can't say why, I had done very well in Chinese up north." Ted was in Palo Alto and Stephanie (Diane was in Seattle and her parents lived in a suburb of San Francisco. Stephanie (Diane) was going to summer school at the UW but she did come down for her birthday in July. "But I couldn't get into class. I couldn't get into studying. I wasn't applying myself. I couldn't 't focus and I found myself - I bought a bicycle - and I found myself riding around. Oh, this is great. La de da. I'm playing lots of tennis. I had never lived in an environment with so much sunshine. I wasn't skipping for class but I wasn't studying for class either. I was just sort of trying to slip by. I started to slip. People were moving ahead with the class work and I wasn't. Then Stephanie (Diane) cane down for her birthday and I stayed at her parent's house. She had really nice parents, nice people. We went to dinner with her friends and went to different places around San Francisco. Stephanie (Diane) and I were just having a great time. I picked her up from the airport when she came in. We just had a fine time. I was still feeling very good, but I shouldn't have been from the way I was doing in school. I just wasn't working at it. I had never failed in school before. Not completely. I had a little bit of difficulty at UPS not applying myself but I had never completely given up, which what I did at Stanford. It was a marvelous opportunity for anybody. I just couldn't apply myself. It wouldn't have mattered what I was studying down there at the time. I can't explain why.

I started to get these flashes of doubt and worry and anxiety about Stephanie (Diane) who'd gone back to Seattle."

Ted had heard that she was playing tennis with some guy and he began worrying that she was going out with him "And I think I got a letter from her that was indifferent or something and all of a sudden, I think I panicked or something about our relationship. I never had a relationship with a girl before or felt this intensely about someone in that way before. I didn't know how to deal with that kind of stuff All of a sudden, a lot of insecurities started. This was severe stuff . Then things really started to fall apart. I was having trouble concentrating in school before but now all I could think about was Stephanie (Diane). I was really feeling maudlin and teary and worried and panic stricken and deserted and lost and ruined and all these things started flooding in on me. It was like [tape was interrupted].

I didn't know what I wanted to do. All of a sudden school was totally meaningless and Chinese was something that just left me. I just lost touch. I couldn't study and then this thing with Stephanie (Diane). All of a sudden, I felt this terrible sense of betrayal, of fear, of loss. She never wrote me a Dear John letter as such. All of this stuff just started flooding in on me. It was frightening. I didn't know what to do. I remember calling her one time almost on the verge of tears telling her I was going to join the Air Force. I was going to just quit school and join the Air Force. I was so lost. I went to that chapel at Stanford. I said I need help. What's going on here. I was really desperate. And at one point - talk about desperate - I borrowed some money from people down there and flew up to Seattle without letting anybody know including Diane because I was so desperately worried about her and about us. I just didn't know how to cope or deal with these feelings or understand what was happening to me. Indeed, she seemed a lot cooler and less enthusiastic about us. Utter loss of direction. I didn't know what was happening. I was frightened about not being able to handle school. That frightened the hell out of me. I was panicked. He didn't start drinking."

Norman asked if he felt he was losing touch with reality. "That's one way of describing it, being fearful of losing touch with reality. I would just wander and walk and walk around campus and I just seemed to be out of touch with everything. Nothing made sense. Nothing seemed to work. I didn't seem to be able to do anything or change anything. I felt helpless and hopeless. Ted said he didn't seek counseling. He had never heard of such a things as a counseling center on campus. I couldn't get it out. I didn't talk to anybody about this. I just kept it all inside me." Ted said he may have given this information to Aynesworth but he didn't get into it as deeply as with Norman. "I didn't even take the final exam. I just kind of petered out and just went back north just totally defeated. I went up to see Diane and we drove around and I think she was sensing my utter sense of desperation and confusion. She was sympathetic but it was clear that something wasn't right and she was saying that maybe we shouldn't be seeing each other, and that kind of thing. Ted wasn't hysterical but he was holding it in. I remember one scene in her car in Seattle. We were talking and I was getting wrought, really emotional, expressing all my fears and whatnot. That was fairly murky. I don't remember exactly what I was saying."

Ted didn't remember exactly what was said but he thinks she was aware that he seemed to be coming apart and "we were just friends." He believes he told her that he wasn't in touch with school anymore and he was really afraid of their relationship and he thought she was a great person and they were drifting apart. He even mentioned that he would like to marry her, but it wasn't a proposal. She was sympathetic but distant. "So then I kind of, having accomplished nothing more than agitate myself, traumatized myself more, I flew back to Stanford and sort of went through the motions of finishing up the summer. It was pretty well shot by then."

He never took the final exams. He went back to Seattle in August of 1967. Everything continued to deteriorate. "I got back up there and decided I was finished with Chinese. I had to start something new. And I wasn't feeling really rational or anything and I was still very, very much feeling sorry for myself about the situation with Diane and feeling so alienated from everything. I couldn't even bring myself to get in touch with her anymore. But, going through all the melodrama of it I decided I was going to become an architect because I that summer I saw a movie about an architect. I imagine it was with Audrey Hepburn and somebody else. I said I'm going to be an architect and I had all these visions of Diane and I and I was going to be an architect and I was going through all these really crazy changes. I couldn't get into the architect school because it was full and I went into the closest thing which was Urban Planning. I enrolled in all these courses which were part of the program for urban planning or prerequisites for the program. Sociology and all the other things. I couldn't live in the dorms because that was too painful. Eventually !just left the university because the whole thing just made me hurt.

So, I went to this other part of town close to the university, called Modely."

Part V: Tests in the Assessment

Where possible, we've included the test results from Ted Bundy's 90-day psychological assessment. We've included two chapters from "The 1976 Psychological Assessment of Ted Bundy" by Dr. Al Carlisle.

EIGHTEEN

Make A Picture Answers

(These are Ted's answers to the Make A Picture test. The images have been redacted.)

1.

Ted: This is a forest scene where the young boy and, well, the servant boy have gone out looking for the boy's sister and the dog who are late to dinner. On seeing the sister, the boy walks over to tell her that she has lost track of time and they have been out in the woods for an hour and they better get back to the house for dinner.

She often likes to go into the woods and play with her dog The boy gets a little bit irritated at times. He always has to come looking for her and this time the servant boy has come along too,

Al: What emotions do they feel?

Ted: Well, the boy's hungry and he wants to get back and eat. The emotion is hunger. This other lady just doesn't care, she wanted an opportunity to get out of the hot kitchen anyway for a walk out the back so she just long for the walk, The girl looks happy, looks like she is smiling. Perhaps she's just that maybe her brother's yelled at her so much before that she just ignores it now. There's really no wrong when she does, this is just something she does before dinner. She occasionally does and she has lost track of time again. Feels a little bit embarrassed that she has forgotten, since dinner was almost ready. But she doesn't, she's sort of reluctant to go back to the house because she sort of likes to walk with her dog. It is about the only time she can find, is just before dinner.

Al: OK, is there an ending to it?

Ted: Yea, the ending is going back for dinner. So, they all troop back together. The dog running between peoples' legs, the girl talking to this other woman, the boy running after the dog.

Al: How about a theme, is there a theme to the story?

Ted: A moral?

Al: Just a type of theme, not necessarily a moral.

Ted: Children losing track of time, I guess, I don't know if that's a theme – a logical theme.

2.

Ted: Well, we have an accident scene here where the man who is down on the street has just been struck by the car. In the lower righthand corner of the picture there is the driver of the car explaining how, explaining to the officer in the picture, how the man stepped out in front of him, the doctor, who is coming down the sidewalk, is going to come to the aid of the man End the man's wife who is starting to come across the street where she has been standing there. She is rather upset. She has her hand up to her head. She is really worried about her husband.

The man explains to the policeman how the man just walked right out in front of him. The man must have been drunk, he didn't look either way or something. He trying to convince the policeman that the guy walked out of this cocktail lounge that appears to be pictured here in this scene. Of course, there is no evidence to show that so the cop seems to be rather irritated, He seems to be waiting for the ambulance and the man driving the car is bending his ear off with his excited denial that he failed to stop for the pedestrian.

The man wasn't hurt badly. Has his head down on his arm in the gutter there.

As he was hit, he was knocked to the ground and banged his head and his face,

The doctor being -- the doctor Is going to get involved, but he doesn't want too because he knows what malpractice suits are nowadays, and his lawyer, or attorney cautioned him not to go the aid of accident victims because so often they get sued as a result.

The woman is just very, very, concerned.

That could be an ambulance there, but I can't tell.

It is a rather routine accident for the policeman, he has seen so many and he knows that the man is not seriously injured and all he wants to do is get this taken care of because it is already near the time, he wants to get off work. This makes his irritation—his irritation is increased by the excited explanations of the driver of the car who seems more concerned about preserving his car insurance than the man who is laying in the street.

It is a warm day; the woman is without a coat. The doctor has his coat over his arm. It is late afternoon and the woman and her husband were on their way to pick up some gifts, to pick up some clothing for a vacation they were going to take--for this is Friday afternoon and this whole thing seems such an abrupt turnaround of events on such a nice day.

It appears that he suffered some lacerations and a concussion but he will be released from the hospital. While they won't go on their vacation, they are just happy that it wasn't more serious.

I guess the theme in this particular scene is how sometimes people are-at an accident are more concerned about the consequences of their own involvement, rather than injuries suffered.

3.

Ted: This right down in the episode of Superman. I guess if we are going to do fiction, we might as well do fiction. If you recall, Superman had this sidekick, Jimmy, I think his name was Jimmy. Then there was this woman who worked in the office, Jane. Anyway. We have a heavy in the picture who is just robbed a jewelry store of several million dollars' worth of diamonds. In the process this —- has lured this Jimmy and Jane out to the bridge in exchange for an opportunity to talk to Superman. When Superman arrives, he drops him over the side of the bridge which is where Jane is now looking. It seems that instead of actually dropping the diamonds over the bridge, he has dropped a bag full of Kryptonite over the side and he hopes that Superman will go over and pick up the bag and of course, we all know the Kryptonite makes Superman whatever, weak, In the course of Superman retrieving the bag will drown. He is one of the local heavies in the crime syndicate who is constantly plagued by Superman's super-human efforts to thwart crime in Gotham City or wherever, the man was.

This fails, of course. Jimmy is peeved in this picture. He is very upset it seems and Jane somewhat aghast that all that has gone down the tube. Superman isn't going to fall for it because with his x-ray vis ion he has seen that the bag actually contained something else. He knows what the guy is up too.

I wouldn't have been a very good script writer if Superman hadn't gotten out.

Al: How does it end now?

Ted: Jimmy runs and calls the police to come and pick up this man and Superman flies off and becomes Clark Kent again, I could never figure out how they could never identify him, but such is life.

Al: Any theme?

Ted: Don' t trick Superman.

4.

Al: This is the fourth one, the living room scene.

Ted: The father, the owner of the house is opening the door to find his daughter and his son-in-law at the door. He has had a long day. He is a professional man. He is a businessman, he's had a long day and he is very tired and it is quite obvious from his sort of tired appearance on his face, but he hasn't seen his daughter now for a year and with her is her husband who was injured in the war. Things have not been going well. She is very tired and she has come back to her dad to ask for some help. He doesn't seem to be in the mood to talk and while she is pleading, her husband is quite defiant because he has had a hard time finding work because of his injury which has left him s lightly paralyzed from the waist down, but he still refuses to take any handouts or help from her father. This makes it very hard for her but she finally in exasperation has come and brought him along and he is still not willing to yield. She is pleading with her father for some financial help and he in a moment of sarcasm has pulled a quarter out of his pocket and offered it to her and asking if that will be enough,

It is too bad because their relationship used to be much better, but through a misunderstanding they have been unable to reconcile themselves He is a very hard, strong-willed man and it is an especially bad time of day for him to be dealing with this kind of a situation. They're not in the mood for compromise or reconciliation. She is caught in the middle between the two of them, they are unable to reach any kind of absolution, so they leave and he somewhat disconsolately goes back and has a nap or whiskey or something, which (rest of sentence missing)

The theme of this if such a theme--the emotional barriers / keeps people apart when those barriers are so easily overcome and when the people involved under slightly different circumstances would be able to get so much. Would be able to gain so much from each other, not just materially but father and daughter shouldn't be separated when there is really no logical reason why they should continue to hate like this.

5.

Al: This one is the fifth one, the bedroom scene.

Ted: A day in the life of myself actually, I am in bed, which is normally the case, and Liz is getting dressed and Molly has just come into the room. And the moral of the story is that Liz always gets mad at Ted when he sleeps in and she has to get up and go to work and he doesn't have to be to school until 10 o'clock. And Molly, looks something like Molly, who is kind of ten (?) has come into the room. She's grumpy in the morning because she doesn't have her hot chocolate and wants Mommy to come fix it right away. Oh no, she's not grumpy, she always wants her Mommy, she wants her hot chocolate first thing in winter.

And Liz is wondering why I can't get up and get it for her. That is why she has that look on her face.

I have the habit of loving to sleep in during the week when she has to get up early and getting up early on the weekends when she likes to sleep in. which makes for a kind of conflict.

Liz is, no... Liz is always in a hurry in the morning. She likes to take a lot of time to get dressed and to get ready for work and she also has to take care of Molly and she can't understand why I can't get up in time to do that. I usually have to jolt out of bed and finally end up fixing Molly's hot chocolate whereupon Liz hops on her bicycle and rides to work.

Molly and I walk to school.

The moral of the story is that Ted had better learn how to behave, the moral of the story, no the theme is that Ted likes to sleep late, let's put it that way. This upsets Liz.

6.

Al: OK, this one is the shanty.

Ted: The days of summer, goofing up boys exploring some deserted area of town that they haven't seen before and they come upon this old shack and try to get into it. The boy on the l eft is at the door, which is ajar, slips and pinched his fingers and he is crying and his friend is screaming at him because he is ruined the door and they were going to make this into a club house.

The other boy on the far right is running to see what happened. They thought about the existence of this place for a long time. They never really had the courage to go in it because they always thought that some old bums lived in there. and were afraid of intruding on them.

Soon the fellow who has pinched his finger has recovers and they go inside to find the standard litter: old wine bottles, couple of bed springs, an old mattress. They feel like they have discovered a new world when they walked in there like they were Lewis and Clark exploring this house for the first time. They decide, however, that this place is too messed up, but they save the bottles, because they collect bottles during the summer and turn them in and they pack the bottles away and explore now hoping to find more goodies and look under the floor boards. There is a lot of talk of coming back and putting in new windows, refurbishing the roof and putting the door back on its hinges. They always talk that way and they are just sort of dreaming of having the place, a place to come and call their own arid make it into a club house. So as young boys do, they quickly lose their interest in the place run to the nearest Safeway store and turn in their bottles and are well fortified now with gum drops and soda pop, their back on their way and looking for new things to discover.

The theme is adventure of being young and finding adventure in things that other people have discarded,

7.

Al: This is the raft, number 7.

Ted: This is the scene after several days on a raft, well actually just a few hours on a raft which is--three people: a prince, a monk, and a pirate. Seems these three unlikely characters have been stranded on the same raft after a battle between the ship on which the pirate was captain, pilot and the prince was a passenger on another vessel that the pirate attacked. The monk was also on the prince's ship.

both ships were sunk, the three survivors scrambled upon the holds of a ship and find themselves very, very different people with one thing in common-survival. The pirate is contemptuous to find himself on a raft with a man of the cloth and a man of royalty. The prince is somewhat arrogant because he feels hostility towards the pirate who sunk his ship but, there is a loss of dignity with being adrift and his power and his influence. He is just one man trying to survive. The priest stands as a mediator between these two. He finds, well he doesn't think they are foolish enough to start fighting.

knows that only if they work together are we going to survive. Still in this picture they haven't been together long enough to discard the social roles, you might say, which holds them apart so the prince is, he is still arrogant, the pi rate is still defiant and the priest finds himself frustrated by the situation. Ultimately, however, the hostility and the circumstances overcome the pettiness of their own differences and all three of them, not just the pi rate and prince, but all three of them recognize they have more in common at the present time than any superficial differences they may have had in the past. They begin to work together and go over ideas. They find a sense of camaraderie that is quite surprising because they never felt that they had that much in common and could really communicate with each other. The prince, for instance, is contemptuous of religion, as the pi rate, you know, he would only use the church to manipulate his own political ends. The priest has always realized this, but through their weeks on the raft they find, well they find that the priest is not only a human being, he represents someone who is a necessary influence in their lives.

Ultimately, they are picked up by a trading vessel from a neutral country. They are taken back to a country that none of them have been in before. While they eventually make their way back to their own homelands, they're changed people to the degree that they shared humbling experiences and exposed to death on a daily way. The experience has mellowed them, mellowed them all toward each other but still they find themselves assuming the role that they had had prior to this experience.

And I guess the theme seems to me to be that people thrown together from widely different individual experiences, backgrounds, beliefs, find the common element of survival, of living, and of just being a human being which would be more powerful than position, roles which they occupied before which seemed to make them miles apart.

8.

Al: This is the eighth one, the landscape.

Ted: The landscape is that of a very barren, arid, desert like existence with some very abstract kinds of objects; rocks and some stick-like things sticking in the ground in the sand. With that kind of background there are very few people who are dressed for this experience or sightseeing or anything else. So, we have another ________. Here is a young couple who have been on vacation from the east coast and they are traveling to the west coast to this desert region and decided to take a side road to-just to do exploring as tourists do. After driving for a number of mi les, their car broke down. They couldn't get it to start. They begin walking back in the direction they thought that the highway was in. Unfortunately, their sense of direct ion was not that good and they became lost in this very trackless, directionless reg on. It is hot. The man has succumbed at least temporarily to exhaustion, dehydration as well as the woman t

They are both holding their stomachs because they feel nauseous from the heat and lack of water, they see in the distance there are some mountains and they recognize some point in their driving and they are trying to make their way back, the woman has to help her husband up, he is bigger than her, they make their way slowly across this extremely hot dungeon (?).

Fortunately, after a couple of hours when both of them could nearly wouldn't be able to move any longer some young people on dune buggies who like to scramble around in this open sandy reg ion saw the two and picked them up and took them to the sheriff Iso

There is really no moral to this only then not to drive into unknown regions unprepared.

9.

Al: Number nine, the cemetery scene.

Ted: Every year at this time the older woman and her three daughters come to pay their respects to their dead father, He died two years ago before the girls were ready to leave the home, they are quite old in terms -- they are in high school so that the death of their father was felt very deeply by them all because they were old enough to understand the significance of his loss. And now while they're all two of them are going to college, one is married and they are feeling great devotion not only to their mother but to the memory of their father, well more than once a year, a couple of them come as often as two or three times, The old woman is quite loyal and tries to come once a month to pay her respects to her dead husband,

It's harder for them because they are younger and they are not perhaps as wise in the ways of living and dying as their mother is, so while she is sad, they are extremely sad, two are crying and one seems to be very upset.

I guess it sort of reflects a philosophy, a point of view

about paying respects to people who have passed away and they feel that so much of their life is owed to their father that they feel that it is respect not only to his memory but out of respect out of what he has made them that they come to visit him at his grave site, it makes them—it reminds them of who they are and what their father was.

I guess the theme would be that those who pass away never really leave use they dwell. The mourning at the gravesite is one way of remembering someone who relives in the kind of people they have made us before they left,

10.

Ted: This is a dream, number 10. And he made the comment that if she had her clothes on “l would rather use her with her clothes on”. Right?

Al: Yea

Ted: Well, there’s no disguising it, I dream a great deal and I think a great deal and mostly I think about Liz and it’s hard and think about the things we have done and how they’re doing now. I think about how Molly’s life is now that she has turned 10. How she has changed, she's maturing, And I think about Liz and all the sad lonely time she is having now, I think about how she has changed—changing. She writes me so frequently about how having been involved in a number of different things, becoming more active and trying to develop a more assertive personality, more honest approach towards things, Being honest and outspoken about her feelings.

Becoming involved and feeling good about herself. Trying to feel good about herself. And I like the thought about what is happening to her, but I always long to see her and wish that was there and see this all going on.

It’s hard to picture their faces after you think about them

so often, but I can still remember Liz's face very vividly and Molly's too, it just hurts to think about them and feel that you might not see each other for a long time.

Now what are we going to cover here? I wasn't aware that we were going to record this.

NINETEEN

Thematic Apperception Test

(Extracted from "The 1976 Psychological Assessment of Ted Bundy" by Al Carlisle.)

The Thematic Apperception Test, commonly known simply as the TAT, is a projective personality test comprised of a number of black and white pictures of various situations, most of them of people interacting in some manner. A person taking the test is asked to make up stories for the pictures. The TAT is a "projective test" because when a person tells a story to match a picture, he "projects" aspects of himself into the picture. He is saying something about himself through the story. An analysis of a set of stories reveals information about a person's motives, fears, hopes, and anticipations.

It was clear at this point of the evaluation that Ted had some serious emotional problems. I wanted to see what a projective test would tell me about the inner workings of Ted Bundy.

I'm putting the stories and my suggested interpretation of

the stories in this chapter for historical reasons. The interpretations of the stories are my own.

There are multiple ways to consider each story and you may want to devise your own. Where necessary I have given a brief description of the picture Ted was looking at when he told his story. The pictures are copyrighted and publication of them is illegal so I can't include the images here.

NAME: Theodore Bundy
DATE: April 28, 1976

Picture number 1: A boy sitting at a table looking at a violin. There is a white object under the violin which appears to be sheet music.

This is a young man who has been practicing all afternoon on his violin. He looks tired if not sleepy. He's been at school all day and has been up since early in the morning and came home and practiced his violin and has set it down now and appears to be so sleepy that he's about ready to nod off. To me there appears to be an element of being tired on his face, which could also be boredom, but he looks like the kind that would faithfully practice his violin because he looks like the kind of boy who would want to learn how to play it. I suppose he's just about finished because when you're so tired you can't… he couldn't practice anymore anyway, but he'll keep at it because it's important to him and it's important to those around him.

Interpretation: Ted has been struggling with his legal problems since he was first arrested on the evening of August 16th, 1975. Also, Ted was struggling with his attempt to get through college with a law degree. The boy in the picture is about to give up because he's too worn out to continue, but "it's important to him and it's important to those around him," so he won't stop.

Theme: You can't give up no matter how tired you get.

Picture number 2: (His story describes the picture.)

This is a family, a father, a mother leaning on the tree, the father tilling the fields in the springtime, a young daughter whose interests are not in the fields and not in a family life on the farm, but perhaps in the city with another occupation: being a teacher or a nurse or a doctor. She's pained inside because she doesn't want to leave her parents, but she knows that she must find her own life and she's trying to think of the best way to initiate the subject of her leaving with them. She has a feeling that they wouldn't agree with her, or they would try to convince her to stay, which would hurt her very much because she wouldn't want to go against their wishes and yet eventually she does talk to them and finds to her surprise that they know that she is looking for something else and to find a place for her in the city with relatives so that she can attend school.

Interpretation: He is identifying with the girl in this picture. The girl is not interested in "the family life on the farm." Ted wanted a career that was different from family tradition. Also, he was not satisfied that Liz was good enough to be a politician's wife. He was always seeking someone different. He was never able to stay with jobs, schools, or other relationships. The "farm life" is not spectacular enough for him. He has always been looking for something elsewhere to satisfy him but has failed. He has to keep looking. The "family" in this story could be his mother, his girlfriend Liz, Marjorie, or anyone who have attempted to satisfy him. They all realize that he has to make his own decisions but there is nothing in the story that says they are happy about it.

Theme: One has to look somewhere else other than where he is to find satisfaction.

Picture number 3: Woman sitting with her head down on a seat. She could be crying or is simply tired. There is a small object beside her.

Here is a woman who is very distraught or at least appears resigned and tired. She has a gun that lays on the floor, which she dropped there in utter defeat, so as it were, knowing that death was not the answer but very frustrated about living. Perhaps realizing in her own mind that because her husband left, because things seem hard was not a reason to give up and that she still has her family to think of. She may fall asleep there and wake up later and maybe even wonder what drove her to such lengths to… what made her so unhappy with herself or life to want to go so far. She'll go on living and it won't be easy but she'll pick up that gun and throw it away and do the best she can.

Interpretation 1: Ted was frustrated with the way life had turned out for him up to this point. He had achieved only a taste of success in a career. Relationships have not worked out for him. Now he is in prison. He won't give up but from here on it won't be easy.

Interpretation 2: There's another possibility. *If* Ted had killed several women and *if* he was unable to stop, he could feel defeated and totally worn out and "unhappy with [himself] or with life." Perhaps he has considered suicide.

Theme: Life is extremely troubling but you can't give up no matter how much you want to.

Picture number 4: A man and a woman. She is holding on to him and he is pulling away from her. He has an intense look on his face. In the background off to the side is a picture of a woman with bare legs showing.

Both of them have interesting expressions on their faces. The one of the woman is of admiration almost, and of passion. The look on the man's face is one where he looks eager and confident. He may be leaving for some—for a trip or an adventure and she, proud of what he is about to do, wants to kiss him one more time before he leaves. He is dressed in the shirt of a working man but may not have his tie on. They're married and they haven't been married long, but she appears to be very much in love with him and he appears very eager to do what he has to do. It ends up that he was prepared for what he had to do because he had that confidence and he was ready and he came back and now with that job off his mind, he could turn to her and have the same love in his eyes that she has for him.

Interpretation: He sees a couple who have been married only a short time. She is very much in love with him and she is trying to hold on to him. He, however, can't return that passion towards her. There is something that he has to do before he can reciprocate her love. He is eager (driven) and he is confident (he is skilled in doing it). Only after he does what he has to do and has satisfied that unmentioned need can he turn his attention to his wife and her needs. This suggests something that has become an obsession and a compulsive drive for Ted and he has to give in to it. Only after he has achieved what he has to do can he stop thinking about it. When he has done "the job" he can once again "have the same love in his eyes that she has for him." This is similar to Kim reporting that Ted couldn't stop driving in the back areas of Lake Sammamish, looking for something and not being able to settle down until he found it.

Theme: There are some needs that are more necessary than being home with his passionate wife. My take on it is that he is speaking of his drive to find victims.

Picture number 5: An elderly woman is standing by a window but she is looking straight ahead rather than out the window. A younger man with a shirt and tie and a coat is holding onto his hat. He is looking down rather than at the woman.

The woman in the picture is the man's mother. She is an older woman in her 60s. The man has just returned home to find that his father has just died. She has cried all her tears. There is very little she can do. She has been ready and prepared for this and he, younger and not quite prepared, is taking it very much harder than she. It is difficult for them both, but because he came to her, they'll both gain—they'll both be able to support each other and make the initial separation easier than it would have been otherwise. I suppose I would hope that he would ask her to come live with his family because she would be alone—all the children have moved away. And she will.

Interpretation: This may be about him being born illegitimate. His mother had several months to prepare herself for his birth after she was deserted by Ted's father. Ted wasn't informed about it and so he wasn't prepared for it when he did learn about it as a teenager. He is taking it very hard [which he did] but if he comes to her about it, both can gain from it.

Theme: The loss of a father is difficult. He needs to take care of his mother.

Picture number 6: An elderly man is talking to a younger man. The older man is leaning towards the younger man. The younger man is staring off in space as he appears to be listening. The younger man appears to be afraid.

Two attorneys at a friend's table—well actually it looks more like an attorney and a client. The attorney being the gentleman with the mustache, the light hair, dark suit; the client dark hair, younger, light suit. They have just heard testimony from a damaging witness and the attorney is about to whisper to his client to take it easy, that it's not as bad as it sounds, to try to comfort him to try to calm him down. The young man appears bitter like an accomplice has testified against him or like a friend who said something that hurt him very deeply but also angered him. And yet he has restrained himself. So, his attorney tells him this and he tries to understand, although he can't fully, but he trusts his attorney and this makes it easier for him. He is definitely found innocent in my stories. There is no doubt about it. Yes, well the attorney looks like a good one, but looks are deceiving. There can be no happier ending.

Interpretation: This one is fairly easy to interpret. Ted had a good defense attorney who likely tried to encourage him by telling him that it wasn't as bleak as it appeared. Who was the friend who said something that hurt and angered him? Ted came to the attention of the police when his girlfriend Liz informed them that her boyfriend Ted might be the person they were looking for. There were a couple of others who knew Ted fairly well and were friends with him who called the police on him.

Theme: People he has trusted have turned against him and he's not fully certain that he can even trust his attorney. The more general theme is that one can't really trust anyone.

Picture number 7: A young boy by what appears to be a cabin. The door is open and it's dark inside. The boy is sitting on the landing in what appears to be overalls. He has bare feet and he seems to be daydreaming.

He's a little boy that lives in the neighborhood of an old pioneer fort and on bright school days finds it great entertainment to go and sit in the old log cabins and watch the tourists who pay to see what he can see every day. He loves going there because that is part of summer. I thought he was eating something, but he doesn't have anything. He just sits there and watches the tourists come from California and

New Jersey and points all across the United States to his hometown to see a fort which is to him just like home. He comes there every day and tells them stories about the fort that he has heard from his parents and is really quite a curiosity for the tourists, and he enjoys it and loves this strange old place which is so rich in stories, and will come there nearly every day that summer to be an unofficial guide with the people.

Interpretation: Ted seemed to enjoy telling me about the time when he was a child and he had two friends he had fun with. He called the three of them the "three musketeers." That seemed to be an adventurous and fun time in his life.

Theme: The memories of the freedom and friends he had as a child were wonderful. In the story, the boy is an important authority. It's a story of freedom and nostalgia.

Picture number 8: This entire picture is dark other than a man who appears to be looking out an open window. It's light outside and he is silhouetted against the light as if he is about to climb out.

A man staring out of an open window. It is difficult for me to tell anything more about him or about what his expression is or what the room is like. It is an entirely dark picture. Sometimes it reminds me of staring out my window or the windows of the prison looking at the freeway, but there are no bars there so it can't be that. He's looking out across the view he has from his upstairs window. It's been a long hot summer day. He has opened the window to cool off his apartment. The sun is very, very low in the sky and yet he sees a brilliant sunset which he always enjoys watching when one can be seen. He'll stand there by the window with the cool air rushing in until his apartment is cooled and the sun is set and he can rest in comfort in his apartment. The man is staring, not looking out his window, suggesting a strong desire to be out there. Normally he could walk out the door and be away from the heat, but something is preventing him from doing so.

Interpretation: This could be referring to being in prison. There are no bars on his window in this story yet it reminds him of looking out the prison window at the freeway. It's a dark picture as Ted sees it. He can open his window but something has to happen from the outside ("cool air rushing in") that gives him the rest and comfort he is seeking. There are a number of possibilities as to what the "cool air" might be referring to. It's dark inside but beautiful and refreshing outside. When the sun goes down it will be dark inside but that's all right now that something from the outside has comforted him.

Theme: It's been a long hot summer day (his legal problems) but he can see that which created the heat turn into something beautiful—the sunset.

Picture number 9. Man in cemetery, looking down at a grave.

There is a sinister gentleman standing in the middle of the graveyard, it would appear. In spite of his solid face and his rather bizarre dress, and even because it appears by the light it's late in the day and it's getting dark, he's come to pray for a child and lay flowers on the grave of a child who was his—who belonged to he and his wife before their divorce. People don't give him much credit for sentiment but underneath the rather evil, rather sinister, sad face, there is someone who can feel a great deal of loss—and come late at night so people won't mock him so he can be alone in the quiet and think his own thoughts. Perhaps it's because he doesn't want to show the goodness that is inside of him and reveal the weakness (which he thinks is a weakness) that he has for sorrow and sadness. He comes there once a week, stops and thinks about the life he could have had but he knows it is long past time for that life as long as it has passed, and yet he still cares very much and only wishes that things had been different.

Interpretation: This one is especially interesting. The combination of the words "sinister" and "gentleman" suggests a person who has two sides to his personality—one menacing (sinister) and the other an aristocrat (gentleman). Ted was a killer who wanted people to see him as an up and coming politician.

Who is the child? Is he referring to the abortion Liz had? Or, could he possibly be referring to himself as an illegitimate child? Or still, could it be Ann Burr, the girl who went missing (and who Ted was suspected of killing) when he was a teenager? Regardless, he is feeling a deep loss of the child.

There are two strong themes in the story. One theme is that the person is seen as evil by others but there is goodness and the capability for sorrow in him.

Another major theme is that the person feels bad about his life and wishes it could have been different.

But it's too late.

Theme: Even an evil person can feel sorrow and wish that things had been different.

Picture number 10: Woman standing on a bridge looking down into the water.

This scene is a scene along a riverbank in France. It's one of those large commercial rivers that's there to transport the produce—the vegetables, goods of France. It's in France's internal regions, a bridge over the river meant routinely for unloading sacks of potatoes from a barge to a large storage mill. And on that bridge over the river quietly, mid-day, a woman stands to watch the river, contemplating her own life during her lunch hour. She is thinking of the many thoughts that one thinks when one sees a river run by: the places that it goes to, the fun—the good times that have been had with other people. It's like a stream of thought. She remembers, with happiness and some sadness, the people she has known and looks forward with some expectation but has some indecision about the future. She's lonely, but only because the person she wants to be with is not there to be with her. But he will return. She comes here each day because it's the kind of place she can stand to think and deal with her thoughts and feel relaxed.

Interpretations: Ted has conflicting feelings of happy memories but he's not part of it. In the TAT a person can speak of himself whether the picture is of a man or a woman. In this picture, Ted is standing off to the side watching progress occur but he's not part of it. He's thinking about happy memories but with some sadness. He's looking forward to the future with some indecision. He's lonely because the person he wants to be with (Liz?) is not there. However, he will return to her.

Theme: Wishing for something he once had but doesn't have now and isn't sure about the decisions he will have to make in the future.

Picture number 11: Woman looking in the door of a room.

The young woman is obviously crying or in some sort of pain. She's holding her head, her face that is. It's hard to understand just why it is that she feels that way. She's received some news and is very startled by it. Her son it seems was killed in a bicycle accident with a car and she was in another room and just came into this room and is holding the door open, but is unable to go any further. Her grief is too great. She can't think. She can only cry and let emotion take its course. But she is a young mother and she'll have more children and one that will compensate. Her grief will certainly diminish, but she will always remember her son and will always be very fond of him because he was her first.

Interpretation: Ted seems to be talking about the grief his mother is feeling over him. After all, he was her first. There's a finality to it. Her son is dead, not just injured. His career has ended.

Theme: Mother grieves over a permanent loss of her first-born son.

Picture number 12: House in snowstorm.

It's a small mountain village—either some remote section of the Alps where each winter the snows pile high and the small village cottages become covered and overcome, drifted in snow. It's snowing, so apparently the weather is quite fierce even now, as the snowdrifts indicate. But inside it looks warm as the glow around the windows seems to be light inside. It may even be Christmas although I can't tell. It looks like some of the windows are decorated. It's always nice to celebrate Christmas under these conditions because it makes being together and it makes home all that much warmer and all that much more secure when the weather outside is so threatening and so fierce. It looks like the storm is raging still by the way the clouds have gathered in the distance, but there's nothing better than being inside on a night like this. Reminds me of a house that some skiing directors, friends of mine have. They have a very comfortable cabin in Park City. It's always nice to go inside from outside.

Interpretation: He's talking about his current circumstances where he's facing being put in prison and the loss of his future. It's "threatening and fierce" and "the storm is raging still." How nice it would be to be away from the storm, in a comfortable cabin, where there are friends, happiness, and it's "secure." Christmastime is a time when love and companionship is particularly enjoyable.

Theme: He needs a place where he can get away from the fierce storm going on around him. A place where he can be accepted by friends. The violent storm is still going on and he is out in it.

MAKE UP PICTURE: In this one, the person is handed a blank card and is asked to make up a picture and then tell a story to it.

Well, the picture that's in my mind the most—all the time--is a picture of a girl I love very much. It's a picture of her apartment and the memories of us being together. But the one that occurs most often in my mind is the picture of her kneeling, cleaning the oven. Just standing there in the doorway watching her clean the oven when she didn't know I was there, really marveling about how in spite of all the grease around her elbows, the smudges on her face, that I really cared for her--knowing that I could take her any way she was, dirty or clean or any way. In that picture of her when I came over to her, and how happy we were to see each other. And I only hope I know how it ends.

Interpretation: There appears to be two things going on here. First, Ted is aware of the purpose of this test and what it is that I'm trying to discover about him, so he's trying to tell me how much he loves Liz. It's the same as telling the police and others that he and Liz are engaged and will be getting married in December.

On one hand it's contrived, but I think not totally so. Ted had tears in his eyes when he told this story. It indicates that the girl in the picture, whom he suggests is Liz, is someone the man in the picture—Ted—is deeply in love with. In the picture, he is separated from her—he sees her in her home but he isn't there. He's been off somewhere and he's coming home.

Unlike his statements about Liz not being a politician's wife type of person, he is now willing to accept her with all her faults. In this picture, Liz is working hard to take care of the home. It's interesting that he puts the next to the last sentence in the past tense: "When I *came* over to her…" and "… how happy we *were* to see each other." His last statement that "… I only hope I know how it ends" is a deep desire for this reunion. I felt his tears were genuine and not a manipulation to make me feel sorry for him.

Theme: He longs to be back with Liz and he is willing to accept her the way she is. He recognizes how much effort she puts into making a home and right now he really needs her.

Overall, these tests reveal deep emotions of longing, despair, death, discouragement, and hope. He needed Liz but it was often only when he was hurting.

TWENTY

The TWIST Assessment

(Extracted from "The 1976 Psychological Assessment of Ted Bundy" by Al Carlisle.)

Personality and IQ tests are part of a battery of tests that can be used in a psychological assessment. I administered several of these tests to Ted. He scored in the Superior range on an IQ test I gave him, which I could have predicted. After speaking with him for a short time, I could see he was intelligent.

He was given a personality test that asks a person to read a sentence and then mark the sentence either true or false as he sees himself. The test measures levels of anger, depression, and anxiety as well as other emotional and personality factors.

Ted scored very low on each of these dimensions, meaning he did not have any of the personality traits being assessed. By scoring low, he was telling me that he had none of these problems. This is not an easy achievement because the test is designed to cross-reference different dimensions of one's personality, thus making the test hard to fool. His results were not entirely surprising, however, because he had previously been given the Minnesota Multi-phasic Personality Inventory (MMPI), a similar true-false personality test where he had scored low on all of the scales, which would indicate no presence of an emotional problem. This didn't seem accurate, however, because a person who is, or may be, spending a lot of time in prison just doesn't score this low in all of these areas. Either Ted was telling the truth and he was trouble-free, or he was exceptionally good at lying about it.

When Ted's scores didn't match the normal profile of a convicted felon facing prison time, it made the evaluation much harder. I had no choice but to conclude that something was wrong and that Ted was working hard—and well—to hide something. The personality test couldn't indicate what he was hiding. I had to dig deeper.

Another test I gave Ted was the Two Word Incomplete Sentences Test (TWIST), a sentence completion test created by Dr. Allan Roe of Psychological Resources, Inc. This test consists of 38 beginnings of sentences of varying length, and the subject is asked to finish each sentence using one or two words only. This is a projective test in which a person says things about his personality without always being fully aware of just what he is saying about himself, and is thus harder to fool. For the most part, if a person taking this test does not want to appear violent, he will obviously not give an answer such as:

I consider myself to be a… "violent person."

On the other hand, even if the subject of the test is trying hard to conceal a personality problem, the likelihood is that he will write some answers that hint at the truth. The value of this test is not only in the individual answers themselves, but in the pattern across answers, which reflects the person's thoughts and concerns beyond what a single answer will give.

When a person finishes the sentences in a sentence completion test, there may be multiple levels of meaning representing multiple levels of awareness or consciousness within the person. The first level may be an answer given to comply with the demands of the evaluation but also one designed to avoid revealing himself. However, there is sometimes a deeper, more hidden meaning. I have no doubt that when Ted took the TWIST, he attempted to write his answers in a way that would keep me from observing anything that would suggest anger or violence. He wanted to make a good impression for the court. Naturally, this is to be expected. If an offender is taking a psychological assessment that could possibly make the difference between leniency and harsh punishment, he will take whatever approach that seems most logical in order to achieve this outcome.

The following is Ted's sentence completion items on this test, administered on April 1, 1976 at the Utah State Prison. The spelling is his. He printed his answers in capital letters. (Please note, Ted didn't follow the instructions to answer with only two words. In fact, it is common for the subject of this test to overlook that instruction.)

1. I feel: "CHALLENGED."
2. My mind is: "ACTIVE."
3. A good way to relax is: "TO LISTEN TO MUSIC."
4. A person just isn't himself when: "AFRAID."
5. It would be too easy to: "BE DEPRESSED."
6. It's hard to express feelings of: "PRISON LIFE."

7. The only thing that really matters in this world is: "HAPPINESS AND PEACE."
8. Things would be great if I could: "BE ACQUITTED."
9. I've never: "HURT ANYONE."
10 I need: "FREEDOM."
11 I feel I have to: "KEEP LEARNING."
12. A person is most helpless when: "WITHDRAWS FROM OTHERS."
13. My mother was usually: "LOVING."
14. Most people think I am: "(WHO KNOW ME) INNOCENT."
15. Marriage is: "INTIMATE PARTNERSHIP."
16. I can't: "STOP STRUGGLING."
17. I wish I hadn't: "COME TO UTAH."
18. It's easy to get into trouble when: "OTHERS AREN'T CONSIDERED."
19. When I was a child I felt: "CONSTANT ADVENTURE."
20. I want to know why: "ABOUT EVERYTHING."
21. I am: "CONFIDENT."
22. Drugs are: "DESTRUCTIVE."
23. Worse than being lonely is being: "UNLOVED."
24. Women are: "MEN'S EQUALS."
25. I hate: "PREJUDICE."
26. When frustrated I: "I DESENSITIZE."
27. The thing I remember about my father was: "BOUNDLESS ENERGY."
28. In the future there will be: "NEW OPPORTUNITIES."
29. Compared to most families mine usually: "WAS CLOSE."
30. What excites me is: "SPRING-TIME."
31. I don't like people who are: "SOLICITOUS."

32. I think most girls should: "BE THEMSELVES."
33. My greatest weakness is: "PROCRASTINATION."
34. Someday I will become: "AN ATTORNEY."
35. I wish I could lose the fear of: "HYPODERMIC NEEDLES."
36. I was proud of myself when: "FINISHED COLLEGE."
37. I couldn't live without: "CARING PEOPLE."
38. Tests like this are: "OBLIGATORY; OBTUSE."

(Editor's Note: Appendix V contains an image of the actual test response sheet filled out by Ted.)

Analysis

According to the assessment, Ted felt challenged (item 1) about what the court's final conclusions might be regarding him doing time in prison. It would be easy to be depressed about it (item 5). However, he needed his active intelligent mind (item 2) to be free from distractions if he was going to devise solutions to the obstacles facing him. If he allowed himself to feel much fear (item 4), it might diminish his mental capability to be successful in facing his challenges. However, it won't be easy and he can't stop struggling (item 16) even though he feels confident (item 21).

So, how does Ted handle the situation when he feels it might not turn out well for him? How does he keep himself from being controlled by the normal fear and anxiety that most people would feel if they were in his shoes? He desensitizes (item 26). It's a technique he likely learned in one of the psychology classes he took in college.

Desensitization is a psychological process used to help a person reduce a fear that is controlling him. It's commonly used to get rid of a fear of snakes, or of flying, or of having a panic attack when around crowds.

At first, I didn't catch on to what Ted meant by desensitizing. A few days later when I was interviewing him about his history, I asked him if there was anything he was afraid of. He suddenly had an angry look on his face, his voice was loud, and he looked into my eyes and said,

> "I don't have fears! Fear, pain, and punishment don't stick with me!"

It wasn't the words that stood out, it was the intensity of the anger in his voice. It appeared that he viewed fear as a weakness and was determined that he would have none of it. It appeared that Ted might have applied the process of desensitizing to get rid of fear (and possibly guilt).

There were other items in the sentence completion test that seemed to have meaning as well. Sometimes a person will carry a thought from one item to the next. Items 6 to 11 appear to possibly share a common thought.

He had difficulty with prison (item 6). It would be an extension of his jail time, but even worse. He desperately needed happiness and peace (item 7). This is particularly important because the beginning of the sentence is, "The *only* thing that really matters in this world is..." In spite of him attempting to convince me (and probably himself) that fear, pain, and punishment didn't stick with him, he couldn't find peace.

He hoped to be acquitted (item 8). He wanted to tell me he had never hurt anyone (item 9) and he needed freedom (item 10). And, in order to get what he was after in life, he had to keep learning (item 11).

Item 12 is particularly interesting. He is saying that a person is *most* helpless when he withdraws from others. This seems to be a repetition in meaning to item 4. A person withdraws from others when he is depressed or afraid. Ted seemed to be saying that when he withdrew from the association and support of others, he was most helpless.

Item 18 is also interesting. It's easy to get into trouble when "others aren't considered." This item appears to have multiple meanings. From what I saw, Ted was lonely when he was young. This suggests that maybe he wasn't "considered" or loved as much as he wanted or needed. If this is accurate it could have resulted in him getting involved in inappropriate things. Also, if he did kill the girls the police were beginning to blame him for, it would be because he didn't consider their lives to be important. This would suggest self-centered thinking.

Item 23 is an extension of items 7, 37, and 16. He is saying (item 23) that he is fearful of not being loved. Perhaps he didn't feel loved when he was growing up. Or perhaps he might have been seriously hurt when a particular girl (or girls in general) that he loved didn't love him back. He can't find the "happiness and peace" he requires (item 7) unless he has "caring people" (item 37). This may be *part* of the reason he can't "stop struggling" (item 16). There is also a contradiction between this item saying he can't stop struggling and his statement that he doesn't have any fears.

The findings from the TWIST say something about Ted's personality and could give collateral support to the conclusion that Ted is violent. Still, nothing here indicated clearly that he was.

I had to look elsewhere for answers.

TWIST

Two Word Incomplete Sentences Test

Complete these sentences with one or two words. Try to express your feelings. Try to do every one.

Name TED BUNDY No. 0522 Sex MALE Date 4-1-76

1. I feel CHALLENGED. 2. My mind is ACTIVE.
3. A good way to relax is LISTEN TO MUSIC.
4. A person just isn't himself when AFRAID.
5. It would be too easy to BE DEPRESSED.
6. It's hard to express feelings of PRISON LIFE.
7. The only thing that really matters in this world is HAPPINESS AND PEACE.
8. Things would be great if I could BE ADMITTED.
9. I've never HURT ANYONE. 10. I need FREEDOM.
11. I feel I have to KEEP LEARNING.
12. A person is most helpless when WITHDRAWS FROM OTHERS.
13. My mother was usually LOVING.
14. Most people think I am (WHO KNOW ME) INNOCENT.
15. Marriage is INTIMATE PARTNERSHIP. 16. I can't STOP STRUGGLING.
17. I wish I hadn't COME TO UTAH.
18. It's easy to get into trouble when OTHERS AREN'T CONSIDERED.
19. When I was a child I felt CONSTANT [illegible].
20. I want to know why ABOUT EVERYTHING.
21. I am CONFIDENT. 22. Drugs are DESTRUCTIVE.
23. Worse than being lonely is being UNLOVED.
24. Women are MEN'S EQUALS. 25. I hate PREJUDICE.
26. When frustrated I DESENSITIZE.
27. The thing I remember about my father was BOUNDLESS ENERGY.
28. In the future there will be MANY OPPORTUNITIES.
29. Compared to most families mine usually WAS CLOSE.
30. What excites me is SPRING-TIME.
31. I don't like people who are SUSPICIOUS.
32. I think most girls should BE THEMSELVES.
33. My greatest weakness is PROCRASTINATION.
34. Some day I will become AN ATTORNEY.
35. I wish I could lose the fear of HYPODERMIC NEEDLES.
36. I was proud of myself when FINISHED COLLEGE.
37. I couldn't live without CARING PEOPLE.
38. Tests like this are OBLIGATORY, I SUPPOSE.

Psychological Resources

725 West 120 North
Orem, Utah 84057

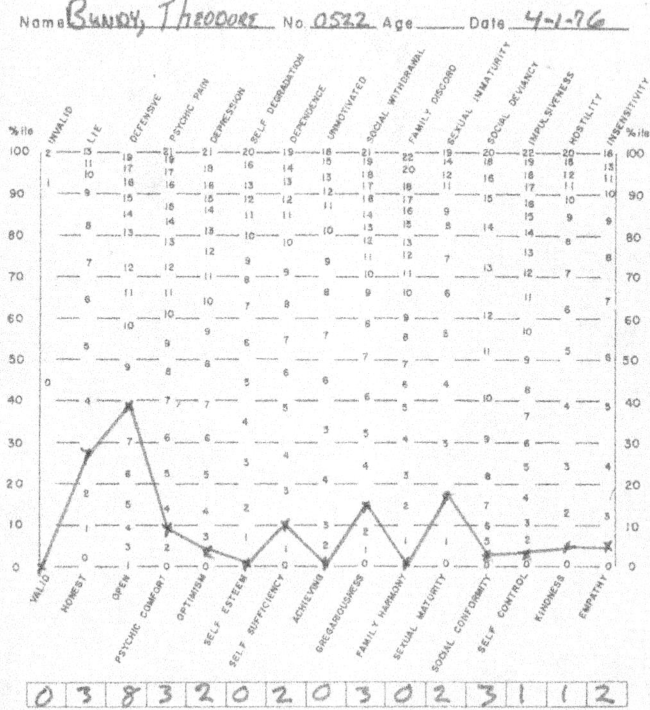

BIPOLAR PSYCHOLOGICAL INVENTORY

OFFENDER NORMS — FORM A

MALE

Name Bundy, Theodore No. 0522 Age ____ Date 4-1-76

0	3	8	3	2	0	2	0	3	0	2	3	1	1	2

December 27, 1976 Theodore Bundy

Psychology Staff,

Sorry for the delay in responding to your request to take this inventory.

The results from the original bi-polar test I took should be in your files somewhere.

Whether or not you can locate these findings, I can see no point in responding a second time to the 300 true/false items in the bi-polar inventory. During the period of my diagnostic evaluation there was some justification for me to respond to an assessment instrument of such questionable validity. At that time I complied seriously and honestly. Presently, I see no need to subject myself to 300 out-of-context statements many of which are so obtuse and so loaded that even the most sincere response to them would permit the conscious or unconscious bias of the interpretor to significantly manipulate the final analysis.

Theodore Bundy

THE CALIFORNIA LIFE GOALS EVALUATION SCHEDULES

PERSONAL PROFILE FORM

By

MILTON E. HAHN, Ph.D.

University of California, Los Angeles

Published by

WPS WESTERN PSYCHOLOGICAL SERVICES
PUBLISHERS AND DISTRIBUTORS
12031 WILSHIRE BOULEVARD
LOS ANGELES, CALIFORNIA 90025

A DIVISION OF MANSON WESTERN CORPORATION

NAME (please print) Bundy (Last) Ted (First) (Middle) Date

HIGHEST GRADE COMPLETED

AGE SEX: M F MARITAL STATUS: Single Married Divorced Separated Widowed

PERSONAL PROFILE

		Small Scores		Middle Scores		Large Scores			Total Scores	Schedule Number
	Percentile	10%	25%	40%	60%	75%	90%			
1. ESTEEM	M	15	24 X	31	37	43	52	M	27	1
	F	13	22	31	34	41	50	F		
2. PROFIT	M	13	20 X	31	34	39	47	M	26	2
	F	11	20	27	32	37	46	F		
3. FAME	M	1	X 11	19	23	31	41	M	10	3
	F	0	9	16	20	26	37	F		
4. POWER	M	3	12	21	X 25	32	41	M	25	4
	F	6	13	20	25	32	40	F		
5. LEADERSHIP	M	17	25	32	37	X 43	52	M	41	5
	F	13	21	31	35	42	50	F		
6. SECURITY	M	8	17	23	28	37	40 X	M	42	6
	F	0	17	25	29	36	53	F		
7. SOCIAL SERVICE	M	7	15	25	29	X 36	44	M	34	7
	F	10	18	26	29	37	45	F		
8. INTERESTING EXPERIENCES	M	11	23	29	X 34	40	53	M	34	8
	F	13	20	29	32	41	49	F		
9. SELF-EXPRESSION	M	10	19	26	31	X 39	43	M	38	9
	F	9	23	28	32	38	53	F		
10. INDEPENDENCE	M	10	19	26	31	X 37	46	M	37	10
	F	3	17	26	29	37	53	F		

See Reverse Side for Interpretation and Construction of Profile.

EVALUATIONS

SUGGESTIONS

Al Rie — Psychologist or Counselor 4/22/76 — Date

W-90B

$\frac{CA}{Score}$ 64 = 122 I.Q.

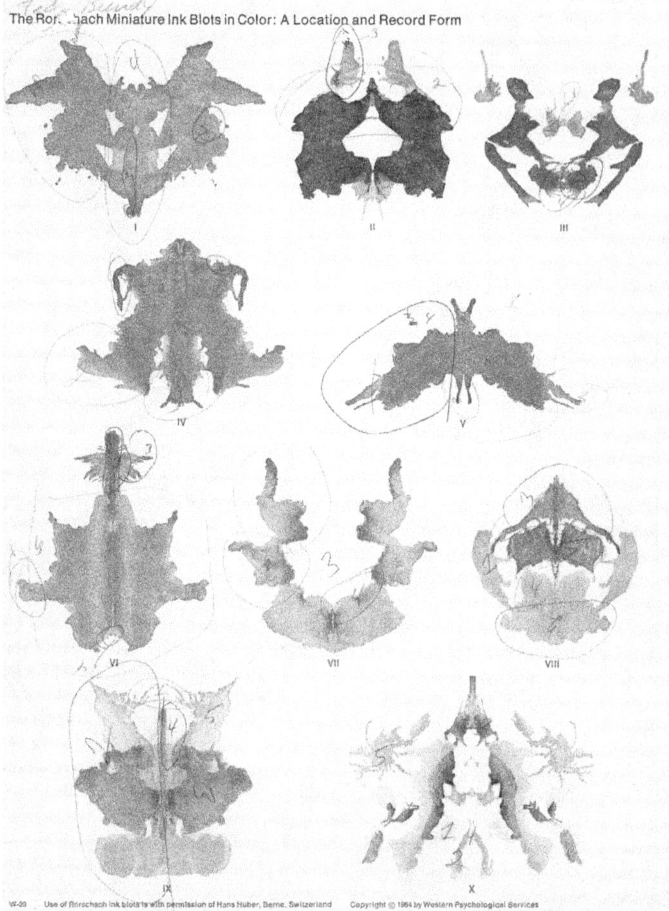
The Rorschach Miniature Ink Blots in Color: A Location and Record Form
I
II
III
IV
V
VI
VII
VIII
IX
X
W-20 Use of Rorschach ink blots is with permission of Hans Huber, Berne, Switzerland
Copyright © 1964 by Western Psychological Services

Part VI: Additional information

These are other things gathered by Dr. Carlisle.

The timeline may have originated from "My Phantom Prince," but we believe it was added to by Dr. Carlisle.

TWENTY-ONE

Quotes from Richard Larsen Interview

(From the Richard Larsen Tapes 11-12-1990 Tape 1. Side A.)

The following are quotes from a taped conversation I had with Richard Larsen in Seattle on 11-12-90. I learned today (11-13-2001) from his wife that Richard died last April. These conversations took place in Richard's home.

Richard had written the book on Ted Bundy. Which was turned into a movie with Mark Harmon. Mrs. Larsen said that both she and Richard are in the movie — in the court room scene in Florida. They are in the second or third row.

He had felt that there was something cyclical about Bundy's crimes. "The patterns that one could detect looking at his gas purchases, after a crime would occur there would be kind of a lull and then you would notice that he was starting to drive a bit, then driving quite a lot then a lot of driving activity, building up then would come another crime. It's wasn't precisely a monthly cycle, maybe there was about three weeks or something like that, but there was a real consistent pattern. So far as our northwest crimes were concerned up here, there was about one a month. Ted would talk on occasion subsequently about the urge and I often wondered if it was associated to a testosterone, but there seemed to be a kind of an emotional, or psychiatric buildup of some sort that seemed to crest and come in cycles." He was an active masturbater.

"Over a period of time you get the sense of somewhat lessening of his planning and control and conduct of the crimes. They tended to get very disorganized towards the latter states, taking on different forms. In the case in Florida, first of all the multiple victims in the sorority house, totally out of character, out of keeping with his past behavior. The window peaking, the voyeurism I think has always been part of Ted's conduct."

The lady on Dunwoody street, after the Chi Omega homicides may have been planned instead of the Chi Omega killings. "There's some indication that he had gone to the Dunwoody Street house and had seen that girl dancing either in her undies or perhaps totally nude because she liked to dance that way her friends said. So, he had seen her. And the indications he gave in some conversations was that on that night his plan was to go to Dunwoody street. That was it. He didn't plan the Chi Omega things, that was incidental. In trying to reconstruct that whole night where he began from his apartment nearby and wound up over at the little tavern and bar near the Chi Omega house. He went in there to have a couple of drinks, apparently to get himself bolstered. Alcohol also plays throughout this. He seemed to be highly susceptible to alcohol, would get intoxicated quite readily, obviously had a very low threshold. I think he got triggered there and went immediately out of control. Again, perhaps the combination of the alcohol, the triggering and the buildup that had occurred. The rampage in the Sorority House emerged and then went on over to Dunwoody (or Dinwoody) street to that victim, which he indicated was his original plan all along." (Who did he indicate this to?) He chatted with a psychologist and

Richard wasn't clear if this was confidential or not. Nonetheless, it was shared to him.

(Why didn't the Chi Omega killings satisfy him? Why did he have to go to the other?) "It's hard to understand other than the fact he was in a complete state of disorganization, I think by that time. I think he probably tried — and we know he did on several occasions — there would come times that he would try to control his impulse. And apparently, he tried and tried and I think that one side of him felt just awful after the crime had been committed and then this , obviously, great state of depression would set in. By this time, I think he probably, at all levels, had concluded that he was out of control. There simply was no hope. I would think that having done everything he had done at the Chi Omega House which was so extreme, so unusual, such high risk, that he was in depression but it was not debilitating insofar as his urge was concerned. The urge by this time had just taken over and he had surrendered any hope of control. He still had this survivor's instinct. He had a sense of danger and a sense of getting the hell out of there, especially when he heard a phone ring. Then he went on to being totally out of control, leaving that scene and then taking the stolen van up to northern Florida and trying to pick up a girl in Jacksonville and going to Lake City. And these were young girls. Why did he do it? I just felt that by that time a lot had snapped and all these things were running out of control."

"My theory is that one of the victims in the Chi Omega was Margaret Bowman. When I first saw her picture I thought, Wow! This is his original love, the girl from California, because they looked alike. A beautiful, beautiful, girl. Radiant smile, flashing dark eyes. Margaret was a very gregarious girl and apparently loved to dance and she would move from partner to partner to partner and be very vivacious. That kind of girl illuminates a room. So, I think of Ted sitting there in that bar and seeing her and he's immediately triggered into that action. I think that just by chance he dropped into that bar that same night, was fortifying himself (with alcohol) for his walk over to Dunwoody street a few blocks away and here's this girl. He's already in the mood and he would see her and would be reminded of Diane. My theory is that Margaret became his fixation at that time. He could have observed that girl as she would have left that bar going through that side door of the Chi Omega Sorority House, which was unlocked and Ted noticed it.

"He may possibly have done some voyeuristic checking out of the Chi Omega House and other sorority houses beforehand. He might have had some sense of it. But there's no indication that that's the case. In fact, those sorority houses are pretty discrete. They are accustomed to Peeping Tom activities and they have their defenses up against it, so I doubt very much that he had scoped that house beforehand. But that's been my theory all along."

He thinks she was one of the latter ones. The first was Lisa. Richard thinks she was going from room to room searching for her. However, he did go to one other victim after her. He isn't positive, but he thinks there were four girls assaulted in that house and Margaret was number three. "The description of his behavior in the nightclub that night was one of kind of a sleazy, strange, alien sort of a person with strange eyes."

One of the things that would be fun to explore would be the physiological changes that go with this transformation. I think they are visible. I think something changes in the eyes and in the mannerism. I've had conversation with a couple of girls. Number one is the girl who escaped from the Fashion Mall [Carol DaRonch] who is not very verbal, but she communicated you have no way knowing the sudden terror that hit her. There was a sudden change in the look and the manner and everything. She first saw it after she got in the car and he had told her to put on her seat belt. She was starting then to become aware of something wrong here and began feeling very uneasy. This was going on for a matter of minutes now. And she felt this rising concern but when he pulled the car over to the curb and then came at her with a gun. At that moment, the look, the sense she had, the look of his eyes. I had interviewed another girl who didn't realize she had an encounter with Ted, but I'm sure she did.

TWENTY-TWO

Letter to Jim Massie

Mr. Jim Massie
Louisville, KY 40218

Dear Jim.

Here is the letter I promised you. This is the second time I am writing it. I had it completely written before (A week ago) When my Apple computer developed a problem and wiped out all memory and destroyed the entire letter. So, I borrowed my brother's computer and am starting again. Much of this information you may already know, but I hope there will be something new that you can use. Since I am not sure where the issue lies on using the test an interview data I collected on him, It will be easier to give an account of the manner in which I feel his personality developed rather than say Ted said this or that. Does that make sense? Also, I can't find the large file I have on him (I put it somewhere for safekeeping) So this information comes largely from the review file that I use for talks I give on him.

As a child, Ted experienced both happiness and sadness. His family was fairly poor and he compared himself to other family members who were more wealthy. He was somewhat out of place in his environment and at times he was led to believe he didn't belong. At one point in his early school career Ted lived among Italians and he would run from them, To avoid fights. He wasn't of the same religion nor race. He experienced a dividing line between himself and them. During this period of his life, He had a teacher who "put the fear of God in you. "

He had a grandfather who had an intense interest in literature and science. He was a well-educated person and Ted wanted to pattern his life after him. It may well be that he began at this early age to attempt to find an identity through achievement. At one point, he longed to be able to achieve like some of the other children, but he couldn't, which bothered him.

While in junior high school, he ran for student body president, and he lost - and it appears that while he helped others run for some office when he was in high school, he

never attempted such himself. He started dating while in junior high, but for same reason he stopped and didn't until he was in his senior year. Part of the reason may be that he didn't have a car nor did he have much money. While in Junior high, he became less dependent on friends and more of an individualist. He became more interested in

academics and memorized things he heard on the radio. In high school, he felt somewhat left behind as his friends went in other directions.

• • •

After he graduated, he went to the University of Puget Sound. He longed for a beautiful coed, but he didn't feel he had the social skills to cope with it. He had a desire to achieve and he had some fairly noble goals. When he went to the University of Washington, he wanted to major in Asian studies. He wanted to develop his knowledge and skills to the point that he could gain a position of authority and improve relations between China and the USA. However, he found that he couldn't comfortably settle on a suitable major, so this didn't work out for him.

He finally met his beautiful coed. She was well dressed, well-groomed and was socially skilled. She had poise and confidence, and her family was very wealthy. She had everything that Ted wanted to balance off his lack of self-confidence and his lack of social skills. If he could get her to fall in love with him, it would help him to develop the powerful, competent and respected self-image that he had always wanted. If someone so beautiful; So rich and so impressive could fall in love with him, it would mean that he was really the diamond in the rough that he wanted to feel he was, and that she was seeing beyond the outer grain into the truly great soul that was hidden within.

However, she saw him as "Pitifully weak ", As a person who would not stand up for himself, and as a person she Could not respect. She broke off the relationship which hurt Ted very much. He later left the area and went back east. He again contacted her when he returned and she saw him as a totally different person. He now had self-confidence, poise, was outgoing and showed power behind his personality.

During this period of time, Ted developed another relationship which he continued with until he came to Utah. This was not always a smooth relationship and at one point he was deeply hurt by her. He dated other girls as well, and attempted to put them on a pedestal, only to try to pull them off again. Some women felt their relationship with him was a power struggle. He was developing definite problems by this time as indicated by the boating incident and the incident when he shoved a girl's head under the water in a river and held it there until her air was almost gone.

By the Fall of 1973 two opposite personalities were seen in him, depending on the mood he was in or the amount of stress he was under. On one hand, he was outgoing, confident, verbal, had poise and was able to relate well in a salesman-like manner. On the other hand. he was angry, jealous, seemed to have a secret life that he kept hidden from others, and was engaging in some aggressive sexual practices that got out of hand.

Some feel that Edna Cowell was his first victim. This is not logical to me. The person who committed that crime was skilled and had confidence about what he was doing.

This was not the act of a novice. By this time, Ted must have become a victim to his own obsessive thoughts and fantasies. The personality of a rapist-murderer was well developed through hundreds of hours of living and reliving fantasies of acts he would later be committing with all of the excitement and inherent feelings of power, control and mastery that come through such a fantasy life. While me may well have regretted the acts he committed he found that he could not get away from the overpowering obsessions until he acted them out. This led him from one crime to the next until he was finally caught.

. . .

While probably not a true multiple personality Ted has two sides to him. On one hand, he was be very friendly, warm and showed tender feelings. I saw him with tears in

his eyes more than once, and I do not feel that this was just an attempt to make an impression on me. He needed to be loved and accepted and approved of by others. He was lonely and was dependent on women for the feelings of closeness he so needed.

On the other hand, he was distant, cold, calculating. He lived his life in a compulsive manner that was well ordered and exact. Events and actions as well as conversations were planned and rehearsed many times before they took place. It was very important for him to never be caught off his guard. Life was like a chess game to him.

He was always mentally two moves ahead of his opponent so no matter what move was made he always had several suitable countering actions that could assure him success. However, outward appearing stability was countered by inward instability. Incarceration and continuous pressure broke down his controls until he ended up where he is today.

I hope this is of some use to you.

It appears as if the prison won't come through with the finances for me to come back there for the two-day conference on serial murders. It would have been nice.

Thank you anyway for the invitation. Good luck with your chapter. I would like to get a copy of the book when it is done and would appreciate it if you would send me the name of the book and publisher when it is finished.

. . .

Sincerely,

A.L. Carlisle, Ph.D.
Clinical Psychologist

TWENTY-THREE

Multi Agency Investigative Team Report

U.S. Department of Justice
Federal Bureau of Investigation

Ted Bundy Multiagency Investigative Team Report 1992

FBI/DOJ
DIRECTOR'S COMMENTS

Theodore Robert Bundy has become, perhaps, society's most infamous and notorious serial killer. By committing his crimes in many different jurisdictions, he wittingly or unwittingly complicated. the investigative efforts to identify, locate, and prosecute him.

Unfortunately, such cases are becoming more commonplace in today's society. It is only through cooperation and communication that we in the law enforcement community can hope to stem the growing tide of violence. The following pages represent the product of just such a collaborative effort. This exhaustive documentation of Bundy's activities was prepared in the hope that Bundy's suspected participation in crimes other than those he has confessed to can be clarified. We may never know the total extent of his devastation but through the efforts of the Bundy Task Force we now have one document with which to compare Bundy's whereabouts with crimes he may be suspected of committing.

I wish to express my gratitude to the individuals and agencies involved. Through the spirit of cooperation, the law enforcement community now has definitive documentation of Bundy's activities.

On January 24, 1989, serial killer THEODORE ROBERT BUNDY had been convicted of killing two coeds on January 15, 1978, at Florida State University in Tallahassee. Also, on that date he bludgeoned three other women who miraculously survived his attacks.

His final death warrant resulted from his slaying a 12-year-old girl who disappeared from school cm February 9, 1978; her remains were discovered on April 7, 1978.

During the last years of his life, BUNDY confided to investigators directly and indirectly regarding the motivation, victim selection, modus operandi, etc. for his crimes. In his last days on death row, in an unsuccessful attempt to prolong life, BUNDY requested certain investigators meet with him.

Investigators from the Federal Bureau of Investigation and the states of Colorado, Idaho, Utah, and Washington traveled to the prison to talk to BUNDY about a number of unsolved murders in which he was a suspect. At BUNDY's request, all the interviews were conducted in the presence of a member of the FBI's national Center for the Analysis of Violent Crime (NCAVC) who had become

BUNDY'S confidant over the years. Based on BUNDY's

communications with this FBI Agent over several years, and the information provided during the final days and hours of his life, BUNDY discussed thirty homicides.

BUNDY'S homicidal activities spanned at least five years and reportedly .claimed the lives of thirty females in at least seven states. Although every effort has been made and every available resource has been utilized throughout the years to arrive at a comprehensive account of his victims, the true toll may never be known.

In March 1989, under the auspices of the FBI's NCAVC Violent Criminal Apprehension Program, investigators involved in BUNDY's final revelations and other knowledgeable law enforcement officials attended the BUNDY Multi-Agency Investigative Team conference at the FBI Academy in Quantico, Virginia. The purpose of this meeting was to assess and share intelligence among the participants, inasmuch as the Bundy interviews at the prison preceding his execution are specific as to individual crimes. Following the Quantico meeting, specialists from the FBI's Visual Investigative Analysis Unit consulted with investigators throughout the country in attempt to formulate a singular database reflecting BUNDY's documented whereabouts over the years. They hope that such information, coupled with information derived by investigation and BUNDY's own revelations, might lead to the solution of additional unsolved murders.

The NCAVC and BUNDY conference members who responded to numerous inquiries from investigators who are attempting to determine BUNDY's culpability in unsolved matters. It is the purpose of this report to share, within the law enforcement community, information relative to BUNDY's crimes, furnish insight into his activities, and provide the most accurate timeline possible for establishing his whereabouts during any known period.

HOMICIDE ADMISSIONS

BUNDY admitted to the murder of at least 30 women between 1973 and 1978 in the following states: California (1), Colorado (3), Florida (3), Idaho (2), Oregon (2), Utah (8), and Washington (11).

MODUS OPERANDI

BUNDY was involved in voyeuristic activities throughout his life and actually studied his victims without their knowledge through surveillance and occasional clandestine entry of their residences.

In discussions regarding the development of his method of operation, BUNDY differentiated between "dry runs" and "abductions." He defined a dry run as picking up a woman and releasing her unharmed to test his skills. An abduction was an incident in which intended victim managed to escape.

Although BUNDY had sex with most of his victims, it is doubtful that he committed only rapes. He was more interested sexually in semi-conscious or unconscious victims.

BUNDY termed 1 of his modes as a "predator mode." When operating in this mode, he was most organized. His planning included preselection of our body disposal site, discrete research regarding his victim, preparation of necessary paraphernalia, and complete planning of the assault to include flight, evidence disposal, and alibi. Only then would he approach the victim and put his plan into action.

Generally, BUNDY's crimes followed a particular pattern he would feign injury and indicate he needed assistance or he would portray an authority figure such as a police officer. He thus persuaded the victim to voluntarily accompany him to his Volkswagen where he secreted a crowbar near the rear of the vehicle. Upon reaching the vehicle, he would retrieve the crowbar and strike the victim over the head, rendering her unconscious. He would then handcuff her and place her in the passenger side of the vehicle which he had modified by removing the seat.

BUNDY would often drive 4 hours with the victim in the car. If the victim regained consciousness while he was driving, he would calm her down by talking to her. He commented that the victim was often so disoriented that he could convince her that she had been injured and he was transporting her to a hospital.

When BUNDY got to his preselected dumpsite, he would again hit the victim (if she had regained consciousness) and strangle her with a ligature while raping her. Although his first murder was reportedly performed by meeting and manual strangulation, he most often used a ligature he had prepared solely for that purpose. Victims were strangled from the rear.

Being voyeuristic, it was important that BUNDY be able to see what he was doing. He selected sites where the moon shone brightly, or he would "operate" in front of the headlights of his vehicle. He commented that there were times that he thought he should have been caught because the headlights of his vehicle would have been visible to people driving in the area.

BUNDY advised that he made return visits to nearly all of his crime scenes.

There is little evidence to indicate BUNDY recorded his murders or assaults in any particular fashion. He indicated he had, at one time, a box of Polaroid photographs of victims that he kept hidden but subsequently destroyed after becoming a suspect. It is known that he would sometimes keep ski brochures that were apparently marked to signify homicides. Also found was a brochure from the high school play where 1 of his victims was abducted. BUNDY advised he would discard everything belonging to his victims and would sometimes discard his possessions, such as his props or tools, connected with the incidents. He would later have to replace those items.

BUNDY gave the impression that he committed most of his assault outdoors, except in Utah and Florida. In Utah, he was able to take his victims back to his apartment, where he could reenact scenarios depicted on the covers of Detective magazines.

Of the thirty victims BUNDY claimed to have killed, he reportedly buried about ten. He would always attempt to bury the bodies two or three feet deep and place rocks on top of the gray. He also claimed to have disposed of victims in bodies of water.

BUNDY reported he severed the heads of about a dozen of his victims. He would sometimes retain the heads for longer periods than the bodies and not necessarily dispose of the body and head in the same location. Actually, body parts, clothing, and other victim possessions were dispersed, perhaps, hundreds of miles from the discarded torso.

BUNDY clearly followed media reports of his crimes as well as the reports of others who killed. He was interested in other people's murders and the possibility that he was being copied. He followed his own cases to glean as much intelligence as possible regarding suspects, evidence, leads, etc. He felt he was helped quite a bit with the abundance of information from investigators' quotes available through the media and his perceived lack of cooperation among law enforcement agencies.

Although ligature strangulation was BUNDY's favorite method of killing, the manual strangulation of his first murder is consistent behavior in an evolving serial murderer. That is, the serial killer is disorganized when he starts but improve significantly as he progresses, choosing his victims, murder and body disposal sites, and methodology more carefully. He becomes more sophisticated.

BUNDY exhibited this evolution toward sophistication. Finally, however, under the stress of being a fugitive, he regressed. He resorted to using his bare hands and a blunt weapon and selected sleeping victims or young girls as targets.

When asked about the whiteboards he inflicted on his victims at one of his last crime scenes, and whether he had done anything like that before, BUNDY did not respond fully. However, he did say that when he was in an extremely aggravated state, biting took place.

Unfortunately, there remain, and perhaps forever will remain, many unanswered questions about BUNDY's activities.

CONCLUSION

Of the homicides examined at the BUNDY Multi-Agency Investigative Team conference, BUNDY claims responsibility for thirty. As a result of information provided by BUNDY and an independent verification of that information by investigators, it was possible to associate BUNDY with twenty cases.

THEODORE ROBERT BUNDY TIMELINE

THEODORE ROBERT BUNDY DOB: 11-24-1946

PLACE OF BIRTH: BURLINGTON, VERMONT

WHITE/MALE 5'11", 170 POUNDS

BROWN HAIR, BLUE EYES, ALL ON, SCAR ON SCALP, LEFT-HANDED, HAD VEERED OFF AND ON, HAD WORN HORN-RIMMED GLASSES (I-159)

GOOD PRONUNCIATION-ARTICULATE, INTERMITTENT STARTER, EYELIDS FLUTTER WHEN STUTTERING.

BLOOD TYPE: TYPE "O" SECRETOR-ERYTHROCYTE ACID PHOSPHATASE TYPE CA (EAP-CA), PHOSPHOGLUTOMATASE TYPE 2-1 (PGM 2-1),ADENYLATE KINASE TYPE 1 (AK-1),AND ESTERASE D TYPE (ESD 2-1) (I-34/429)

CRIMINAL INFORMATION NUMBERS:

COLORADO # NO STATE NUMBER EXIST
FBI # 2511632P2
FLORIDA # FL01294198
SALT LAKE COUNTY, UTAH # 78058
UTAH STATE PRISON# 13819

FINGERPRINT CLASSIFICATION:

PI 54 08 13 11
L9 12 05 11 13

ALIAS INFORMATION:

NAMES USED:
BUNDY, REX
BUNDY, TEDDY
BUNDY, TED
BUNDY, THEODORE R.
COWELL, TED
EVANS, MR.
HAMMOND, GARY

MISNER, KEN
MISNER, KENNETH RAYMOND
NELSON, THEODORE, ROBERT

ALIAS DATES OF BIRTH:
02-07-49

ALIAS SOCIAL SECURITY NUMBERS USED:
xxx-xx-xxxx

RESIDENCES where LIVED:

MCMAHON HALL, UNIVERSITY OF WASHINGTON, TACOMA, WASHINGTON — 1963

UNKNOWN ADDRESS: PALO ALTO, CALIFORNIA

16TH ST., SEATTLE, WA —1967

16TH ST., SEATTLE, WA — 1968

20TH, TACOMA, WASHINGTON — 1968

SOUTHWARNER, LAFAYETTE HILL, PENNSYLVANIA — 1969

215TH AVE., MARINCOUNTY, CALIFORNIA — 1970

12TH NORTHEAST, SEATTLE, WASHINGTON — 1970 — 1974

16TH NE., SEATTLE, WASHINGTON — DATE UNKNOWN

EIGHTEENTH NE., SEATTLE, WASHINGTON — DATE UNKNOWN

15TH AVE., SEATTLE, WA — DATE UNKNOWN (GIVEN TO POLICE 8-20-70)

ELMORE, SEATTLE, WASHINGTON — LATE 1973

1ST AVE., SALT LAKE CITY, UT — 1976 (BUNDY LIBRARY CARD)

"B" STREET, SALT LAKE CITY, UTAH — 3-22-76

Douglas St., Salt Lake City, UT — 1976
College Ave., Tallahassee, FL — 1978

DRIVER LICENSE NUMBERS:
UTAH — Axxxxxx
WASHINGTON — BUNDY TRxxxxx

OCCUPATIONS:
BELLBOY
BUSBOY
COOK'S HELPER
DISHWASHER
HOTEL WORKER
JANITOR
LAW SCHOOL STUDENT
LEGAL MESSENGER
OFFICE WORKER
PARKING ATTENDANT
POLITICAL CAMPAIGN WORKER
PSYCHIATRIC SOCIAL WORKER
SALESMAN
SAW MILL WORKER
SECURITY GUARD
YACHT CLUB WORKER

ITEMS USED OR TAKEN DURING CRIMES:
BADGE — GOLD IN COLOR
BAGS — GREEN PLASTIC "GLAD" TYPE

BICYCLES MODEL — GIRLS MAKE — TIGER COLOR — YELLOW SERIAL NUMBER P-290 OWNER: JANICE OTT BICYCLE HAS NEVER BEEN RECOVERED

BRIEFCASE FULL OF BOOKS
CLOTHING BELONGING TO VICTIMS

CREDIT CARDS
CROWBAR
CRUTCHES
DRIVERS LICENSE
FLASHLIGHT
GLOVES
HANDCUFFS
ICE PICK
LICENSE PLATES, FLORIDA 13D11300
NYLON PANTYHOSE WITH MOUTH HOLE AND EYEHOLES CUT OUT
PISTOL — CALIBER UNKNOWN
RADIOS
ROPE
RIFLE
SHEETS — TORN INTO STRIPS
SHOPLIFTED ITEMS FROM SUPERMARKETS
SKI MASK
SLING FOR ARM
TELEVISION
TYPEWRITER
VEHICLES
WALLETS

VEHICLES:

1968 VOLKSWAGEN - PURCHASED 1973, OWNED UNTIL OCTOBER 3, 1975

TAN IN COLOR WITH SUNROOF

WASHINGTON TAG IBH-xxx - VIN #xxxxxxxxx

FIRST — UTAH TAG LJB-xxx - VIN #xxxxxxxxx

SECOND — UTAH TAG xxx-xxx - VIN #xxxxxxxxx

VEHICLE FRONT SEAT REMOVABLE, NO FRONT BUMPER, NO FRONT TAG

1973 — LIGHT BLUE - VOLKSWAGEN - WASHINGTON TAG OPM-xxx

WASHINGTON - TAG C-xxxxx (3-9-xx) OWNED BY KING COUNTY, WASHINGTON, MAKE/MODEL UNKNOWN

WASHINGTON TAG OYU-xxx (8-18-xx) OWNED BY FRIEND OF BUNDY, KING COUNTY, WASHINGTON MAKE/MODEL UNKNOWN

WASHINGTON TAG ICI-xxx (8-29-xx) NO RECORD COULD BE LOCATED

WASHINGTON TAG BTR-xxx (9-2-xx) OWNED BY REPUBLICAN STATE CENTRAL COMMITTEE, WASHINGTON MAKE/MODEL UNKNOWN

WHITE FORD PICKUP TRUCK — PURCHASE DATE UNKNOWN, OWNED UNTIL NOVEMBER/DECEMBER 1975 WASHINGTON TAG L-xxxxx

1978 WHITE VAN — FLORIDA — STOLEN FROM FLORIDA STATE UNIVERSITY

1976 WHITE DODGE VAN, VIN BxxABxXxxx-xxx WITH FLORIDA TAG 13D-xxxx

1966 BROWN VOLKSWAGEN, WASHINGTON PLATES AQB – xxx

1966 BLUE CADILLAC, COLORADO ZG-xxxx 6-13-xx, STOLEN/RECOVERED

HERTZ TRUCKS 08-30-xx

USED STOLEN BICYCLES WHILE IN FLORIDA

WHITE MAZDA-STOLEN IN FLORIDA

GREEN TOYOTA-STOLEN IN FLORIDA

BLUE VOLKSWAGEN-STOLEN IN FLORIDA

ORANGE VOLKSWAGEN-STOLEN IN FLORIDA

HOMICIDES TO WHICH BUNDY CONFESSED:

CALIFORNIA, CONFESSED TO ONE HOMICIDE CASE, NEVER IDENTIFIED

COLORADO:
KAREN CAMPBELL 1-12-75 — LOCATED
JULIE CUNNINGHAM 3-15-75
Denise OLIVERSON 4-6-75

FLORIDA:
MARGARET BOWMAN 1-15-78 — LOCATED
LISA LEVY 1-15-78 — LOCATED
KIMBERLY LEACH 2-9-78 — LOCATED

IDAHO:
UNKNOWN HITCHHIKER EARLY SEPTEMBER 1974

LYNETTE CULVER 5-6-75 — BASED ON BUNDY'S DESCRIPTION OF VICTIM

OREGON: CONFESSED TO TWO HOMICIDES, ONLY ONE IDENTIFIED
ROBERTA PARKS 5-6-74 —**

UTAH: CONFESSED TO EIGHT HOMICIDES, ONLY FIVE IDENTIFIED
LYNDA HEALY 1-31-74 — LOCATED
DONNA MANSON 3-12-74
SUSAN RANCOURT 4-17-74 — LOCATED
ROBERTA PARKS 5-6-74 —**
BRENDA BALL 6-1-74 — LOCATED
GEORGEANN HAWKINS 6-12-74
JANICE OTT 7-14-74 — LOCATED
DENISE NASLUND 7-14-74 — LOCATED

**ABDUCTED FROM OREGON, LOCATED IN WASHINGTON

TIMELINE:

1946

11-24-46 (00:00) BUNDY IS BORN IN BURLINGTON VERMONT. BORN UNDER THE DOOR ROBERT COWELL (COWELL WAS HIS MOTHER'S MAIDEN NAME).

1950

10-06-50 (00:00) BUNDY, BORN UNDER CAL, HAD NAME CHANGED TO NELSON

1951

00-00-51 (00:00) BUNDY AND MOTHER MOVED TO BROWN'S POINT, WASHINGTON.

03-19-51 (00:00) BUNDY'S MOTHER, MS. COWELL, GOT MARRIED; TED FROM THIS POINT FORWARD WAS KNOWN AS TED BUNDY.

1952

00-00-52 (00:00) BUNDY IN SCHOOL, TACOMA, WASHINGTON

1953

00-00-53 (00:00) BUNDY IN SCHOOL, TACOMA, WASHINGTON

1954

00-00-54 (00:00) BUNDY IN SCHOOL, TACOMA, WASHINGTON

1955

00-00-55 (00:00) BUNDY IN SCHOOL, TACOMA, WASHINGTON

06-10-55 (00:00) BUNDY IN SCHOOL, TACOMA, WASHINGTON

1962

09-00-62 (00:00) BUNDY ATTENDED WOODROW WILSON HIGH SCHOOL, TACOMA HIGH SCHOOL WASHINGTON

1963

09-00-63 (00:00) BUNDY ATTENDED WOODROW WILSON HIGH SCHOOL, TACOMA HIGH SCHOOL WASHINGTON

1964

09-00-64 (00:00) BUNDY ATTENDED WOODROW WILSON HIGH SCHOOL, TACOMA HIGH SCHOOL WASHINGTON

1965

00-00-65 (00:00) GRADUATED FROM WOODROW WILSON HIGH SCHOOL, TACOMA HIGH SCHOOL WASHINGTON

06-00-65 (00:00) BUNDY WORKED FOR TACOMA CITY LIGHT, TACOMA, WASHINGTON

07-00-65 (00: 00) BUNDY WORKED FOR TACOMA CITY LIGHT, TACOMA, WASHINGTON

08-00-65 (00:00) BUNDY WORKED FOR TACOMA CITY LIGHT, TACOMA, WASHINGTON

09-00-65 (00:00) BUNDY WORKED FOR TACOMA CITY LIGHT UNTIL HE STARTED SCHOOL AT UNIVERSITY OF PUGET SOUND, TACOMA,

WASHINGTON

09-26-65 (00:00) ENROLLED AND ATTENDED PUGET SOUND COLLEGE, WASHINGTON

1966

01-00-66 (00:00) ATTENDED UNIVERSITY OF PUGET SOUND, WASHINGTON LAST SESSION, ENDED 4-66

09-26-66 (00:00) ENROLLED AND ATTENDED UNIVERSITY OF WASHINGTON THROUGH 12-31-66, SEATTLE, WASHINGTON

1967

00-00-67 (00:00) BUNDY ATTENDED UNIVERSITY OF WASHINGTON, SEATTLE, WASHINGTON

03-17-67 (00:00) BUNDY ATTENDED UNIVERSITY OF WASHINGTON, SEATTLE, WASHINGTON

06-00-67 (00:00) BUNDY ATTENDED STANFORD UNIVERSITY, PALO ALTO, CALIFORNIA

06-25-67 (17:50) BUNDY ARRIVED IN SAN FRANCISCO, CALIFORNIA

06-26-67 (00:00) BUNDY ARRIVED BACK AT STANFORD UNIVERSITY, PALO ALTO, CALIFORNIA

07-00-67 (00:00) BUNDY HAD DINNER, SAN FRANCISCO, CALIFORNIA

08-00-67 (00:00) BUNDY ATTENDED STANFORD UNIVERSITY, PALO ALTO, CALIFORNIA

09-00-67 (00:00) BUNDY WORKED AT SEATTLE YACHT CLUB, SEATTLE, WASHINGTON

1968

01-18-68 (00:00) DISCONTINUED HIS SCHOOLING, TOOK UP TRAVELING. TRAVELED TO: SAN FRANCISCO, CALIFORNIA, DENVER AND ASPEN,

COLORADO, HE TOOK UP SKIING, PHILADELPHIA, PENNSYLVANIA AND ARKANSAS

03-00-68 (00:00) BUNDY WORKED AT OLYMPIC HOTEL, BUT WAS LET GO BECAUSE OF THEFTS FROM LOCKERS, SEATTLE, WASHINGTON

04-12-68 (00:00) BUNDY WORKED AT SAFEWAY UNTIL 7-26-68, SEATTLE, WASHINGTON

1969

01-00-69 (00:00) ENROLLED FOR ONE SEMESTER TEMPLE UNIVERSITY, PHILADELPHIA, PENNSYLVANIA

05-00-69 (00:00) TRAVELED TO SAN FRANCISCO, CALIFORNIA, AND STAYED WITH FRIENDS FOR TWO OR THREE WEEKS

05-00-69 (00:00) MOVED TO AND WORKED IN SAWMILL, TACOMA, WASHINGTON

09-00-69 (00:00) MOVED TO SEATTLE, WASHINGTON

09-00-69 (00:00) BUNDY WORKED AS LEGAL MESSENGER, SEATTLE, WASHINGTON

09-31-69 (00:00) MET GIRLFRIEND, SEATTLE, WASHINGTON

12-25-69 (00:00) WENT TO OGDEN, UTAH

1970

06-05-70 (00:00) BUNDY WORKED FOR MEDICAL INSTRUMENT COMPANY, QUIT ON 12-31-71, SEATTLE, WASHINGTON

06-00-70 (00:00) ENROLLED UNIVERSITY OF WASHINGTON, SEATTLE, WASHINGTON

08-20-70 (00:30) BUNDY GIVEN TICKET BY HIGHWAY PATROL FOR HITCHHIKING SOUTHBOUND ON HIGHWAY 101, MARIN COUNTY,

WASHINGTON; GAVE HOME ADDRESS AS 1252 15TH AVE., SEATTLE, WA

08-29-70 (00:00) BUNDY AND GIRLFRIEND LEAVE SEATTLE, DRIVE TO OGDEN, UTAH; TRAVEL TO YAKIMA, WASHINGTON; BAKER, OREGON; AND OGDEN, UTAH

09-04-70 (00:00) BUNDY AND GIRLFRIEND ARRIVED BACK IN SEATTLE, WASHINGTON

10-29-70 (00:00) BUNDY IN SEATTLE, WASHINGTON

10-30-70 (00:00) BUNDY IN SEATTLE, WASHINGTON

10-31-70 (00:00) BUNDY IN SEATTLE, WASHINGTON

11-01-70 (00:00) BUNDY IN SEATTLE, WASHINGTON

11-02-70 (00:00) BUNDY IN SEATTLE, WASHINGTON

11-03-70 (00:00) BUNDY IN SEATTLE, WASHINGTON

11-04-70 (00:00) BUNDY IN SEATTLE, WASHINGTON

1971

01-00-71 (00:00) BUNDY AT SCHOOL, UNIVERSITY OF WASHINGTON, THROUGH 12-00-71, SEATTLE, WASHINGTON

12-31-71 (00:00) BUNDY LEFT HIS JOB WITH THE MEDICAL INSTRUMENT COMPANY, SEATTLE, WASHINGTON

1972

04-15-72 (00:00) BUNDY BOUGHT GAS, SEATTLE, WASHINGTON

(00:00) BUNDY BOUGHT GAS, NEAH BAY, WASHINGTON

04-28-72 (00:00) 05-05-72 (00:00) Bundy bought gas, Seattle, Washington

05-18-72 (00:00) BUNDY BOUGHT GAS, COEUR D'ALENE, IDAHO

06-00-72 (00:00) BUNDY WENT TO WORK FOR H.V.H. MENTAL HEALTH CENTER, SEATTLE, WASHINGTON

06-00-72 (00:00) BUNDY HIRED BY THE SEATTLE CRIME COMMISSION, SEATTLE, WASHINGTON

06-04-72 (00:00) BUNDY BOUGHT GAS, SEATTLE WASHINGTON

06-09-72 (00:00) BUNDY BOUGHT GAS, SEATTLE WASHINGTON

06-10-72 (00:00) GRADUATED WITH A BS DEGREE IN PSYCHOLOGY FROM THE UNIVERSITY OF WASHINGTON, SEATTLE, WASHINGTON

06-17-72 (00:00) BUNDY BOUGHT GAS, SEATTLE, WASHINGTON

07-00-72 (00:00) BUNDY WORKED AT H.V.H. MENTAL HEALTH CENTER, SEATTLE, WASHINGTON

07-04-72 (00:00) BUNDY BOUGHT GAS, HOQUIAM, WASHINGTON

07-10-72 (00:00) BUNDY BOUGHT GAS, SEATTLE, WASHINGTON

07-16-72 (00:00) BUNDY BOUGHT GAS, SEATTLE, WASHINGTON

07-24-72 (00:00) BUNDY BOUGHT GAS, SEATTLE, WASHINGTON

08-00-72 (00:00) BUNDY WORKED AT H.V.H. MENTAL HEALTH CENTER, SEATTLE, WASHINGTON

08-19-72 (00:00) BUNDY BOUGHT GAS, ISSAQUAH, WASHINGTON

08-23-72 (00:00) BUNDY BOUGHT GAS, SEATTLE WASHINGTON

08-25-72 (00:00) BUNDY BOUGHT GAS, TACOMA, WASHINGTON

08-28-72 (00:00) BUNDY BOUGHT GAS, SEATTLE, WASHINGTON

09-00-72 (00:00) BUNDY WENT TO WORK FOR CITIZENS GROUP TO ELECT A GOVERNOR, SEATTLE, WASHINGTON

09-01-72 (00:00) BUNDY BOUGHT GAS, SEATTLE WASHINGTON

09-03-72 (00:00) BUNDY BOUGHT GAS, CLE ELUM, WASHINGTON

09-07-72 (00:00) BUNDY BOUGHT GAS, SEATTLE WASHINGTON

09-15-72 (00:00) BUNDY BOUGHT GAS, SEATTLE WASHINGTON

09-16-72 (00:00) BUNDY BOUGHT GAS, SEATTLE WASHINGTON

09-17-72 (00:00) BUNDY BOUGHT GAS, CLE ELUM WASHINGTON

09-19-72 (00:00) BUNDY BOUGHT GAS, SEATTLE, WASHINGTON

09-24-72 (00:00) BUNDY BOUGHT GAS, SEATTLE WASHINGTON

09-26-72 (00:00) BUNDY BOUGHT GAS, SEATTLE WASHINGTON

09-28-72 (00:00) BUNDY BOUGHT GAS, SEATTLE WASHINGTON

10-00-72 (00:00) BUNDY WORKED FOR CITIZENS GROUP TO ELECT A GOVERNOR, SEATTLE, WASHINGTON

10-05-72 (00:00) BUNDY BOUGHT GAS, SEATTLE WASHINGTON

10-07-72 (00:00) BUNDY BOUGHT GAS, SEATTLE WASHINGTON

10-10-72 (00:00) BUNDY BOUGHT GAS, SEATTLE WASHINGTON

10-19-72 (00:00) BUNDY BOUGHT GAS, SEATTLE WASHINGTON

10-20-72 (00:00) BUNDY BOUGHT GAS, SEATTLE WASHINGTON

10-23-72 (00:00) BUNDY BOUGHT GAS, RICHLAND, WASHINGTON

(00:00) BUNDY BOUGHT GAS, SEATTLE WASHINGTON

10-24-72 (00:00) BUNDY BOUGHT GAS, SEATTLE WASHINGTON

10-26-72 (00:00) BUNDY BOUGHT GAS, SEATTLE WASHINGTON

11-00-72 (00:00) BUNDY WORKED FOR CITIZENS GROUP TO ELECT A GOVERNOR, SEATTLE, WASHINGTON

11-07-72 (00:00) BUNDY BOUGHT GAS, SEATTLE WASHINGTON

12-26-72 (00:00) BUNDY BOUGHT GAS, SPOKANE, WASHINGTON

12-27-72 (00:00) BUNDY BOUGHT GAS, SEATTLE WASHINGTON

12-30-72 (00:00) BUNDY BOUGHT GAS, SEATTLE WASHINGTON

1973

01-00-73 (00:00) BUNDY ON CONTRACT WITH CRIMINAL JUSTICE PLANNING. BUNDY COMPANY NAME IS T.R.B., SEATTLE, WASHINGTON

01-10-73 (00:00) BUNDY BOUGHT GAS, DRIVING WASHINGTON OPM-001, SEATTLE, WASHINGTON

01-19-73 (00:00) BUNDY BOUGHT GAS, SEATTLE WASHINGTON

01-29-73 (00:00) BUNDY BOUGHT GAS, DRIVING WASHINGTON OPM-001, SEATTLE, WASHINGTON

02-10-73 (00:00) BUNDY BOUGHT GAS, DRIVING WASHINGTON OPM-001, SEATTLE, WASHINGTON

03-00-73 (00:00) ARRESTED FOR TICKET WARRANTS, SEATTLE, WASHINGTON

03-05-73 (00:00) BUNDY BOUGHT GAS, DRIVING WASHINGTON OPM-001, SEATTLE, WASHINGTON

03-09-73 (00:00) BUNDY BOUGHT GAS, DRIVING WASHINGTON C-26464, SEATTLE, WASHINGTON

03-16-73 (00:00) BUNDY TURNED IN PROGRESS REPORT TO CRIMINAL JUSTICE PLANNING, SEATTLE, WASHINGTON

03-26-73 (00:00) BUNDY BOUGHT GAS, DRIVING WASHINGTON OPM-001, SEATTLE, WASHINGTON

03-29-73 (00:00) BUNDY BOUGHT GAS DRIVING WASHINGTON IBH-521, SEATTLE, WASHINGTON

03-30-73 (13:30) BUNDY HAD HIS VOLKSWAGEN REPAIRED AND A KEY MADE, PLUS HAD A KEY TO HIS GIRLFRIEND'S CAR MADE, SEATTLE, WASHINGTON

03-30-73 (00:00) BUNDY'S GIRLFRIENDS VOLKSWAGEN WAS STOLEN, SEATTLE, WASHINGTON

04-03-73 (00:00) BUNDY BOUGHT GAS DRIVING WASHINGTON IBH-521, SEATTLE, WASHINGTON

04-08-73 (00:00) BUNDY BOUGHT GAS DRIVING WASHINGTON IBH-521, SEATTLE, WASHINGTON

04-12-73 (12:30) BUNDY HAD GAS LEAK REPAIRED ON HIS VOLKSWAGEN, SEATTLE, WASHINGTON

(00:00) BUNDY BOUGHT GAS DRIVING WASHINGTON IBH-521, SEATTLE, WASHINGTON

04-13-73 (00:00) BUNDY IN SEATTLE, WASHINGTON

04-16-73 (00:00) BUNDY BOUGHT GAS DRIVING WASHINGTON IBH-521, SEATTLE, WASHINGTON

04-18-73 (00:00) BUNDY IN SEATTLE, WASHINGTON

04-19-73 (00:00) BUNDY BOUGHT GAS, SEATTLE WASHINGTON

04-20-73 (00:00) BUNDY BOUGHT GAS DRIVING WASHINGTON IBH-521, SEATTLE, WASHINGTON

(00:00) BUNDY BOUGHT GAS, TUMWATER, WASHINGTON

04-22-73 (00:00) BUNDY BOUGHT GAS, SEATTLE, WASHINGTON

04-23-73 (00:00) BUNDY IN SEATTLE, WASHINGTON

04-24-73 (00:00) BUNDY BOUGHT GAS DRIVING WASHINGTON IBH-521, DUPONT, WASHINGTON

(00:00) BUNDY TOOK PLANE FROM SEATTLE TO SPOKANE, WASHINGTON

(00:00) BUNDY CHECKED INTO SIESTA MOTEL ROOM #8, COLFAX, WASHINGTON

04-26-73 (00:00) BUNDY IN OLYMPIA, WASHINGTON

(00:00) BUNDY BOUGHT GAS DRIVING WASHINGTON IBH-521, SEATTLE, WASHINGTON

04-29-73 (00:00) BUNDY BOUGHT GAS, DRIVING WASHINGTON OPM-001, SEATTLE, WASHINGTON

04-30-73 (00:00) BUNDY IN OLYMPIA, WASHINGTON

05-00-73 (00:00) BUNDY CLAIMED HE COMMITTED HIS FIRST HOMICIDE: VICTIM

UNKNOWN. PICKED UP HITCHHIKER TUMWATER/OLYMPIA: WASHINGTON. NOT CONFIRMED

05-01-73 (00:00) BUNDY IN OLYMPIA, WASHINGTON

(00:00) BUNDY BOUGHT GAS DRIVING WASHINGTON IBH-521, SEATTLE, WASHINGTON

05-04-73 (00:00) Bundy in Olympia, Washington

05-07-73 (00:00) BUNDY BOUGHT GAS, SEATTLE, WASHINGTON

05-08-73 (00:00) BUNDY IN SEATTLE, WASHINGTON

05-09-73 (00:00) BUNDY IN OLYMPIA, WASHINGTON

(00:00) BUNDY BOUGHT GAS DRIVING WASHINGTON IBH-521, SEATTLE, WASHINGTON

05-10-73 (00:00) BUNDY IN OLYMPIA, WASHINGTON

(00:00) BUNDY BOUGHT GAS DRIVING WASHINGTON IBH-521, SEATTLE, WASHINGTON

05-12-73 (00:00) BUNDY BOUGHT GAS DRIVING WASHINGTON IBH-521, SEATTLE, WASHINGTON

05-14-73 (00:00) BUNDY BOUGHT GAS DRIVING WASHINGTON IBH-521, SEATTLE, WASHINGTON

05-16-73 (00:00) BUNDY IN SEATTLE, WASHINGTON

05-17-73 (00:00) BUNDY IN DAVENPORT HOTEL, SPOKANE, WASHINGTON

05-18-73 (00:00) BUNDY IN OLYMPIA, WASHINGTON

05-19-73 (00:00) BUNDY BOUGHT GAS DRIVING WASHINGTON IBH-521, ENUMCLAW, WASHINGTON

(00:00) BUNDY BOUGHT GAS DRIVING WASHINGTON IBH-521, SEATTLE, WASHINGTON

05-22-73 (00:00) BUNDY IN OLYMPIA, WASHINGTON

(00:00) BUNDY BOUGHT GAS DRIVING WASHINGTON IBH-521, SEATTLE, WASHINGTON

05-25-73 (00:00) BUNDY IN SEATTLE, WASHINGTON

05-26-73 (00:00) BUNDY IN OLYMPIA, WASHINGTON

(00:00) BUNDY BOUGHT GAS DRIVING WASHINGTON IBH-521, SEATTLE, WASHINGTON

05-31-73 (00:00) BUNDY BOUGHT GAS DRIVING WASHINGTON IBH-521, SEATTLE, WASHINGTON

06-01-73 (00:00) BUNDY IN OLYMPIA, WASHINGTON

06-02-73 (00:00) BUNDY BOUGHT GAS DRIVING WASHINGTON IBH-521, SEATTLE, WASHINGTON

06-03-73 (00:00) BUNDY RENTED AN UNKNOWN MAKE OF VEHICLE FROM NATIONAL RENTAL CAR, SEATTLE, WASHINGTON

06-04-73 (00:00) BUNDY IN OLYMPIA, WASHINGTON

(00:00) BUNDY BOUGHT GAS DRIVING WASHINGTON IBH-521, SEATTLE, WASHINGTON

06-05-73 (00:00) BUNDY IN OLYMPIA, WASHINGTON

(00:00) BUNDY BOUGHT GAS DRIVING WASHINGTON IBH-521, SEATTLE, WASHINGTON

06-06-73 (00:00) BUNDY BOUGHT GAS, SEATTLE, WASHINGTON

06-09-73 (00:00) BUNDY BOUGHT GAS DRIVING WASHINGTON IBH-521, SEATTLE, WASHINGTON

06-10-73 (00:00) BUNDY IN OLYMPIA, WASHINGTON

06-11-73 (00:00) BUNDY IN SEATTLE, WASHINGTON

06-12-73 (00:00) BUNDY BOUGHT GAS DRIVING WASHINGTON IBH-521, SEATTLE, WASHINGTON

06-13-73 (00:00) BUNDY STAYED AT MARK HOPKINS HOTEL, SAN FRANCISCO, CALIFORNIA

06-14-73 (00:00) BUNDY STAYED AT MARK HOPKINS HOTEL, SAN FRANCISCO, CALIFORNIA

06-15-73 (00:00) BUNDY IN SAN FRANCISCO, LEFT FOR SEATTLE, WASHINGTON

06-18-73 (00:00) BUNDY BOUGHT GAS DRIVING WASHINGTON IBH-521, SEATTLE, WASHINGTON

06-19-73 (00:00) BUNDY BOUGHT GAS, SEATTLE, WASHINGTON

06-20-73 (00:00) BUNDY IN SEATTLE & TUMWATER & OLYMPIA, WASHINGTON

(00:00) BUNDY BOUGHT GAS DRIVING WASHINGTON IBH-521, TACOMA, WASHINGTON

06-25-73 (00:00) BUNDY IN OLYMPIA, WASHINGTON

(00:00) BUNDY BOUGHT GAS DRIVING WASHINGTON IBH-521, TUMWATER, WASHINGTON

06-27-73 (00:00) BUNDY IN SEATTLE & OLYMPIA, WASHINGTON

06-29-73 (00:00) BUNDY IN SEATTLE, WASHINGTON

(00:00) BUNDY BOUGHT GAS, SEATTLE, WASHINGTON

06-30-73 (00:00) BUNDY BOUGHT GAS, SEATTLE, WASHINGTON

07-02-73 (00:00) Bundy in Olympia & Seattle, Washington (I-229)

07-03-73 (00:00) Bundy in Seattle & Olympia, Washington

07-04-73 (00:00) BUNDY RENTED ROOM AT EDGEWATER INN, SEATTLE, WASHINGTON

(00:00) BUNDY BOUGHT GAS DRIVING WASHINGTON IBH-521, SEATTLE, WASHINGTON

07-05-73 (00:00) BUNDY IN OLYMPIA, WASHINGTON

07-06-73 (00:00) BUNDY IN SEATTLE, WASHINGTON

07-07-73 (00:00) BUNDY BOUGHT GAS DRIVING WASHINGTON OPM-001 SEATTLE, WASHINGTON

07-08-73 (00:00) BUNDY IN SEATTLE & OLYMPIA, WASHINGTON

07-09-73 BUNDY BOUGHT GAS DRIVING WASHINGTON OPM-001, DUPONT, WASHINGTON

07-10-73 (00:00) BUNDY IN OLYMPIA, WASHINGTON

07-12-73 (00:00) BUNDY IN OLYMPIA, WASHINGTON

(00:00) BUNDY BOUGHT GAS DRIVING WASHINGTON IBH-521, DUPONT, WASHINGTON

07-13-73 (00:00) BUNDY BOUGHT GAS, SEATTLE, WASHINGTON

07-14-73 (00:00) BUNDY BOUGHT GAS DRIVING WASHINGTON IBH-521, UNKNOWN CITY, WASHINGTON

07-15-73 (00:00) BUNDY IN SEATTLE, WASHINGTON

07-17-73 (00:00) BUNDY BOUGHT GAS, SEATTLE, WASHINGTON

07-18-73 (00:00) BUNDY IN SEATTLE, WASHINGTON

(00:00) BUNDY BOUGHT GAS, TUMWATER, WASHINGTON

07-19-73 (00:00) BUNDY IN SEATTLE, WASHINGTON

07-20-73 (00:00) BUNDY IN SEATTLE, WASHINGTON

07-23-73 (00:00) BUNDY IN SEATTLE, WASHINGTON

(00:00) BUNDY BOUGHT GAS DRIVING WASHINGTON IBH-521, TUMWATER, WASHINGTON

07-24-73 (00:00) BUNDY IN OLYMPIA, WASHINGTON

07-25-73 (00:00) BUNDY IN SEATTLE WASHINGTON

07-26-73 (00:00) BUNDY PART OF VEHICLE, SEATTLE, WASHINGTON

07-27-73 (00:00) BUNDY IN SEATTLE, WASHINGTON

07-28-73 (00:00) BUNDY IN SEATTLE & ELLENSBURG, WASHINGTON

07-29-73 (00:00) BUNDY IN SEATTLE & OLYMPIA, WASHINGTON

07-30-73 (00:00) BUNDY BOUGHT GAS DRIVING WASHINGTON IBH-521, TUMWATER, WASHINGTON

08-01-73 (00:00) BUNDY IN SEATTLE, WASHINGTON

08-02-73 (00:00) BUNDY BOUGHT GAS DRIVING WASHINGTON IBH-521, TUMWATER, WASHINGTON

08-03-73 (00:00) BUNDY IN SEATTLE, WASHINGTON

08-04-73 (00:00) BUNDY IN SEATTLE, WASHINGTON

(00: 00) BUNDY BOUGHT GAS, TUMWATER, WASHINGTON

08-06-73 (00:00) BUNDY BOUGHT GAS DRIVING WASHINGTON IBH-521, SEATTLE, WASHINGTON

08-07-73 (00:00) BUNDY PART OF VEHICLE, SEATTLE, WASHINGTON

08-10-73 (00:00) BUNDY IN SEATTLE, WASHINGTON

08-11-73 (00:00) BUNDY IN SEATTLE & TUMWATER, WASHINGTON

08-15-73 (00:00) BUNDY BOUGHT GAS DRIVING WASHINGTON IBH-521, SEATTLE, WASHINGTON

08-16-73 (00:00) BUNDY IN SEATTLE, WASHINGTON

08-17-73 (00:00) BUNDY BOUGHT GAS DRIVING WASHINGTON IBH-521, SEATTLE, WASHINGTON

08-18-73 (00:00) BUNDY BOUGHT GAS DRIVING WASHINGTON OYU-149, TACOMA, WASHINGTON

08-20-73 (13:15) BUNDY HAD A CLUTCH REPAIRED ON HIS VOLKSWAGEN, SEATTLE, WASHINGTON

08-22-73 (00:00) BUNDY IN SEATTLE, WASHINGTON

08-23-73 (00:00) BUNDY BOUGHT GAS, TUMWATER, WASHINGTON

08-24-73 (00:00) BUNDY IN OLYMPIA, WASHINGTON

(00: 00) BUNDY GOT IN ACCIDENT WITH GIRLFRIENDS OF VEHICLE, SEATTLE, WASHINGTON

08-28-73 (00:00) BUNDY BOUGHT GAS DRIVING WASHINGTON IBH-521, DUPONT, WASHINGTON

08-29-73 (00:00) BUNDY BOUGHT GAS DRIVING WASHINGTON ICI-418, TUMWATER, WASHINGTON

08-30-73 (12:00) BUNDY DROVE A HERTZ RENTAL TRUCK, OLYMPIA, WASHINGTON

(00:00) BUNDY BOUGHT GAS DRIVING WASHINGTON 17241V, TUMWATER, WASHINGTON

(20:00) BUNDY RETURNED RENTAL TRUCK, OLYMPIA, WASHINGTON

08-31-73 (00:00) BUNDY IN SEATTLE, WASHINGTON

(PM.HR) BUNDY AT SEA-TAC AIRPORT, SEATTLE, WASHINGTON

09-00-73 (00:00) BUNDY HAD SPRAINED ANKLE EXAMINED, SEATTLE, WASHINGTON

09-01-73 (00:00) BUNDY PART OF VEHICLE, SEATTLE, WASHINGTON

09-02-73 (00:00) BUNDY BOUGHT GAS DRIVING WASHINGTON BTR-416, ISSAQUAH, WASHINGTON

09-03-73 (00:00) BUNDY BOUGHT GAS, SEATTLE, WASHINGTON

09-04-73 (00:00) BUNDY IN SEATTLE & OLYMPIA, WASHINGTON

09-05-73 (00:00) BUNDY IN SEATTLE, WASHINGTON

09-06-73 (00:00) BUNDY BOUGHT GAS DRIVING WASHINGTON IBH-521, SEATTLE, WASHINGTON

09-07-73 (00: 00) BUNDY IN SCHOOL, UPS, TACOMA, WASHINGTON

09-10-73 (00:00) BUNDY IN SCHOOL, UPS, TACOMA, WASHINGTON

09-11-73 (00:00) BUNDY IN TUMWATER, WASHINGTON

09-12-73 (00:00) BUNDY IN SCHOOL, UPS, TACOMA, WASHINGTON

09-14-73 (00:00) BUNDY IN SCHOOL, UPS, TACOMA, WASHINGTON

09-17-73 (00:00) BUNDY HAD SPRAINED ANKLE

CHECKED AT ORTHOPEDIC CLINIC, SEATTLE, WASHINGTON

09-18-73 (00:00) BUNDY IN SCHOOL, UPS, TACOMA, WASHINGTON

09-19-73 (00:00) BUNDY IN SCHOOL, UPS, TACOMA, WASHINGTON

09-20-73 (00:00) BUNDY PART OF VEHICLE, SEATTLE, WASHINGTON

09-21-73 (00:00) BUNDY IN SCHOOL, UPS, TACOMA, WASHINGTON

09-24-73 (00:00) BUNDY IN SCHOOL, UPS, TACOMA, WASHINGTON

09-25-73 (00:00) BUNDY BOUGHT GAS DRIVING WASHINGTON IBH-521, TUKWILLA, WASHINGTON

09-26-73 (00:00) BUNDY IN SCHOOL, UPS, TACOMA, WASHINGTON

09-27-73 (00:00) BUNDY IN SCHOOL, UPS, TACOMA, WASHINGTON

09-28-73 (00:00) BUNDY BOUGHT GAS DRIVING WASHINGTON IBH-521, SEATTLE, WASHINGTON

10-01-73 (00:00) BUNDY IN SCHOOL, UPS, TACOMA, WASHINGTON

10-03-73 (00:00) BUNDY IN SCHOOL, UPS, TACOMA, WASHINGTON

10-04-73 (00:00) BUNDY PARKED A VEHICLE, SEATTLE, WASHINGTON

10-05-73 (00:00) BUNDY IN SCHOOL, UPS, TACOMA, WASHINGTON

10-06-73 (00:00) BUNDY BOUGHT GAS, SEATTLE, WASHINGTON

10-08-73 (00:00) BUNDY IN SCHOOL, UPS, TACOMA, WASHINGTON

10-10-73 (00:00) BUNDY IN SCHOOL, UPS, TACOMA, WASHINGTON

10-12-73 (00:00) BUNDY IN SCHOOL, UPS, TACOMA, WASHINGTON

10-13-73 (00:00) BUNDY BOUGHT GAS DRIVING WASHINGTON IBH-521, SEATTLE, WASHINGTON

10-15-73 (00:00) BUNDY IN SCHOOL, UPS, TACOMA, WASHINGTON

10-17-73 (00:00) BUNDY IN SCHOOL, UPS, TACOMA, WASHINGTON

10-18-73 (00:00) BUNDY PARKED A VEHICLE, SEATTLE, WASHINGTON

10-19-73 (00:00) BUNDY IN SCHOOL, UPS, TACOMA, WASHINGTON

10-21-73 (00:00) BUNDY BOUGHT GAS DRIVING WASHINGTON IBH-521, SEATTLE, WASHINGTON

10-24-73 (00:00) BUNDY IN SCHOOL, UPS, TACOMA, WASHINGTON

10-26-73 (00:00) BUNDY IN SCHOOL, UPS, TACOMA, WASHINGTON

10-29-73 (00:00) BUNDY IN SCHOOL, UPS, TACOMA, WASHINGTON

10-31-73 (00:00) BUNDY IN SCHOOL, UPS, TACOMA, WASHINGTON

11-01-73 (00:00) BUNDY VISITED UNEMPLOYMENT OFFICE, SEATTLE, WASHINGTON

11-02-73 (00:00) BUNDY IN SCHOOL, UPS, TACOMA, WASHINGTON

11-05-73 (00:00) BUNDY BOUGHT GAS DRIVING WASHINGTON IBH-521, SEATTLE, WASHINGTON

11-07-73 (00:00) BUNDY VISITED UNEMPLOYMENT OFFICE, SEATTLE, WASHINGTON

11-09-73 (00:00) BUNDY IN SCHOOL, UPS, TACOMA, WASHINGTON

11-12-73 (00:00) BUNDY BOUGHT GAS DRIVING WASHINGTON IBH-521, SEATTLE, WASHINGTON

11-13-73 (00:00) BUNDY VISITED UNEMPLOYMENT OFFICE, SEATTLE, WASHINGTON

01-12-74 (00:00) Bundy wrote a check to Aurora plumbing, SEATTLE, WASHINGTON

1974

01-13-74 (00:00) BUNDY WROTE A CHECK TO SAFEWAY, SEATTLE, WASHINGTON

01-14-74 (00:00) BUNDY IN SCHOOL, UPS, TACOMA, WASHINGTON

01-15-74 (00:00) BUNDY BOUGHT GAS, SEATTLE, WASHINGTON

01-16-74 (00:00) BUNDY IN SCHOOL, UPS, TACOMA, WASHINGTON

01-17-74 (00:00) BUNDY VISITED UNEMPLOYMENT OFFICE, SEATTLE, WASHINGTON

01-18-74 (00:00) BUNDY IN SCHOOL, UPS, TACOMA, WASHINGTON

01-19-74 (00:00) BUNDY WROTE CHECK TO OFFICE OF THE ATTY. GEN. FOR A WORKSHOP, SEATTLE, WASHINGTON

01-20-74 (00:00) BUNDY IN SCHOOL, UPS, TACOMA, WASHINGTON

01-21-74 (00:00) BUNDY DEPOSITED MONEY IN BANK, SEATTLE, WASHINGTON

(00:00) BUNDY IN SCHOOL, UPS, TACOMA, WASHINGTON

01-22-74 (00:00) BUNDY PARKED THE VEHICLE AT THE OLY HOTEL, SEATTLE, WASHINGTON

01-23-74 (00:00) BUNDY BOUGHT GAS, SEATTLE, WASHINGTON

01-25-74 (00:00) BUNDY IN SCHOOL, UPS, TACOMA, WASHINGTON

01-26-74 (00:00) BUNDY WROTE A CHECK TO SAFEWAY, SEATTLE, WASHINGTON

01-28-74 (00:00) BUNDY MADE BANKING DEPOSIT, SEATTLE, WASHINGTON

(00:00) BUNDY IN SCHOOL, UPS, TACOMA, WASHINGTON

01-29-74 (00:00) BUNDY CHARGED GAS 1200 BLOCK DENNY, SEATTLE, WASHINGTON

(00:00) BUNDY VISITED UNEMPLOYMENT OFFICE, SEATTLE, WASHINGTON

01-30-74 (00:00) BUNDY IN SCHOOL, UPS, TACOMA, WASHINGTON

01-31-74 (00:00) BUNDY WROTE CHECK AT SAFEWAY STORE AT 49TH AND BROOKLYN, CLOSE TO HEALY RESIDENCE.

(00:01) BUNDY ABDUCTED LINDA ANNE HEALY FROM HER HOME IN SEATTLE, WASHINGTON

(00:00) BUNDY IN SCHOOL, UPS, TACOMA, WASHINGTON

02-01-74 (00:00) HEALY REPORTED MISSING TO POLICE, SEATTLE, WASHINGTON

(00:00) BUNDY DEPOSITED MONEY INTO BANK, SEATTLE, WASHINGTON

(00:00) BUNDY IN SCHOOL, UPS, TACOMA, WASHINGTON

(00:00) BUNDY CHARGED GAS AT FORTY-THIRD AND ROOSEVELT, SEATTLE, WASHINGTON

(00:00) BUNDY MADE BANKING DEPOSIT, SEATTLE, WASHINGTON

02-04-74 (00:00) BUNDY IN SCHOOL, UPS, TACOMA, WASHINGTON

02-06-74 (00:00) BUNDY IN SCHOOL, UPS, TACOMA, WASHINGTON

02-07-74 (00:00) BUNDY BOUGHT GAS FOR HIS

GIRLFRIEND'S VOLKSWAGEN, SEATTLE, WASHINGTON

02-08-74 (00:00) BUNDY WROTE CHECK, SEATTLE, WASHINGTON

02-09-74 (00:00) BUNDY WROTE CHECK, SEATTLE, WASHINGTON

02-10-74 (00:00) BUNDY WROTE CHECK, SEATTLE, WASHINGTON

02-11-74 (00:00) BUNDY BOUGHT GAS, SEATTLE, WASHINGTON

02-13-74 (00:00) BUNDY VISITED UNEMPLOYMENT OFFICE, SEATTLE, WASHINGTON

02-14-74 (00:00) BUNDY IN SCHOOL, UPS, TACOMA, WASHINGTON

02-15-74 (00:00) BUNDY BOUGHT SHOES AT NORDSTROM, SEATTLE, WASHINGTON

(00:00) BUNDY IN SCHOOL, UPS, TACOMA, WASHINGTON

02-16-74 (00:00) BUNDY WROTE CHECK, SEATTLE, WASHINGTON

02-17-74 (00:00) BUNDY WROTE CHECK, SEATTLE, WASHINGTON

02-19-74 (00:00) BUNDY WROTE CHECK, SEATTLE, WASHINGTON

02-22-74 (00:00) BUNDY IN SCHOOL, UPS, TACOMA, WASHINGTON

02-27-74 (00:00) BUNDY VISITED UNEMPLOYMENT OFFICE, SEATTLE, WASHINGTON

02-28-74 (00:00) BUNDY WROTE CHECK, SEATTLE, WASHINGTON

03-01-74 (00:00) BUNDY IN SCHOOL, UPS, TACOMA, WASHINGTON

03-03-74 (00:00) BUNDY WROTE CHECK TO NORTHWEST COPY, SEATTLE, WASHINGTON

03-04-74 (00:00) BUNDY DEPOSITED MONEY INTO BANK, SEATTLE, WASHINGTON

(00:00) BUNDY IN SCHOOL, UPS, TACOMA, WASHINGTON

03-05-74 (00:00) BUNDY BOUGHT GAS, SEATTLE, WASHINGTON

03-06-74 (00:00) BUNDY IN SCHOOL, UPS, TACOMA, WASHINGTON

03-07-74 (00:00) BUNDY BOUGHT GAS, SEATTLE, WASHINGTON

(00:00) BUNDY IN SCHOOL, UPS, TACOMA, WASHINGTON

03-08-74 (00:00) BUNDY IN SCHOOL, UPS, TACOMA, WASHINGTON

03-09-74 (00:00) BUNDY PURCHASED SHOES FROM NORDSTROM, SEATTLE, WASHINGTON

03-11-74 (00:00) BUNDY BOUGHT GAS, SEATTLE, WASHINGTON

03-12-74 (00:00) BUNDY WROTE CHECK, SEATTLE, WASHINGTON

(19:00) BUNDY ABDUCTED DONNA MANSON FROM THE EVERGREEN STATE COLLEGE, OLYMPIA, WASHINGTON

03-13-74 (00:00) BUNDY IN SCHOOL, UPS, TACOMA, WASHINGTON

03-14-74 (00:00) BUNDY BOUGHT GAS, SEATTLE, WASHINGTON

03-15-74 (00:00) BUNDY IN SCHOOL, UPS, TACOMA, WASHINGTON

03-17-74 (00:00) BUNDY WROTE A CHECK TO QFC, SEATTLE, WASHINGTON

03-18-74 (00:00) BUNDY VISITED UNEMPLOYMENT OFFICE, SEATTLE, WASHINGTON

03-19-74 (00:00) BUNDY BOUGHT GAS, SEATTLE,

WASHINGTON

03-21-74 (00:00) BUNDY DEPOSITED MONEY INTO BANK, SEATTLE, WASHINGTON

(00:00) BUNDY IN SCHOOL, UPS, TACOMA, WASHINGTON

03-22-74 (00:00) BUNDY IN SCHOOL, UPS, TACOMA, WASHINGTON

03-24-74 (00:00) BUNDY BOUGHT GAS, SEATTLE, WASHINGTON

03-25-74 (00:00) BUNDY BOUGHT GAS, SEATTLE, WASHINGTON

03-26-74 (00:00) BUNDY BOUGHT GAS, SEATTLE, WASHINGTON

03-27-74 (00:00) BUNDY VISITED UNEMPLOYMENT OFFICE, SEATTLE, WASHINGTON

03-29-74 (00:00) BUNDY BOUGHT GAS, SEATTLE, WASHINGTON

03-30-74 (00:00) BUNDY IN SCHOOL, UPS, TACOMA, WASHINGTON

04-01-74 (00:00) BUNDY BOUGHT GAS, SEATTLE, WASHINGTON

04-02-74 (00:00) BUNDY WROTE CHECK, SEATTLE, WASHINGTON

04-03-74 (00:00) BUNDY IN SCHOOL, UPS, TACOMA, WASHINGTON

04-05-74 (00:00) BUNDY WROTE CHECK, SEATTLE, WASHINGTON

04-06-74 (00:00) BUNDY WROTE CHECK, SEATTLE, WASHINGTON

04-07-74 (00:00) BUNDY WROTE CHECK, SEATTLE, WASHINGTON

04-08-74 (00:00) BUNDY WROTE CHECK, SEATTLE, WASHINGTON

04-09-74 (00:00) BUNDY WITHDREW FROM UPS

LAW SCHOOL, SEATTLE, WASHINGTON

04-10-74 (00:00) BUNDY VISITED UNEMPLOYMENT OFFICE, SEATTLE, WASHINGTON

04-11-74 (00:00) BUNDY WROTE CHECK, SEATTLE, WASHINGTON

04-12-74 (00:00) BUNDY BOUGHT GAS, SEATTLE, WASHINGTON

04-13-74 (00:00) BUNDY WROTE CHECK, SEATTLE, WASHINGTON

04-15-74 (18:00) BUNDY ROAD IN CARPOOL TO TAKE EXAM AT UPS LAW SCHOOL, SEATTLE, WASHINGTON

(00:00) BUNDY WROTE A CHECK TO FREEWAY VOLKSWAGEN, SEATTLE, WASHINGTON

(00:00) BUNDY BOUGHT GAS, SEATTLE, WASHINGTON

04-16-74 (00:00) BUNDY WROTE CHECK, SEATTLE, WASHINGTON

(13:30) BUNDY HAD NEW MUFFLER PUT ON HIS VOLKSWAGEN, SEATTLE, WASHINGTON

04-17-74 (00:00) Bundy wrote check to Freeway Volkswagen, Seattle, Washington

(00:00) BUNDY WROTE CHECK TO QFC, SEATTLE, WASHINGTON

(PM.HR) BUNDY BOUGHT GAS AT STANDARD STATION, SEATTLE, WASHINGTON

(21:30) BUNDY WITH ARM IN SLING WAS IDENTIFIED ON THE CENTRAL STATE COLLEGE CAMPUS, ELLENSBURG, WASHINGTON

(22:00) BUNDY ABDUCTED SUSAN ELAINE RANCOURT FROM CENTRAL STATE COLLEGE, ELLENSBURG, WASHINGTON

04-18-74 (00:00) BUNDY DEPOSITED PAYCHECK, SEATTLE, WASHINGTON

04-19-74 (00:00) BUNDY WROTE CHECK TO NESS FLOWERS, SEATTLE, WASHINGTON

04-20-74 (00:00) BUNDY WROTE CHECK TO SAFEWAY, SEATTLE, WASHINGTON

04-22-74 (00:00) BUNDY WROTE CHECK, SEATTLE, WASHINGTON

04-23-74 (00:00) BUNDY IN SEATTLE, WASHINGTON

04-24-74 (00:00) BUNDY VISITED UNEMPLOYMENT OFFICE, SEATTLE, WASHINGTON

(00:00) APPLICATION TO THE UNIVERSITY OF UTAH LAW SCHOOL IN SALT LAKE CITY, UTAH

04-27-74 (00:00) BUNDY WROTE CHECK, SEATTLE, WASHINGTON

04-29-74 (00:00) BUNDY WROTE CHECK, SEATTLE, WASHINGTON

04-30-74 (00:00) BUNDY WROTE CHECK, SEATTLE, WASHINGTON

05-02-74 (00:00) BUNDY BOUGHT GAS, SEATTLE, WASHINGTON

05-03-74 (00:00) BUNDY STARTED WORK AT DEPARTMENT OF EMERGENCY SERVICES, SEATTLE, WASHINGTON

(00:00) BUNDY BOUGHT GAS, SEATTLE, WASHINGTON

05-06-74 (00:00) BUNDY BOUGHT GAS TWICE AT STANDARD STATION, SEATTLE, WASHINGTON

(00:00) BUNDY WROTE CHECK TO SAFEWAY, SEATTLE, WASHINGTON

(00:00) BUNDY WROTE CHECK TO PAY AND SAVE, SEATTLE, WASHINGTON

(23:00) BUNDY ABDUCTED ROBERTA KATHLEEN PARKS FROM OREGON STATE UNIVERSITY, CORVALLIS, OREGON

05-09-74 (00:00) BUNDY WROTE CHECK, SEATTLE, WASHINGTON

05-10-74 (00:00) BUNDY MAY DEPOSIT, SEATTLE, WASHINGTON

05-12-74 (00:00) BUNDY WROTE CHECK, SEATTLE, WASHINGTON

05-14-74 (00:00) BUNDY WROTE CHECK, SEATTLE, WASHINGTON

(00:00) BUNDY BOUGHT SHOES AT NORDSTROM'S, SEATTLE, WASHINGTON

05-15-74 (00:00) BUNDY BOUGHT GAS, SEATTLE, WASHINGTON

05-16-74 (00:00) BUNDY BOUGHT GAS, SEATTLE, WASHINGTON

05-19-74 (00:00) BUNDY WROTE CHECK, SEATTLE, WASHINGTON

05-20-74 (00:00) BUNDY BOUGHT GAS, SEATTLE, WASHINGTON

05-21-74 (00:00) BUNDY MADE BANK DEPOSIT, SEATTLE, WASHINGTON

05-22-74 (00:00) BUNDY BOUGHT GAS, SEATTLE, WASHINGTON

05-23-74 (00:00) BUNDY RECEIVED ACCEPTANCE LETTER FROM UNIVERSITY OF UTAH. BUNDY LIVING IN SEATTLE, WASHINGTON AT THE TIME

05-24-74 (00:00) BUNDY WROTE CHECK, SEATTLE, WASHINGTON

(00:00) BUNDY BOUGHT GAS, TUKWILA, WASHINGTON

05-27-74 (00:00) BUNDY BOUGHT DRESS AT NORDSTROM AT SOUTHCENTER, SEATTLE, WASHINGTON

05-28-74 (00:00) BUNDY BOUGHT GAS, SEATTLE,

WASHINGTON

05-29-74 (00:00) BUNDY BOUGHT GAS, SEATTLE, WASHINGTON

05-30-74 (00:00) BUNDY WORKED IN SEATTLE, WASHINGTON

05-31-74 (00:00) BUNDY DEPOSITED MONEY IN BANK, SEATTLE, WASHINGTON

(PM.HR) BUNDY IN SEATTLE, WASHINGTON

(00:00) BUNDY BOUGHT GAS, OLYMPIA, WASHINGTON

06-01-74 (00:00) BUNDY ABDUCTED BRENDA CAROL BALL, SEATTLE, WASHINTON

(17:20) BUNDY GOES TO HIS GIRLFRIEND'S DAUGHTER'S BAPTISM, SEATTLE, WASHINGTON

06-03-74 (00:00) BUNDY BOUGHT GAS, OLYMPIA, WASHINGTON

06-04-74 (00:00) BUNDY BOUGHT GAS, OLYMPIA, WASHINGTON

06-05-74 (00:00) BUNDY IN SEATTLE, WASHINGTON

(00:00) BUNDY IN TACOMA, WASHINGTON

06-07-74 (00:00) BUNDY BOUGHT GAS, OLYMPIA, WASHINGTON

06-08-74 (12:00) BUNDY WITH FRIEND, SEATTLE, WASHINGTON

06-09-74 (05:00) BUNDY LEFT FRIEND, SEATTLE, WASHINGTON

(00:00) BUNDY WROTE TWO CHECKS IN THE UNIVERSITY AREA OF SEATTLE, WASHINGTON

06-10-74 (DAYHR) BUNDY CHARGED GAS AT STANDARD STATION, OLYMPIA, WASHINGTON

06-11-74(DAYHR) BUNDY CHARGED GAS AT STANDARD STATION, OLYMPIA, WASHINGTON

06-12-74 (01:00) BUNDY ABDUCTED

GEORGEANNE HAWKINS FROM AN ALLEY BEHIND THE KAPPA ALPHA THETA SORORITY HOUSE WHERE SHE WAS LIVING, SEATTLE, WASHINGTON

(PM.HR) Bundy charged gas at standard station, Olympia, Washington

(17:00) BUNDY RETURNED TO ABDUCTION SITE AND PICKED UP EVIDENCE

06-13-74 (00:00) BUNDY BOUGHT GAS, OLYMPIA, WASHINGTON

06-14-74 (00:00) BUNDY BOUGHT GAS, OLYMPIA, WASHINGTON

06-15-74 (00:00) BUNDY RETURNED TO HAWKINS DUMPSITE AND REMOVED MORE EVIDENCE, SEATTLE, WASHINGTON

BUNDY RETURN ONE MORE TIME ONE WEEK OR TEN DAYS FROM THIS DATE

06-16-74 (12:34) Bundy rented power mower, SEATTLE, WASHINGTON

06-17-74 (00:00) BUNDY BOUGHT GAS, OLYMPIA, WASHINGTON

06-19-74 (00:00) BUNDY BOUGHT GAS, OLYMPIA, WASHINGTON

(PM.HR) BUNDY HAD DINNER WITH FRIEND, TACOMA, WASHINGTON

06-21-74 (00:00) BUNDY BOUGHT GAS, TUMWATER, WASHINGTON

06-23-74 (00:00) BUNDY IN SEATTLE, WASHINGTON

06-24-74 (00:00) BUNDY OFF SICK FROM WORK AT DEPARTMENT OF EMERGENCY SERVICES, SEATTLE, WASHINGTON

(00:00) BUNDY BOUGHT GAS, OLYMPIA, WASHINGTON

06-28-74 (00:00) BUNDY BOUGHT GAS, OLYMPIA, WASHINGTON

(PM.HR) BUNDY HAD DINNER IN BELLEVUE, WASHINGTON

06-29-74 (00:00) BUNDY WENT ON RAFT TRIP DOWN YAKIMA RIVER PUT RAFT IN AT I-90 AND HIGHWAY NINETY-SEVEN, ELLENSBURG, WASHINGTON

(00:00) BUNDY BOUGHT GAS, SEATTLE, WASHINGTON

(PM.HR) BUNDY HAD DINNER IN NORTH BEND, WASHINGTON

07-00-74 (00:00) FIRST WEEK, BUNDY REMOVED SKI RACK FROM GIRLFRIEND'S KLOEPFER'S VEHICLE AND PLACED IT ON HIS CAR, SEATTLE, WASHINGTON

07-01-74 (00:00) BUNDY ON LEAVE WITHOUT PAY FROM DEPARTMENT OF EMERGENCY SERVICES, SEATTLE, WASHINGTON

(00:00) BUNDY DEPOSITED MONEY IN BANK, WASHINGTON

(00:00) BUNDY BOUGHT GAS, SEATTLE, WASHINGTON

07-02-74 (00:00) BUNDY BOUGHT GAS, SEATTLE, WASHINGTON

07-03-74 (00:00) BUNDY BOUGHT GAS, OLYMPIA, WASHINGTON

07-05-74 (00:00) BUNDY BOUGHT GAS, TUMWATER, WASHINGTON

07-06-74 (00:00) BUNDY BOUGHT GAS, SEATTLE, WASHINGTON

(00:00) BUNDY BOUGHT GAS, NORTH BEND, WASHINGTON

07-07-74 (00:00) BUNDY SEEN AT LAKE

SAMMAMISH STATE PARK NEAR ISSAQUAH, WASHINGTON

(00:00) BUNDY BOUGHT GAS, MERCER ISLAND, WASHINGTON

07-09-74 (00:00) BUNDY BOUGHT GAS, OLYMPIA, WASHINGTON

07-10-74 (00:00) BUNDY BOUGHT GAS, OLYMPIA, WASHINGTON

07-11-74 (00:00) BUNDY OFF SICK FROM DEPARTMENT OF EMERGENCY SERVICES, SEATTLE, WASHINGTON

(00:00) BUNDY BOUGHT GAS, SEATTLE, WASHINGTON

07-12-74 (00:00) BUNDY OFF SICK FROM DEPARTMENT OF EMERGENCY SERVICES, SEATTLE, WASHINGTON

07-13-74 (00:00) BUNDY WROTE CHECK FOR CASH, SEATTLE, WASHINGTON

07-14-74 (00:00) BUNDY SHOWED UP AT HIS GIRLFRIEND'S HOME AND HAD A FIGHT, THEN HE LEFT, SEATTLE, WASHINGTON

(00:00) BUNDY BOUGHT GAS, SEATTLE, WASHINGTON

(12:15) BUNDY, ARM IN SLING, APPROACHED WOMAN FOR HELP, SAMMAMISH STATE PARK NEAR ISSAQUAH, WASHINGTON

(13:00) DENISE MARIE NASLUND ARRIVED AT SAMMAMISH STATE PARK, WASHINGTON

(15:00) BUNDY, ARM IN SLING, APPROACHED WOMAN FOR HELP, SAMMAMISH STATE PARK NEAR ISSAQUAH, WASHINGTON

(16:00) BUNDY ABDUCTED DENISE MARIE NASLUND FROM LAKE SAMMAMISH STATE PARK NEAR ISSAQUAH, WASHINGTON

(18:00) BUNDY'S GIRLFRIEND RETURNED HOME, THEN BUNDY ARRIVED AND REMOVED SKI RACK FROM HIS CAR AND PUT IT ON HER CAR, SEATTLE, WASHINGTON

(20:15) BUNDY WENT HOME, SEATTLE, WASHINGTON

07-15-74 (00:00) BUNDY OFF SICK FROM DEPARTMENT OF EMERGENCY SERVICES SEATTLE, WASHINGTON

07-16-74 (00:00) BUNDY OFF SICK FROM DEPARTMENT OF EMERGENCY SERVICES SEATTLE, WASHINGTON

07-17-74 (00:00) BUNDY BOUGHT GAS, OLYMPIA, WASHINGTON

07-18-74 (00:00) BUNDY BOUGHT GAS, OLYMPIA, WASHINGTON

07-21-74 (00:00) BUNDY BOUGHT GAS, SEATTLE, WASHINGTON

07-25-74 (00:00) BUNDY PICKED UP RUG CLEANER, SEATTLE, WASHINGTON

07-27-74 (00:00) BUNDY BOUGHT GAS, SEATTLE, WASHINGTON

07-28-74 (00:00) BUNDY WENT TO SEATTLE STATE PARK, SEATTLE, WASHINGTON

07-31-74 (00:00) BUNDY BOUGHT GAS, SEATTLE, WASHINGTON

08-00-74 (00:00) MOVED TO SALT LAKE CITY, UTAH

08-01-74 (00:00) BUNDY DEPOSITED MONEY IN BANK, SEATTLE, WASHINGTON

08-02-74 (00:00) BUNDY BOUGHT GAS AT STANDARD STATION, OLYMPIA, WASHINGTON

08-04-74 (00:00) BUNDY BOUGHT GAS, OLYMPIA, WASHINGTON

08-07-74 (00:00) BUNDY BOUGHT GAS, OLYMPIA, WASHINGTON

08-11-74 (00:00) BUNDY BOUGHT GAS, OLYMPIA, WASHINGTON

08-15-74 (00:00) BUNDY BOUGHT GAS, TACOMA, WASHINGTON

08-18-74 (00:00) BUNDY BOUGHT GAS, OLYMPIA, WASHINGTON

08-22-74 (00:00) BUNDY BOUGHT GAS, OLYMPIA, WASHINGTON

08-24-74 (00:00) BUNDY BOUGHT GAS, OLYMPIA, WASHINGTON

08-25-74 (00:00) BUNDY BOUGHT GAS, OLYMPIA, WASHINGTON

08-28-74 (00:00) BUNDY TERMINATED WORK AT DEPARTMENT OF EMERGENCY SERVICES, SEATTLE, WASHINGTON

08-29-74 (00:00) BUNDY BOUGHT GAS, SEATTLE, WASHINGTON

08-30-74 (00:00) Bundy in Seattle, Washington

09-01-74 (00:00) BUNDY BOUGHT ITEM AT NORDSTROM, TACOMA, WASHINGTON

09-02-74 (00:00) BUNDY BOUGHT ITEM AT NORDSTROM, PORTLAND, OREGON

(00:00) BUNDY BOUGHT GAS, SEATTLE, WASHINGTON

(00:00) BUNDY BOUGHT GAS, YAKIMA, WASHINGTON

(00:00) BUNDY BOUGHT GAS, BOISE, IDAHO

(00:00) BUNDY, WHILE MOVING FROM SEATTLE, WASHINGTON, TO SALT LAKE CITY, UTAH, DROVE THROUGH BOISE, IDAHO, AND PICKED UP AN UNKNOWN HITCHHIKER AND KILLED HER. HE THEN DUMPED HER BODY IN THE

SNAKE RIVER. VICTIM'SIDENTIFICATION IS UNKNOWN, BODY HAS NEVER BEEN LOCATED.

09-03-74 (00:00) BUNDY BOUGHT ITEM AT NORDSTROM, TACOMA, WASHINGTON

09-04-74 (00:00) BODIES OF JANICE AND OTT AND DENISE MARIE NASLUND LOCATED, ISSAQUAH, WASHINGTON

(00:00) BUNDY BOUGHT GAS, BURLEY, IDAHO

09-06-74 (00:00) BUNDY BOUGHT GAS, SALT LAKE CITY, UTAH

(00:00) MONEY DEPOSITED IN BUNDY'S BANK ACCOUNT, SEATTLE, WASHINGTON

09-07-74 (00:00) BUNDY FLEW FROM SEATTLE TO SALT LAKE CITY, UTAH

09-11-74 (00:00) BUNDY BOUGHT GAS, SALT LAKE CITY, UTAH

09-13-74 (00:00) BUNDY ARRIVED BACK IN SEATTLE, WASHINGTON

09-17-74 (00:00) BUNDY FLEW TO TACOMA, WASHINGTON.

09-18-74 (00:00) BUNDY DEPOSITED MONEY INTO BANK, WASHINGTON

(00:00) BUNDY LEFT SEATTLE AND RETURNED TO SALT LAKE CITY, UTAH

(00:00) BUNDY BOUGHT GAS, NORTH BEND, WASHINGTON

(00:00) BUNDY BOUGHT GAS, YAKIMA, WASHINGTON

(00:00) BUNDY BOUGHT GAS, HERMISTON, OREGON

(00:00) BUNDY BOUGHT GAS, LEGRAND, OREGON

(00:00) BUNDY BOUGHT GAS, BURLEY, IDAHO

(00:00) BUNDY BOUGHT GAS, TREMONTON, UTAH

09-19-74 (19:24) BUNDY ON PHONE, SALT LAKE CITY, UTAH

09-20-74 (00:00) BUNDY BOUGHT GAS, SALT LAKE CITY, UTAH

09-23-74 (00:00) BUNDY BOUGHT GAS, SALT LAKE CITY, UTAH

09-24-74 (00:00) BUNDY BOUGHT GAS, SALT LAKE CITY, UTAH

09-25-74 (17:48) BUNDY ON PHONE, SALT LAKE CITY, UTAH

09-26-74 (00:00) BUNDY BOUGHT GAS, MURRAY, UTAH

09-27-74 (00:00) BUNDY BOUGHT GAS, SALT LAKE CITY, UTAH

09-28-74 (00:00) BUNDY BOUGHT GAS, SALT LAKE CITY, UTAH

09-30-74 (00:00) BUNDY BOUGHT GAS, SALT LAKE CITY, UTAH

FALL -74 (00:00) BAPTIZED A MEMBER OF THE LATTER-DAY SAINTS CHURCH, SALT LAKE CITY, UTAH

10-01-74 (00:00) BUNDY BOUGHT GAS, SALT LAKE CITY, UTAH

10-01-74 (00:00) BUNDY BOUGHT GAS, SALT LAKE CITY, UTAH

(22:25) BUNDY ON THE PHONE, SALT LAKE CITY, UTAH

10-02-74 (00:00) BUNDY ABDUCTED NANCY WILCOX, SALT LAKE CITY, UTAH

(00:00) NANCY WILCOX REPORTED MISSING, SALT LAKE CITY, UTAH

(00:00) BUNDY PURCHASED GAS IN SALT LAKE

CITY, UTAH

10-03-74 (21:58) BUNDY ON THE PHONE, SALT LAKE CITY, UTAH

10-08-74 (14:57) BUNDY ON THE PHONE, SALT LAKE CITY, UTAH

10-09-74 (23:50) BUNDY ON THE PHONE, SALT LAKE CITY, UTAH

10-11-74 (00:00) BUNDY BOUGHT GAS, SALT LAKE CITY, UTAH

10-13-74 (03:24) BUNDY ON THE PHONE, SALT LAKE CITY, UTAH

10-14-74 (00:00) BUNDY BOUGHT GAS, MURRAY, UTAH

(19:55) BUNDY ON THE PHONE, SALT LAKE CITY, UTAH

10-15-74 (00:03) BUNDY ON THE PHONE, SALT LAKE CITY, UTAH

10-16-74 (00:00) BUNDY BOUGHT GAS, SALT LAKE CITY, UTAH

10-18-74 (00:00) BUNDY BOUGHT GAS, SALT LAKE CITY, UTAH

(10:30) BUNDY ON THE PHONE IN SALT LAKE CITY, UTAH, CALLED A UTAH NUMBER, SALT LAKE CITY, UTAH

(21:30) BUNDY ABDUCTED MELISSA SMITH, SALT LAKE CITY, UTAH

(23:17) BUNDY ON THE PHONE IN SALT LAKE CITY, UTAH; CALLED GIRLFRIEND IN SEATTLE, WASHINGTON

10-19-74 (00:00) BUNDY BOUGHT GAS, SALT LAKE CITY, UTAH

10-21-74 (21:29) BUNDY ON THE PHONE, SALT LAKE CITY, UTAH

10-25-74 (00:00) BUNDY BOUGHT GAS, SALT

LAKE CITY, UTAH

10-26-74 (00:00) BUNDY BOUGHT GAS, SALT LAKE CITY, UTAH

10-27-74 (00:00) BODY OF MELISSA SMITH LOCATED, SALT LAKE CITY, UTAH

10-28-74 (00:00) BUNDY BOUGHT GAS, BOUNTIFUL, UTAH

10-31-74 (00:00) BUNDY ARE DUCTED LAURAAIME, SALT LAKE CITY, UTAH

11-01-74 (12:44) BUNDY ON PHONE IN SALT LAKE CITY, UTAH, CALLED GIRLFRIEND IN SEATTLE, WASHINGTON

11-02-74 (09:55) BUNDY ON THE PHONE, SALT LAKE CITY, UTAH

11-04-74 (22:08) BUNDY ON THE PHONE, SALT LAKE CITY, UTAH

11-07-74 (14:56) BUNDY ON THE PHONE, SALT LAKE CITY, UTAH

11-08-74 (00:00) BUNDY BOUGHT GAS, SALT LAKE CITY, UTAH

(19:00) ATTEMPTED ABDUCTION OF CAROL DARONCH, MURRAY, UTAH

(00:00) BUNDY ABDUCTED DEBBIE KEMP, BOUNTIFUL, UTAH

(23:52) BUNDY ON PHONE, SALT LAKE CITY, UTAH; CALLED GIRLFRIEND IN SEATTLE, WASHINGTON

11-14-74 (22:08) BUNDY ON THE PHONE, SALT LAKE CITY, UTAH

11-16-74 (00:00) BUNDY BOUGHT GAS, SALT LAKE CITY, UTAH

11-17-74 (00:00) BUNDY BOUGHT GAS, HEBER, UTAH

11-18-74 (00:00) BUNDY BOUGHT GAS, SALT

LAKE CITY, UTAH

11-19-74 (15:36) BUNDY ON THE PHONE, SALT LAKE CITY, UTAH

11-21-74 (00:00) BUNDY BOUGHT GAS, SALT LAKE CITY, UTAH

(23:03) BUNDY ON THE PHONE, SALT LAKE CITY, UTAH

11-22-74 (00:00) BUNDY BOUGHT GAS, SALT LAKE CITY, UTAH

11-23-74 (00:00) BUNDY ON THE PHONE, SALT LAKE CITY, UTAH

11-25-74 (12:08) BUNDY ON THE PHONE, SALT LAKE CITY, UTAH

11-26-74 (12:00) BUNDY ON PHONE, SALT LAKE CITY, UTAH; CALLED GIRLFRIEND IN SEATTLE, WASHINGTON

11-27-74 (00:00) BODY OF LAURA AIMEWILL FOUND IN MT.,20 MILES AWAY FROM WHERE AIME WAS LAST SEEN, SALEM, UTAH

11-30-74 (00:00) BUNDY BOUGHT GAS, SALT LAKE CITY, UTAH

12-02-74 (00:00) BUNDY BOUGHT GAS, SALT LAKE CITY, UTAH

12-05-74 (14:24) BUNDY ON THE PHONE, SALT LAKE CITY, UTAH

12-06-74 (00:00) BUNDY WROTE CHECK, SEATTLE, WASHINGTON

(00:00) BUNDY WROTE CHECK, SEATTLE, WASHINGTON

12-07-74 (21:11) BUNDY ON THE PHONE, SALT LAKE CITY, UTAH

12-10-74 (20:26) BUNDY ON THE PHONE, SALT LAKE CITY, UTAH

12-11-74 (14:42) BUNDY ON THE PHONE, SALT

LAKE CITY, UTAH

12-12-74 (00:00) BUNDY BOUGHT GAS, SALT LAKE CITY, UTAH

12-13-74 (12:54) BUNDY ON THE PHONE, SALT LAKE CITY, UTAH

12-19-74 (00:00) BUNDY'S UTAH DRIVER'S LICENSE A 957298 IS ISSUED

(13:46) BUNDY ON THE PHONE, SALT LAKE CITY, UTAH

12-20-74 (00:00) BUNDY BOUGHT GAS, SALT LAKE CITY, UTAH

12-21-74 (21:14) BUNDY ON THE PHONE, SALT LAKE CITY, UTAH

12-22-74 (05:59) BUNDY ON THE PHONE, SALT LAKE CITY, UTAH

12-24-74 (00:00) BUNDY BOUGHT GAS, SALT LAKE CITY, UTAH

12-25-74 (16:21) BUNDY ON THE PHONE, OGDEN, UTAH

12-26-74 (16:50) BUNDY ON THE PHONE, SALT LAKE CITY, UTAH

12-31-74 (00:00) BUNDY BOUGHT GAS, OGDEN, UTAH

1975

01-01-75 (21:03) BUNDY ON THE PHONE, SALT LAKE CITY, UTAH

01-03-75 (00:00) BUNDY BOUGHT GAS, SALT LAKE CITY, UTAH

01-07-75 (00:00) BUNDY BOUGHT GAS, SALT LAKE CITY, UTAH

(00:00) BUNDY ON THE PHONE, PROVO, UTAH

01-08-75 (00:31) BUNDY ON THE PHONE, SALT LAKE CITY, UTAH

01-09-75 (00:00) BUNDY APPLIED FOR A UTAH DRIVER'S LICENSE, SALT LAKE CITY, UTAH

01-10-75 (00:00) BUNDY BOUGHT GAS, SALT LAKE CITY, UTAH

01-11-75 (00:00) BUNDY PURCHASED GAS, GLENWOOD SPRINGS, COLORADO

(00:00) CARYN E. CAMPBELL ARRIVED AT SNOWMASS, STAYED AT THE WILDWOOD INN AT SNOWMASS, COLORADO

01-12-75 (00:00) BUNDY PURCHASED GAS, GLENWOOD SPRINGS, COLORADO

(18:00) CAMPBELL HAD DINNER, SNOWMASS, COLORADO

(00:00) BUNDY IDENTIFIED AS BEING IN AREA JUST PRIOR TO ABDUCTION, SNOWMASS, COLORADO

(19:43) BUNDY ABDUCTED CARYN EILEEN CAMPBELL FROM THE WILDWOOD INN, SNOWMASS, COLORADO

(22:30) CAMPBELL REPORTED MISSING, SNOWMASS, COLORADO

01-13-75 (00:00) BUNDY BOUGHT GAS, GREEN RIVER, UTAH

(18:23) BUNDY ON PHONE, SALT LAKE CITY, UTAH, CALLED GIRLFRIEND IN SEATTLE, WASHINGTON

01-14-75 (00:00) BUNDY BOUGHT GAS, SALT LAKE CITY, UTAH

01-23-75 (00:00) BUNDY IN SEATTLE, WASHINGTON

(00:00) BUNDY VISITED GIRLFRIEND IN SEATTLE, WASHINGTON

01-27-75 (21:14) BUNDY ON THE PHONE, SALT LAKE CITY, UTAH

01-28-75 (00:00) BUNDY IN SCHOOL, UU, SALT LAKE CITY, UTAH

01-29-75 (00:00) BUNDY IN SCHOOL, UU, SALT LAKE CITY, UTAH

01-30-75 (00:00) BUNDY IN SCHOOL, UU, SALT LAKE CITY, UTAH

01-31-75 (00:00) BUNDY BOUGHT GAS, SALT LAKE CITY, UTAH

02-00-75 (00:00) BUNDY PURCHASED UTAH LICENSE PLATE LJB-088

02-01-75 (13:49) BUNDY ON PHONE, SALT LAKE CITY, UTAH

02-04-75 (00:00) BUNDY IN SCHOOL, UU, SALT LAKE CITY, UTAH

02-06-75 (00:00) BUNDY IN SCHOOL, UU, SALT LAKE CITY, UTAH

02-08-75 (21:42) BUNDY ON PHONE, SALT LAKE CITY, UTAH

02-09-75 (00:00) BUNDY BOUGHT GAS, SALT LAKE CITY, UTAH

02-10-75 (00:00) BUNDY BOUGHT GAS, SALT LAKE CITY, UTAH

(00:00) BUNDY IN SCHOOL, UU, SALT LAKE CITY, UTAH

02-11-75 (00:00) BUNDY IN SCHOOL, UU, SALT LAKE CITY, UTAH

02-13-75 (22:04) BUNDY ON PHONE, SALT LAKE CITY, UTAH

02-15-75 (13:05) BUNDY ON PHONE, SALT LAKE CITY, UTAH

02-17-75 (01:21) BUNDY ON PHONE, SALT LAKE CITY, UTAH

(00:00) CARYN EILEEN CAMPBELL'S BODY

LOCATED 2.8 MILES FROM ABDUCTION SITE ON OWL CREEK RD., ASPEN, CO

02-19-75 (00:00) Bundy bought gas, Salt Lake City, Utah

(00:00) BUNDY IN SCHOOL, UU, SALT LAKE CITY, UTAH

02-20-75 (00:00) BUNDY IN SCHOOL, UU, SALT LAKE CITY, UTAH

02-21-75 (00:00) BUNDY IN SCHOOL, UU, SALT LAKE CITY, UTAH

02-22-75 (23:48) BUNDY ON PHONE, SALT LAKE CITY, UTAH

02-23-75 (00:00) BUNDY BOUGHT GAS, SALT LAKE CITY, UTAH

02-24-75 (00:00) BUNDY IN SCHOOL, UU, SALT LAKE CITY, UTAH

02-25-75 (00:00) BUNDY IN SCHOOL, UU, SALT LAKE CITY, UTAH

02-27-75 (00:00) BUNDY IN SCHOOL, UU, SALT LAKE CITY, UTAH

02-28-75 (00:00) BUNDY IN SCHOOL, UU, SALT LAKE CITY, UTAH

03-01-75 (00:00) BUNDY BOUGHT GAS, SALT LAKE CITY, UTAH

03-04-75 (00:00) BUNDY BOUGHT GAS, SALT LAKE CITY, UTAH

(00:00) BUNDY IN SCHOOL, UU, SALT LAKE CITY, UTAH

03-05-75 (00:00) BODIES OF LINDA AND HEALY, ROBERTA KATHLEEN PARKS, SUSAN ELAINE RANCOURT AND BRENDA CAROL BALL LOCATED ON TAYLOR MT., WASHINGTON

03-06-75 (00:00) BUNDY IN SCHOOL, UU, SALT LAKE CITY, UTAH

(22:11) BUNDY ON PHONE, SALT LAKE CITY, UTAH; CALLED GIRLFRIEND IN SEATTLE, WASHINGTON

03-07-75 (00:00) BUNDY IN SCHOOL, UU, SALT LAKE CITY, UTAH

03-08-75 (00:00) BUNDY BOUGHT GAS, SALT LAKE CITY, UTAH

03-10-75 (00:00) BUNDY IN SCHOOL, UU, SALT LAKE CITY, UTAH

03-12-75 (00:00) BUNDY IN SCHOOL, UU, SALT LAKE CITY, UTAH

03-13-75 (00:00) BUNDY BOUGHT GAS, SALT LAKE CITY, UTAH

(00:00) BUNDY IN SCHOOL, UU, SALT LAKE CITY, UTAH

03-14-75 (00:00) BUNDY BOUGHT GAS, ROCK SPRINGS, WYOMING

(00:00) BUNDY BOUGHT GAS, LARAMIE, WYOMING

03-15-75 (00:00) BUNDY PURCHASED GAS IN DILLON & SILVERTHORNE COLORADO

(PH.HR) SILVERTON POLICE CHIEF SAW BUNDY WALK INTO HOLIDAY INN, FRISCO, COLORADO, WHICH IS NEAR VAIL, COLORADO

(16:00) BUNDY ARRIVED IN HIS VOLKSWAGEN IN VAIL, COLORADO

(21:00) BUNDY ABDUCTED VICTIM JULIE CUNNINGHAM FROM VAIL, COLORADO AND TRANSPORTED HER BODY 100 MILES AWAY FROM VAIL BEFORE DUMPING BODY

03-16-75 (14:47) BUNDY ON THE PHONE, SALT LAKE CITY, UTAH, CALLED GIRLFRIEND IN SEATTLE, WASHINGTON

(20:42) BUNDY ON PHONE, SALT LAKE CITY,

UTAH, CALLED GIRLFRIEND IN SEATTLE, WASHINGTON

03-18-75 (11:01) BUNDY ON THE PHONE, SALT LAKE CITY, UTAH

03-19-75 (00:00) BUNDY IN SCHOOL, UU, SALT LAKE CITY, UTAH

03-20-75 (00:00) BUNDY BOUGHT GAS, SALT LAKE CITY, UTAH

(00:00) BUNDY IN SCHOOL, UU, SALT LAKE CITY, UTAH

03-21-75 (00:00) BUNDY IN SCHOOL, UU, SALT LAKE CITY, UTAH

03-22-75 (00:00) BUNDY BOUGHT GAS, SALT LAKE CITY, UTAH

03-24-75 (00:00) BUNDY IN SCHOOL, UU, SALT LAKE CITY, UTAH

03-25-75 (00:00) BUNDY IN SCHOOL, UU, SALT LAKE CITY, UTAH

03-26-75 (00:00) BUNDY BOUGHT GAS, SALT LAKE CITY, UTAH

03-27-75 (00:00) BUNDY IN SCHOOL, UU, SALT LAKE CITY, UTAH

03-28-75 (00:00) BUNDY IN SCHOOL, UU, SALT LAKE CITY, UTAH

03-29-75 (15:17) BUNDY ON THE PHONE, SALT LAKE CITY, UTAH

03-31-75 (00:00) BUNDY IN SCHOOL, UU, SALT LAKE CITY, UTAH

04-00-75 (00:00) BUNDY RETURN TO MURDER SITE OF JULIE CUNNINGHAM APPROXIMATELY SIX WEEKS AFTER MURDER AND BURIED THE BODY, GARFIELD COUNTY, COLORADO

04-01-75 (00:00) BUNDY BOUGHT GAS, SALT LAKE CITY, UTAH

(00:00) BUNDY IN SCHOOL, UU, SALT LAKE CITY, UTAH

04-02-75 (00:00) BUNDY IN SCHOOL, UU, SALT LAKE CITY, UTAH

04-03-75 (00:00) BUNDY BOUGHT GAS, SALT LAKE CITY, UTAH

(00:00) BUNDY IN SCHOOL, UU, SALT LAKE CITY, UTAH

04-04-75 (00:00) BUNDY BOUGHT GAS, GOLDEN, COLORADO

(00:00) BUNDY ABDUCTED DENISE OLIVERSON WHILE SHE WAS RIDING HER BICYCLE IN GRAND JUNCTION, COLORADO. BODY NEVER LOCATED, POSSIBLY IN A RIVER IN COLORADO.

04-05-75 (00:00) BUNDY BOUGHT GAS, SILVERTON, COLORADO

(00:00) OLIVERSON BICYCLE WAS SEEN BUT NOT REPORTED TO THE POLICE UNTIL 4-7-75, GRAND JUNCTION, COLORADO

04-06-75 (00:00) BUNDY BOUGHT GAS, GRAND JUNCTION, COLORADO

04-08-75 (00:00) BUNDY IN SCHOOL, UU, SALT LAKE CITY, UTAH

(00:00) BUNDY BOUGHT GAS, GREEN RIVER, UTAH

04-09-75 (00:00) BUNDY IN SCHOOL, UU, SALT LAKE CITY, UTAH

04-10-75 (00:00) BUNDY BOUGHT GAS, SALT LAKE CITY, UTAH

(00:00) BUNDY IN SCHOOL, UU, SALT LAKE CITY, UTAH

04-11-75 (00:00) BUNDY IN SCHOOL, UU, SALT LAKE CITY, UTAH

04-14-75 (00:00) BUNDY BOUGHT GAS, SALT LAKE CITY, UTAH

04-15-75 (00:00) BUNDY IN SCHOOL, UU, SALT LAKE CITY, UTAH

04-17-75 (00:00) BUNDY BOUGHT GAS, SALT LAKE CITY, UTAH

04-20-75 (00:00) BUNDY BOUGHT GAS, SALT LAKE CITY, UTAH

04-22-75 (00:00) BUNDY BOUGHT GAS, SALT LAKE CITY, UTAH

(00:00) BUNDY IN SCHOOL, UU, SALT LAKE CITY, UTAH

04-25-75 (00:00) BUNDY BOUGHT GAS, SALT LAKE CITY, UTAH

4-28-75 (00:00) BUNDY IN SCHOOL, UU, SALT LAKE CITY, UTAH

4-29-75 (00:00) BUNDY IN SCHOOL, UU, SALT LAKE CITY, UTAH

4-30-75 (00:00) BUNDY BOUGHT GAS, SALT LAKE CITY, UTAH

(00:00) BUNDY IN SCHOOL, UU, SALT LAKE CITY, UTAH

05-03-75 (00:00) BUNDY BOUGHT GAS, SALT LAKE CITY, UTAH

05-05-75 (00:00) BUNDY BOUGHT GAS, SALT LAKE CITY, UTAH

(00:00) BUNDY DROVE HIS VOLKSWAGEN TO POCATELLO, IDAHO

(PM.HR) BUNDY WAS CHALLENGED IN DORM ON COLLEGE CAMPUS, POCATELLO, IDAHO

05-06-75 (12:00) BUNDY ABDUCTED A FEMALE FROM POCATELLO, IDAHO. DESCRIPTION FIT LYNETTE CULVER, WHO WAS THE ONLY MISSING FEMALE AT THE TIME, POCATELLO, IDAHO

05-12-75 (00:00) BUNDY BOUGHT GAS, SALT LAKE CITY, UTAH

05-15-75 (00:00) BUNDY BOUGHT GAS, SALT LAKE CITY, UTAH

05-18-75 (00:00) BUNDY BOUGHT GAS, SALT LAKE CITY, UTAH

05-30-75 (00:00) BUNDY BOUGHT GAS, SALT LAKE CITY, UTAH

06-00-75 (00:00) NIGHT MANAGER, BAILIF HALL, UNIVERSITY OF UTAH, SALT LAKE CITY, UTAH

06-05-75 (00:00) BUNDY BOUGHT GAS, SALT LAKE CITY, UTAH

(00:00) BUNDY BOUGHT GAS, BOISE, IDAHO

06-06-75 (00:00) Bundy bought gas, PENDLETON, OREGON

(00:00) BUNDY BOUGHT GAS, ELLENSBURG, WASHINGTON

06-12-75 (00:00) BUNDY BOUGHT GAS, PENDLETON, OREGON

(00:00) BUNDY BOUGHT GAS, BOISE, IDAHO

06-13-75 (00:00) BUNDY BOUGHT GAS, SALT LAKE CITY, UTAH

06-18-75 (00:00) BUNDY IN SCHOOL, UU, SALT LAKE CITY, UTAH

06-23-75 (00:00) BUNDY IN SCHOOL, UU, SALT LAKE CITY, UTAH

06-25-75 (00:00) BUNDY IN SCHOOL, UU, SALT LAKE CITY, UTAH

06-27-75 (00:00) BUNDY ABDUCTED SUSAN CURTIS, BRIGHAM YOUNG UNIVERSITY, PROVO, UTAH

06-30-75 (00:00) BUNDY IN SCHOOL, UU, SALT LAKE CITY, UTAH

07-00-75 (00:00) SECURITY GUARD, UNIVERSITY

OF UTAH, SALT LAKE CITY, UTAH (LAST JOB AUGUST 1975)

07-01-75 (00:00) BUNDY IN SCHOOL, UU, SALT LAKE CITY, UTAH

07-02-75 (00:00) BUNDY IN SCHOOL, UU, SALT LAKE CITY, UTAH

07-03-75 (00:00) BUNDY IN SCHOOL, UU, SALT LAKE CITY, UTAH

07-07-75 (00:00) BUNDY IN SCHOOL, UU, SALT LAKE CITY, UTAH

07-08-75 (00:00) BUNDY IN SCHOOL, UU, SALT LAKE CITY, UTAH

07-09-75 (00:00) BUNDY BOUGHT GAS, SALT LAKE CITY, UTAH

(00:00) BUNDY IN SCHOOL, UU, SALT LAKE CITY, UTAH

07-10-75 (00:00) BUNDY IN SCHOOL, UU, SALT LAKE CITY, UTAH

07-12-75 (00:00) BUNDY BOUGHT GAS, SALT LAKE CITY, UTAH

07-14-75 (00:00) BUNDY BOUGHT GAS, SALT LAKE CITY, UTAH

07-15-75 (00:00) BUNDY BOUGHT GAS, SALT LAKE CITY, UTAH

(00:00) BUNDY IN SCHOOL, UU, SALT LAKE CITY, UTAH

07-16-75 (00:00) BUNDY IN SCHOOL, UU, SALT LAKE CITY, UTAH

07-18-75 (00:00) BUNDY IN SCHOOL, UU, SALT LAKE CITY, UTAH

07-19-75 (00:00) BUNDY IN SCHOOL, UU, SALT LAKE CITY, UTAH

07-21-75 (00:00) BUNDY BOUGHT GAS, SALT LAKE CITY, UTAH

07-23-75 (00:00) BUNDY IN SCHOOL, UU, SALT LAKE CITY, UTAH

07-24-75 (00:00) BUNDY IN SCHOOL, UU, SALT LAKE CITY, UTAH

07-25-75 (00:00) BUNDY IN SCHOOL, UU, SALT LAKE CITY, UTAH

07-26-75 (00:00) BUNDY IN SCHOOL, UU, SALT LAKE CITY, UTAH

07-30-75 (00:00) BUNDY IN SCHOOL, UU, SALT LAKE CITY, UTAH

08-08-75 (00:00) BUNDY BOUGHT GAS, SALT LAKE CITY, UTAH

08-16-75 (02:30) BUNDY ARRESTED; ATTEMPT TO EVADE POLICE, SALT LAKE CITY, UTAH

08-17-75 (00:00) BUNDY BAILED OUT OF JAIL, SALT LAKE CITY, UTAH

08-18-75 (21:16) BUNDY ON PHONE, SALT LAKE CITY, UTAH

08-21-75 (00:00) BUNDY BOUGHT GAS, SALT LAKE CITY, UTAH

(00:00) BUNDY ARRESTED: POSSESSION OF BURGLARY TOOLS, SALT LAKE CITY, UTAH

(19:00) BUNDY APARTMENT WAS SEARCHED. FOUND WAS A PROGRAM FROM A HIGH SCHOOL PLAY IN BOUNTIFUL, UTAH, WHERE DEBBIE KENT WAS LAST SEEN.

08-22-75 (00:00) BUNDY BAILED OUT OF JAIL, SALT LAKE CITY, UTAH

09-02-75 (00:00) BUNDY ON THE PHONE, SALT LAKE CITY, UTAH

09-05-75 (00:00) BUNDY IN COLORADO

09-07-75 (00:00) BUNDY ON PHONE, SALT LAKE CITY, UTAH

09-08-75 (00:00) BUNDY'S VOLKSWAGEN, VIN

#118731185, WAS IDENTIFIED BY CAROL DARONCH.

(10:59) BUNDY ON THE PHONE, SALT LAKE CITY, UTAH

09-12-75 (09:20) BUNDY IN SALT LAKE CITY, UTAH

09-15-75 (11:45) BUNDY IN SALT LAKE CITY, UTAH

(00:00) CUSTODIAL WORKER, UNIVERSITY OF UTAH, SALT LAKE CITY, UTAH

10-01-75 (00:00) CUSTODIAL WORKER, LAST WORKDAY, UNIVERSITY OF UTAH, SALT LAKE CITY, UTAH

10-02-75 (09:00) BUNDY ARRIVED FOR LINEUP. LONG HAIR WAS CUT AND PARTED ON DIFFERENT SIDE. ABDUCTION VICTIM CAROL DARONCH IDENTIFIED BUNDY, SALT LAKE CITY, UTAH

(11:00) BUNDY ARRESTED; AGGRAVATED KIDNAPPING/ATTEMPTED CRIMINAL HOMICIDE, SALT LAKE CITY, UTAH

10-03-75 (00:00) BUNDY RESIDENCE ON DOUGLAS WAS SEARCHED, SALT LAKE CITY, UTAH

10-15-75 (00:00) BUNDY'S VOLKSWAGEN WAS SEARCHED, SALT LAKE CITY, UTAH

10-16-75 (00:00) BUNDY IS SERVED WITH A SEARCH WARRANT FOR HIS BLOOD, SALT LAKE CITY, UTAH

10-20-75 (00:00) BUNDY BAILED OUT OF JAIL, SALT LAKE CITY, UTAH

11-00-75 (00:00) BUNDY FLEW OUT OF SALT LAKE CITY, UTAH, ON THANKSGIVING DAY AND FLEW TO SEA-TAC AIRPORT, SEATTLE, WASHINGTON

12-00-75 (00:00) GOT ENGAGED TO HIS GIRLFRIEND

12-02-75 (18:30) BUNDY DROVE VOLKSWAGEN, LIGHT TAN IN COLOR WITH WASHINGTON TAG, A QB-894, ON I-FIVE AT 320, SEATTLE, WASHINGTON

12-03-75 (10:05) Bundy seen driving in Seattle, Washington

12-04-75 (12:40) BUNDY SEEN IN SEATTLE, WASHINGTON

(15:00) BUNDY AT UNIVERSITY OF WASHINGTON IN CAFETERIA, SEATTLE, WASHINGTON

12-05-75 (20:30) BUNDY IN SEATTLE WASHINGTON

12-06-75 (09:20) BUNDY IN SEATTLE WASHINGTON

12-07-75 (13:15) BUNDY IN SEATTLE WASHINGTON

12-08-75 (16:00) BUNDY IN SEATTLE WASHINGTON

12-09-75 (08:15) BUNDY IN SEATTLE WASHINGTON

12-10-75 (07:47) BUNDY IN SEATTLE WASHINGTON

12-11-75 (09:00) BUNDY PURCHASED BUS TICKET TO AIRPORT, SEATTLE, WASHINGTON

(00:00) BUNDY LEFT FOR SALT LAKE CITY, UTAH

12-13-75 (00:00) BUNDY IN SALT LAKE CITY, UTAH

12-14-75 (00:00) BUNDY IN COURT, SALT LAKE CITY, UTAH

12-15-75 (AM:HR) BUNDY IN COURT, SALT LAKE CITY, UTAH

12-16-75 (00:00) BUNDY IN SALT LAKE CITY, UTAH

12-18-75 (00:00) BUNDY IN SALT LAKE CITY, UTAH

12-19-75 (00:00) BUNDY IN SALT LAKE CITY, UTAH

12-20-75 (00:00) BUNDY IN SALT LAKE CITY, UTAH

12-21-75 (00:00) BUNDY IN SALT LAKE CITY, UTAH

12-22-75 (00:00) BUNDY IN SALT LAKE CITY, UTAH

12-25-75 (00:00) BUNDY VISITED BY GIRLFRIEND, SALT LAKE CITY, UTAH

12-31-75 (AM:HR) BUNDY IN COURT, SALT LAKE CITY, UTAH

1976

01-12-76 (20:00) BUNDY IN SEATTLE, WASHINGTON

01-13-76 (08:30) BUNDY SEEN, SEATTLE, WASHINGTON

(13:32) BUNDY DROVE VOLKSWAGEN WITH WASHINGTON TAG A QB-894, SEATTLE, WASHINGTON

01-29-76 (09:15) INVESTIGATORS LEARNED THAT HARRIS FOUND IN BUNDY'S VOLKSWAGEN CAME FROM HOMICIDE VICTIMS KAREN CAMPBELL AND MELISSA SMITH

01-30-76 (00:00) BUNDY DROVE WASHINGTON OPM-001, SEATTLE, WASHINGTON

02-03-76 (22:21) BUNDY LEFT DRIVING VOLK-

SWAGEN WITH WASHINGTON TAG OPM-001, SEATTLE, WASHINGTON

(00:00) BUNDY IN SEATTLE, WASHINGTON

02-23-76 (00:00) BUNDY TRIAL BEGAN, SALT LAKE CITY, UTAH

03-01-76 (00:00) CONVICTED IN COURT, AGGRAVATED KIDNAPPING, REMANDED TO CUSTODY, SALT LAKE CITY, UTAH

03-22-76 (00:00) COMMITTED TO JAIL/PRISON, SALT LAKE CITY, UTAH

03-23-76 (00:00) CHARGED WITH FRAUDULENT APPLICATION OF MOTOR VEHICLE, SALT LAKE CITY, UTAH

06-22-76 (00:00) CONVICTED IN COURT, EVADING POLICE, SALT LAKE CITY, UTAH

07-06-76 (00:00) PRISON: RECEIVED UTAH STATE PRISON FOR AGGRAVATED KIDNAPPING

10-21-76 (00:00) BUNDY CHARGED WITH MURDER OF KAREN CAMPBELL, PITKIN COUNTY, COLORADO

1977

01-28-77 (00:00) BUNDY RELEASED FROM SALT LAKE CITY, UTAH, TO GLENWOOD SPRINGS, COLORADO

01-29-77 (00:00) BUNDY CHARGED WITH MURDER, ASPEN, COLORADO

06-07-77 (10:48) ESCAPE FROM COURTHOUSE, PITKIN COUNTY JAIL, ASPEN, COLORADO

06-08-77 (00:00) BUNDY BROKE INTO MOUNTAIN CABIN 5 MILES FROM ASPEN AND STOLE RIFLE, CASTLE CREEK ROAD, PITKIN COUNTY, COLORADO

06-13-77 (00:00) BUNDY STOLE 1966 BLUE CADILLAC, COLORADO TAGZG-1765, FROM 805 BONITA, ASPEN, IN PITKIN COUNTY, COLORADO

(02:00) BUNDY ARRESTED; ESCAPE FROM ASPEN, COLORADO, DRIVING STOLEN VEHICLE

06-15-77 (00:00) BUNDY CHARGED WITH ESCAPE, BURGLARY AND FELONY THEFT, PITKIN COUNTY, COLORADO

12-31-77 (00:00) ESCAPE FROM JAIL, GLENWOOD SPRINGS, COLORADO

(00:00) BUNDY STOLE OLD MG, WHICH BROKE DOWN, AND GOT A RIDE TO VAIL, COLORADO

(00:00) BUNDY TOOK BUS FROM VAIL TO DENVER, COLORADO

(00:00) BUNDY TOOK A PLANE FROM DENVER, COLORADO, TO CHICAGO, ILLINOIS

1978

01-01-78 (00:00) BUNDY TOOK TRAIN FROM CHICAGO TO ANN ARBOR, MICHIGAN

(00:00) BUNDY ARRIVED IN ANN ARBOR, MICHIGAN, AND STOLE VEHICLE

01-03-78 (00:00) BUNDY STOLE UNKNOWN VEHICLE, ANN ARBOR, MICHIGAN

01-05-78 (00:00) BUNDY LEFT ANN ARBOR, MICHIGAN, IN STOLEN VEHICLE AND DROVE TO ATLANTA, GEORGIA, WHERE BUNDY LEFT THE STOLEN VEHICLE.

01-06-78 (00:00) BUNDY TOOK BUS FROM ATLANTA, GEORGIA, TO TALLAHASSEE, FLORIDA

01-07-78 (PM.HR) BUNDY ARRIVED IN TALLAHASSEE, FLORIDA SIGNED LEASE AT THE “OAKS”.

01-12-78 (15:55) BUNDY STOLE VAN KEYES

FROM FLORIDA STATE AND HAD THEM COPIED WITH INTENTION OF STEALING A VAN. KEYS WERE REPORTED STOLEN AND VAN WAS BLOCKED IN. BUNDY RETURNED KEYS, WAS UNABLE TO STEAL VAN, TALLAHASSEE, FLORIDA

01-13-78 (00:00) BUNDY STOLE FLORIDA LICENSE TAG 13 D-11300, TALLAHASSEE, FLORIDA

01-14-78 (00:00) BUNDY SEEN NEXT TO CHI OMEGA SORORITY HOUSE, TALLAHASSEE, FLORIDA

01-15-78 (02:00) BUNDY LEFT SHARROD'S BAR, TALLAHASSEE, FLORIDA

(02:30) BUNDY ENTERED CHI OMEGA SORORITY HOUSE, KILLED LISA LEVY, MARGARET BOWMAN, AN INJURED KAREN CHANDLER AND KATHY KLEINER, TALLAHASSEE, FLORIDA

(03:17) NEARY ENTERED CHI OMEGA SORORITY HOUSE AND HEARD NOISES UPSTAIRS. SAW BUNDY COMING DOWN THE STAIRS WITH SOME TYPE OF CLUB IN HIS HAND.

(03:23) TELEPHONE CALL FROM CHI OMEGA SORORITY HOUSE TO LOCAL HOSPITAL REPORTING THE ASSAULTS.

(03:26) OFFICERS ARRIVED AT THE SCENE.

(04:40) TALLAHASSEE POLICE RECEIVED A CALL TO RESPOND TO CHERYL THOMAS HOUSE, TALLAHASSEE, FLORIDA

(05:00) BUNDY BACK AT HIS RESIDENCE, TALLAHASSEE, FLORIDA

01-21-78 (03:02) BUNDY STOLE WALLET AND CREDIT CARDS AT 1940 N. MONROE ST., TALLAHASSEE, FL

01-23-78 (00:00) BUNDY USED CREDIT CARD, TALLAHASSEE, FLORIDA

01-24-78 (00:00) BUNDY USED STOLEN CREDIT CARD, TALLAHASSEE, FLORIDA

01-25-78 (00:00) BUNDY USED STOLEN CREDIT CARD, TALLAHASSEE, FLORIDA

01-26-78 (00:00) BUNDY USED STOLEN CREDIT CARD, TALLAHASSEE, FLORIDA

01-27-78 (00:00) BUNDY USED STOLEN CREDIT CARD, TALLAHASSEE, FLORIDA

01-28-78 (00:00) BUNDY USED STOLEN CREDIT CARD, TALLAHASSEE, FLORIDA

01-29-78 (00:00) BUNDY USED STOLEN CREDIT CARD, TALLAHASSEE, FLORIDA

01-31-78 (00:00) BUNDY USED STOLEN CREDIT CARD, TALLAHASSEE, FLORIDA

02-03-78 (15:00) BUNDY STOLE CREDIT CARD, TALLAHASSEE, FLORIDA

(PM.HR) BUNDY STOLE CREDIT CARD FROM HILTON HOTEL, TALLAHASSEE, FLORIDA

02-04-78 (00:00) BUNDY STOLE CREDIT CARD, LAKE CITY, FLORIDA

02-05-78 (00:00) BUNDY STOLE VAN FROM FLORIDA STATE UNIVERSITY AND PUT STOLEN FLORIDA LICENSE TAG 13D11300 ON IT, TALLAHASSEE, FLORIDA

02-06-78 (00:00) BUNDY LEFT IN STOLEN VAN FROM TALLAHASSEE, FLORIDA

02-07-78 (00:00) BUNDY IN LAKE CITY, FLORIDA

(11:30) BUNDY USED STOLEN CREDIT CARD AT HOLIDAY INN AT ORANGE PARK, FLORIDA

(PM.HR) BUNDY SEEN AT AGRICULTURAL AREA TEN OR 12 MILES NORTH OF LAKE CITY, FLORIDA

(23:00) BUNDY USED STOLEN CREDIT CARD FOR GAS, JACKSONVILLE, FLORIDA

(23:00) CHECKED INTO HOLIDAY INN, JACKSONVILLE, FLORIDA

02-08-78 (00:00) BUNDY USED STOLEN CREDIT CARD TO BUY GAS AND UNMAPPED, JACKSONVILLE, FLORIDA

(00:00) BUNDY USED STOLEN CREDIT CARD, ORANGE PARK, FLORIDA

(12:30) BUNDY BOUGHT BUCK KNIFE AT GREEN ACRES SPORTING-GOODS, JACKSONVILLE, FLORIDA

(12:53) BUNDY USED STOLEN CREDIT CARD AND CHECKED INTO HOLIDAY INN, ORANGE PARK, FLORIDA

(13:30) BUNDY ATTEMPTED TO PICK UP FEMALE IN KMART PARKING LOT. VICTIM'S BROTHER INTERVENED. POSITIVE IDENTIFICATION OF BUNDY AND STOLEN WHITE VAN WITH FLORIDA PLATE 13D11300.

02-09-78 (07:30) CROSSING GUARD SAW WHITE VAN DRIVE BY JUNIOR HIGH SCHOOL, LAKE CITY, FLORIDA

(08:00) CROSSING GUARD SAW WHITE VAN DRIVE BY JUNIOR HIGH SCHOOL, LAKE CITY, FLORIDA

(08:20) CROSSING GUARD SAW WHITE VAN DRIVE BY JUNIOR HIGH SCHOOL, LAKE CITY, FLORIDA

(08:45) KIMBERLY DIANA LEACH WENT TO HOMEROOM, RETURNED TO PICK UP A PURSE SHE'D LEFT BEHIND, LAKE CITY, FLORIDA

(08:55) PARAMEDICS DROVE BY AND SAW BUNDY LEAKING KIMBERLY DIANA LEACH BY THE ARM, LAKE CITY, FLORIDA

(09:00) 110 MILES AWAY FROM TALLAHASSEE,

KIMBERLY DIANA LEACH WAS ABDUCTED IN LAKE CITY, FLORIDA

(18:30) BUNDY ATE AND PAID WITH STOLEN CREDIT CARD, TALLAHASSEE, FLORIDA

02-10-78 (00:00) BUNDY ATE AT CHEZ PIERRE, PAID WITH STOLEN CREDIT CARD, TALLAHASSEE, FLORIDA

(00:00) BUNDY STOLE GREEN TOYOTA, FLORIDA

(22:00) BUNDY SEEN BY POLICE, TALLAHASSEE, FLORIDA

02-11-78 (00:00) BUNDY SEEN AT RESIDENCE, TALLAHASSEE FLORIDA

(00:00) BUNDY USED STOLEN CREDIT CARD AT CHEZ PIERRE, TALLAHASSEE, FLORIDA

02-12-78 (00:00) ORANGE VOLKSWAGEN WAS STOLEN, TALLAHASSEE, FLORIDA

(PM.HR) BUNDY LEFT TALLAHASSEE, FLORIDA

02-13-78 (00:00) STOLEN VAN WAS RECOVERED, TALLAHASSEE, FLORIDA

(00:00) BUNDY USED A STOLEN CREDIT CARD TO CHECK INTO HOLIDAY INN, CRESTVIEW, FLORIDA

02-14-78 (01:30) BUNDY ARRESTED: BUNDY HAD ON SHIRT WITH TORN SLEEVE FIBERS FROM SHIRT MATCHED FIBERS FOUND AT THE LEACH CRIME SCENE, PENSACOLA, FLORIDA

02-16-78 (00:00) BUNDY WAS IDENTIFIED AS TED BUNDY, PENSACOLA, FLORIDA

04-07-78 (00:00) KIMBERLY DIANA LEACH HIS BODY LOCATED 32 MILES FROM THE JUNIOR HIGH IN LAKE CITY, FLORIDA. EVIDENCE AT SCENE INDICATED LEACH WAS PLACED AT DUMP-SITE ON 2-9-78.

04-27-78 (17:00) BUNDY HAD DENTAL IMPRESSIONS TAKEN OF HIS TEETH, TALLAHASSEE, FLORIDA

07-07-78 (00:00) BUNDY INDICTED ON THE CHI OMEGA MURDERS IN TALLAHASSEE, FLORIDA, PENSACOLA, FLORIDA

1979

07-31-79 (00:00) BUNDY GIVEN DEATH SENTENCE FOR THE CHI OMEGA MURDERS IN FLORIDA

1980

02-07-80 (00:00) BUNDY CONVICTED OF THE KIMBERLY LEACH MURDER THAT Took Pl. in Lake City, FL

02-09-80 (00:00) BUNDY GETS MARRIED DURING THE PENALTY STAGE OF THE TRIAL, FLORIDA

02-12-80 (00:00) BUNDY RECEIVED THE DEATH PENALTY FOR THE MURDER OF KIMBERLY LEACH THAT Took Pl. in Lake City, FL

1989

01-24-89 (07:16) BUNDY DIED IN THE ELECTRIC CHAIR, FLORIDA STATE PRISON, FLORIDA

(08:38) postmortem examination of Ted Bundy, FLORIDA

PREPARED BY JAMES F. BELL

800-634-xxxx OR 703-640-xxxx
VICAP-F.B.I. ACADEMY
QUANTICO, VIRGINIA

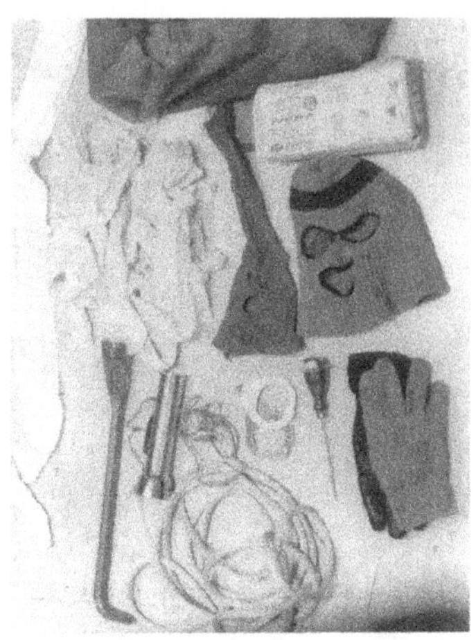

Items located in Bundy's Volkswagen at the time of his arrest in Salt Lake City, Utah, 8/16/75.

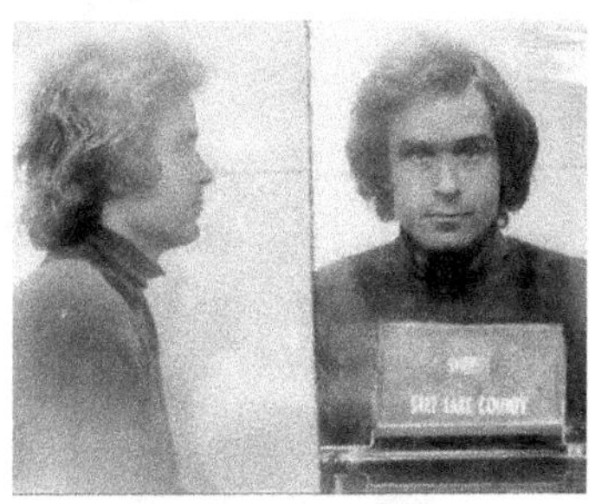

Photo taken of *Bundy when arrested* on 8/16/75.

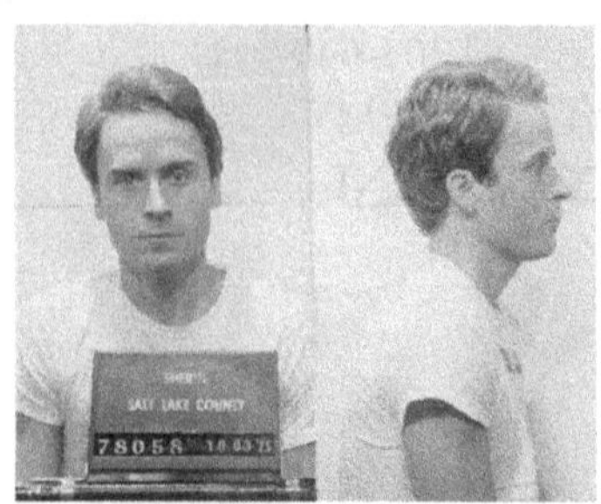

Photo taken of Bundy right after Lineup
on *10/2/75.*

One of Bundy's victims identified him from this line up even after he had cut bis hair and parted it on *the opposite side.*

Photo taken of Bundy after his arrest in Pensacola, Florida, 2/15/78

SSA Bill Hagmaier and Bundy during final confession on *the eve of Bundy's execution, 1/23/89.*

WANTED BY THE FBI

INTERSTATE FLIGHT - MURDER

THEODORE ROBERT BUNDY

DESCRIPTION

Born November 24, 1946, Burlington, Vermont (not supported by birth records); Height, 5'11" to 6'; Weight, 145 to 175 pounds; Build, slender, athletic; Hair, dark brown, collar length; Eyes, blue; Complexion, pale / sallow; Race, white; Nationality, American; Occupations, bellboy, busboy, cook's helper, dishwasher, janitor, law school student, office worker, political campaign worker, psychiatric social worker, salesman, security guard; Scars and Marks, mole on neck, scar on scalp; Social Security Number used, 533-44-4655; Remarks, occasionally stammers when upset; has worn glasses, false mustache and beard as disguise in past; left-handed; can imitate British accent; reportedly physical fitness and health enthusiast.

CRIMINAL RECORD

Bundy has been convicted of aggravated kidnaping.

CAUTION

BUNDY, A COLLEGE-EDUCATED PHYSICAL FITNESS ENTHUSIAST WITH A PRIOR HISTORY OF ESCAPE, IS BEING SOUGHT AS A PRISON ESCAPEE AFTER BEING CONVICTED OF KIDNAPING AND WHILE AWAITING TRIAL INVOLVING A BRUTAL SEX SLAYING OF A WOMAN AT A SKI RESORT. HE SHOULD BE CONSIDERED ARMED, DANGEROUS AND AN ESCAPE RISK.

The FBI Wanted Poster of Bundy.

(Text transcribed for easier reading)

THEODORE ROBERT BUNDY

DESCRIPTION

Born November 24, 1946, Burlington, Vermont (not supported by birth records); Height, 5'11" to 6'; Weight, 145 to 175 pounds; Build, slender, athletic; Hair, dark brown, collar length; Eyes, blue; Complexion, pale/ sallow; Race, white; Nationality, American; Occupations, bellboy, busboy, cook's helper, dishwasher, janitor, law school student, office worker, political campaign worker,

psychiatric social worker, salesman, security guard; Sears and Marks, mole on neck, scar on scalp; Social Security Number used, 533-44-4655; Remarks, occasionally stammers when upset, has worn glasses, false mustache and beard as disguise in past; left-handed; can imitate British accent; reportedly physical fitness and health enthusiast.

CRIMINAL RECORD

Bundy has been convicted of aggravated kidnaping.

CAUTION

BUNDY, A COLLEGE· EDUCATED PHYSICAL FITNESS ENTHUSIAST WITH APRIOR HISTORY OF ESCAPE, IS BEING SOUGHT AS A PRISON ESCAPEE AFTER BEING CONVICTED OF KIDNAPING AND WHILE AWAITING TRIAL INVOLVING A BRUTAL SEX SLAYING OF A WOMAN AT A SKI RESORT. HE SHOULD BE CONSIDERED ARMED, DANGEROUS AND AN ESCAPE RISK.

F81/00J

Bundy Multi Agency Investigation Team Conference 2/21-24/89

Jim Bell - Salt Lake City (UT) Police Department

Jerry M. Blair - State Attorney, FL

Mike Brown - Sonoma County (CA) Sheriff's Department

Alan E. Burgess - FBI

Dennis Couch - Salt Lake County (UT) Sheriff's Office

Paul Decker - Florida Department of Corrections

George R. Dekle (Bob) - Assistant State Attorney, FL

Lee Erickson - Oregon State Police

Bob Evans - Department of Public Safety, Seattle, WA

Mike Fisher - DA's Office, Glenwood Springs, CO

Terence J. Green - FBI

W. Hagmaier, III - FBI

Andrea Hillyer - Office of the Governor, FL

James B. Howlett - FBI

Ken Kahn - Santa Clara County (CA) Sheriff's Office

Robert Keppel - Office of the Attorney General, WA

Bonnie Knapp - FBI

Cynthia J. Lent - FBI

Matt Lindvall - Vail (CO) Police Department

James Sewell - Gulfport (Fl.) Police Department

David Stapleton - FBI
Jerry Thompson - Salt Lake County (UT) Sheriff's Office
David Tubbs - FBI
Jim Whitehead - Idaho Department of Law Enforcement
James A. Wright - FBI
James York - Attorney General's Office, FL

TWENTY-FOUR

Early Indicators of Possible Sexual Abuse Problems

Although there are no definite indicators that would predict a person is going to act out in a sexually aggressive manner, there are some signs that hint of a possibility of a developing problem. Heavy predictive weight cannot be put on any one sign, and there are persons who have many of the following characteristics who do not act out in a sexually aggressive manner. However, a large percentage of sexually aggressive persons demonstrated many of these characteristics when they were in their teens.

1) Low self-image, shyness, feelings of inferiority.

2) Scapegoat or object of jokes by others.

3) Anger toward girls.

4) Non-productive in school.

5) Socially awkward.

6) Constant failure experiences.

7) Early interest or involvement with sexual relations.

8) Broken home, hostile, domineering mother or stepmother, etc.

9) Heavy physical punishment used in home.

10) Lonely.

11) Early involvement with criminal or antisocial activities.

12) Strong rejection experiences by girlfriends, female teachers, etc.

13) Strong tendency toward becoming dependent on others.

14) Easily angered or strong inhibition of emotions.

A.L. Carlisle, Ph.D.
Clinical Psychologist
Utah State Prison

Sept 1946 – illeg birth – [illegible] father

Theodore Robert Cowell –

" " Nelson

age 4½ she md Mr Bundy

Normal childhood

Participation at Wilson High [illegible] – [illegible]

U of Puget Sound (Fall 65) → U of Wash – Chinese studies (Fall 66)

Summer Study at Stanford – prestigious Chinese Institute

U of Wash – Fall 67 – withdrew winter 1968

Ap 68 Seattle Chairman & Assist State Chairman for New
Majority for Rockefeller

Driver for GOP Lieut governor candidate (he lost)

→ Philadelphia → Temple University – 5 mo later → Seattle

met (Liz K) [illegible] (girlfriend)

U of Wash Summer 1970 – Psychology

Seattle Crisis Clinic

Sept 1972 Committee to Re-Elect Dan Evans

Oct – City of Seattle's Crime Prevention Advisory
Commission, left Jan 1973 when he didn't
get the top job

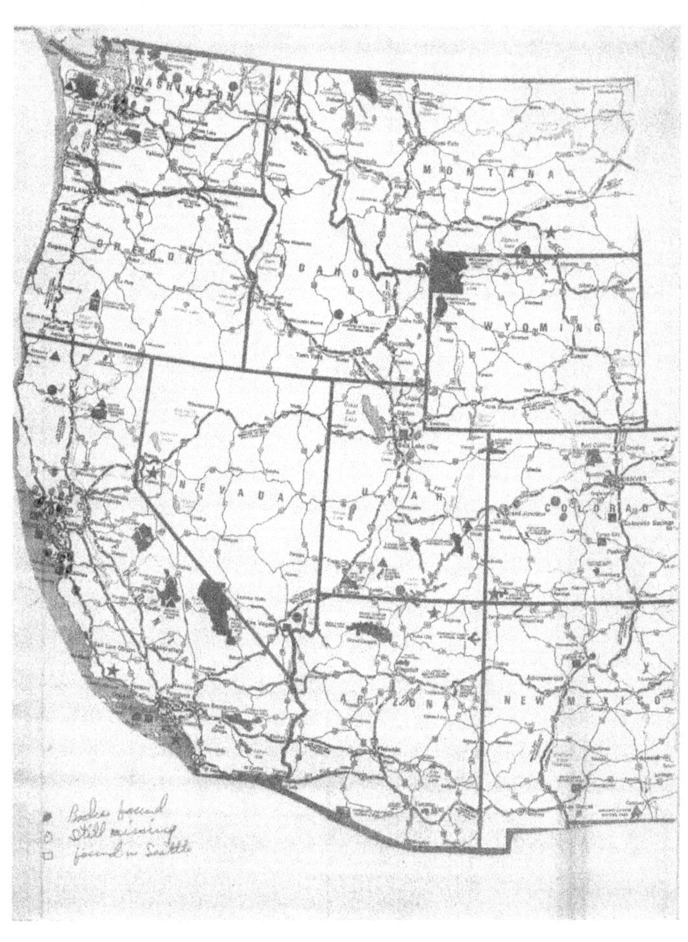
WASHINGTON
PORTLAND
OREGON
IDAHO
MONTANA
WYOMING
NEVADA
UTAH
COLORADO
DENVER
ARIZONA
NEW MEXICO
Bodies found
Still missing
found in Seattle

About the Author

Al Carlisle (1937 - 2018)

Al Carlisle was born and raised in Utah. His interest in serial killers began with Charles Manson. He was fascinated with what made Manson become a cult leader and murderer.

This led him to a lifetime of research on serial killers. He received a BS and MS from Utah State University and a PhD in clinical psychology from Brigham Young University.

He spent 20 years as a clinical psychologist at the Utah State Prison, retiring as the head of the department in 1989. He was part of a team that performed the first psychological assessment of Ted Bundy in 1976 while Ted was being held for a 90-day evaluation at the Utah State Prison.

He was a pioneer in the field of forensic psychology and conducted extensive research on serial killers and interviewed the Hi Fi killers, Arthur Gary Bishop, Westley Allan Dodd, Keith Jesperson, Ted Bundy, and many others.

He was also intensely interested in DID (Dissociative Identity Disorder, formerly Multiple Personality Disorder) and PTSD (Post Traumatic Stress Disorder). He became a specialist in DID and interviewed a number of Veterans to understand and help people with PTSD.

Carrie Anne Keller, anthropologist, acted as his agent and helped get his first four books published.

His daughter, Charlene, became his literary executor after

his death and later his publisher. She and her daughter, Jess, run Carlisle Legacy Books, LLC.

Also by Al Carlisle, PhD

Books in the *Development of the Violent Mind* series:

1: *"I'm Not Guilty!" The Case of Ted Bundy*

2: *Mind of the Devil: The Cases of Arthur Gary Bishop & Westley Allan Dodd*

3: *Broken Samurai: One Marine's Journey from Hero to Hitman*

4: *The 1976 Psychological Assessment of Ted Bundy*

5: *The Ted Bundy Files: A 1976 Companion*

www.ingramcontent.com/pod-product-compliance
Lightning Source LLC
Chambersburg PA
CBHW070053030426
42335CB00016B/1876
9781952043154